Timo Minartz

Power Consumption Measurement in Parallel Systems

Timo Minartz

Power Consumption Measurement in Parallel Systems

Südwestdeutscher Verlag für Hochschulschriften

Impressum / Imprint
Bibliografische Information der Deutschen Nationalbibliothek: Die Deutsche Nationalbibliothek verzeichnet diese Publikation in der Deutschen Nationalbibliografie; detaillierte bibliografische Daten sind im Internet über http://dnb.d-nb.de abrufbar.
Alle in diesem Buch genannten Marken und Produktnamen unterliegen warenzeichen-, marken- oder patentrechtlichem Schutz bzw. sind Warenzeichen oder eingetragene Warenzeichen der jeweiligen Inhaber. Die Wiedergabe von Marken, Produktnamen, Gebrauchsnamen, Handelsnamen, Warenbezeichnungen u.s.w. in diesem Werk berechtigt auch ohne besondere Kennzeichnung nicht zu der Annahme, dass solche Namen im Sinne der Warenzeichen- und Markenschutzgesetzgebung als frei zu betrachten wären und daher von jedermann benutzt werden dürften.

Bibliographic information published by the Deutsche Nationalbibliothek: The Deutsche Nationalbibliothek lists this publication in the Deutsche Nationalbibliografie; detailed bibliographic data are available in the Internet at http://dnb.d-nb.de.
Any brand names and product names mentioned in this book are subject to trademark, brand or patent protection and are trademarks or registered trademarks of their respective holders. The use of brand names, product names, common names, trade names, product descriptions etc. even without a particular marking in this works is in no way to be construed to mean that such names may be regarded as unrestricted in respect of trademark and brand protection legislation and could thus be used by anyone.

Coverbild / Cover image: www.ingimage.com

Verlag / Publisher:
Südwestdeutscher Verlag für Hochschulschriften
ist ein Imprint der / is a trademark of
OmniScriptum GmbH & Co. KG
Heinrich-Böcking-Str. 6-8, 66121 Saarbrücken, Deutschland / Germany
Email: info@svh-verlag.de

Herstellung: siehe letzte Seite /
Printed at: see last page
ISBN: 978-3-8381-3794-0

Zugl. / Approved by: Hamburg, Universität Hamburg, Dissertation, 2010

Copyright © 2014 OmniScriptum GmbH & Co. KG
Alle Rechte vorbehalten. / All rights reserved. Saarbrücken 2014

Abstract

In an effort to reduce the energy consumption of high performance computing centers, a number of new approaches have been developed in the last few years. One of these approaches is to switch hardware to lower power states in promising parallel application phases. A test cluster is designed with high performance computing nodes supporting multiple power saving mechanisms comparable to mobile devices. Each of the nodes is connected to power measurement equipment to investigates the power saving potential under different load scenarios of the specific hardware. However, statically switching the power saving mechanisms usually increases the application runtime. As a consequence, no energy can be saved. Contrary to static switching strategies, dynamic switching strategies consider the hardware usage in the application phases to switch between the different modes without increasing the application runtime. Even if the concepts are already quite clear, tools to identify application phases and to determine impact on performance, power and energy are still rare. This thesis designs and evaluates tool extensions for power consumption measurement in parallel systems with the final goal to characterize and identify energy-efficiency hot spots in scientific applications. Using offline tracing, the metrics are collected in trace files and can be visualized or post-processed after the application run. The timeline-based visualization tools Sunshot and Vampir are used to correlate parallel applications with the energy-related metrics. With these tracing and visualization capabilities, it is possible to evaluate the quality of energy-saving mechanisms, since waiting times in the application can be related to hardware power states. Using the energy-efficiency benchmark eeMark, typical hardware usage pattern are identified to characterize the workload, the impact on the node power consumption and finally the potential for energy saving. To exploit the developed extensions, four scientific applications are analyzed to evaluate the whole approach. Appropriate phases of the parallel applications are manually instrumented to reduce the power consumption with the final goal of saving energy for the whole application run on the test cluster. This thesis provides a software interface for the efficient management of the power saving modes per compute node to be exploited by application programmers. All analyzed applications consist of several, different calculation-intensive compute phases and have a considerable power and energy-saving potential which cannot be exhausted by traditional, utilization-based mechanisms implemented in the operating system. Reducing the processor frequency in communication and I/O phases can also gain remarkable savings for the presented applications.

Acknowledgements

One of the joys of completion is to look over the journey past and remember all the colleagues, friends and family who have helped and supported me.
Undertaking this PhD has been a truly life-changing experience for me and it would not have been possible to do without the support and guidance that I received from many people.
I would like to first say a very big thank you to my supervisor Prof. Thomas Ludwig for all the support and encouragement. Without your guidance and constant feedback, this PhD would not have been achievable.
This thesis was co-funded by the German ministry for education and research (BMBF) and the German research foundations (DFG), and I would like to thank both organizations for their generous support and especially my co-workers Daniel, Stephan and Michael for all the contributed results during the eeClust project.
As a member of the University of Hamburg and the DKRZ, I have been surrounded by friendly, inspirational and supportive colleagues which were always available for a chat or support during the day, evening or night.
Special thanks to the research group founding members Michael and Julian, who kept things ticking over and let me focus on the fun stuff!
But also thanks to the additional group members, especially to Petra for supporting my work with GETM and to my (frequently changing) officemates Gerald, Javier, Raul and Konstantinos. I really enjoyed spending time with you.
I particular, I want to thank Florian, Marius, Christian and Jolene for all their work allowing me to complete this thesis.
To the staff and students at DKRZ, I am grateful for the chance to be a part of the center. Thank you for so many lunch breaks, inspiring talks and memorable conference trips. Especially, I would like to thank Michaele for being such a supportive and wise friend.
I would not have contemplated this road without the support of my family and wife. To my parents and siblings, thank you for everything. Isabell, thank you for your amazing personality. Not only that you accepted several long-distance relationships and relocations, you unburdened our daily life with your uncomplicated character and lovable nature. I am excited about our joint future.

Contents

1. **Introduction**   7
   1.1. Individual Approach 15
2. **Hardware Mechanism**   23
   2.1. Component Overview 23
      2.1.1. Central Processing Unit 24
      2.1.2. General Purpose Graphic Processing Unit 27
      2.1.3. Main Memory 27
      2.1.4. Input/Output System 28
      2.1.5. Interconnection Systems 29
   2.2. Interfaces 31
   2.3. Durability Issues 32
3. **Power and Energy Saving Potential**   35
   3.1. Test Infrastructure 35
   3.2. Evaluation of Hardware Power Saving Modes 39
4. **Strategies for Reducing Parallel Application Power Consumption**   57
   4.1. Application Phases of Interest 57
   4.2. Hardware-centric Approach 60
      4.2.1. Sampling Utilization 60
      4.2.2. Sampling Performance Counters 62
   4.3. Application-centric Approach 63
5. **Management of Power Saving Modes**   69
   5.1. Server Design 70
      5.1.1. Map Processes to Hardware Devices 71
      5.1.2. Switching Hardware Device States 71
      5.1.3. Runtime Overhead 72
      5.1.4. Resource Management 74
      5.1.5. Server configuration 75
   5.2. Application interface 76
   5.3. Software package 78
6. **Correlating Applications and Energy-Related Metrics**   79
   6.1. Tracing Approach 79
      6.1.1. HDTrace 80

	6.1.2. VampirTrace	82
	6.1.3. Intrinsic Tracing Tool Problems	82
6.2.	Integration of Energy-Related Metrics	83
	6.2.1. Power	85
	6.2.2. Device Utilization and Hardware States	86
	6.2.3. Performance Counters	87
	6.2.4. eeDaemon Decisions	88
6.3.	Visualization of Trace Files	89
	6.3.1. Sunshot	90
	6.3.2. Vampir	96

7. Evaluation 101
- 7.1. Synthetic Benchmark . . . 101
  - 7.1.1. Reference Run . . . 103
  - 7.1.2. Memory-bound Instrumentation . . . 104
  - 7.1.3. Operation-based Instrumentation . . . 113
  - 7.1.4. Energy-Performance Tradeoff . . . 116
- 7.2. Application Benchmarks . . . 120
  - 7.2.1. Jacobi PDE Solver . . . 121
  - 7.2.2. Shallow Water Modeling . . . 124
  - 7.2.3. Max-Planck-Institute Ocean Model . . . 127
  - 7.2.4. General Estuarine Transport Model . . . 135
- 7.3. Appraisal of Results . . . 141

8. Related Work and State-of-the-Art 145
- 8.1. Assessing Application Power Consumption . . . 145
  - 8.1.1. System Analysis . . . 145
  - 8.1.2. Application Analysis . . . 146
- 8.2. Exploiting Hardware Power Saving Mechanism . . . 148
  - 8.2.1. Application Power Management . . . 148
  - 8.2.2. System Power Management . . . 149

9. Conclusion 151
- 9.1. Future Work . . . 156

A. Appendix I

Bibliography XV

1. Introduction

Supercomputers combine the performance of several thousands of desktop computers to tackle problems which can not be solved on normal desktop computers or workstations within adequate time. High performance computing (HPC) is an important tool in science and industry to analyze questions in silico. Instead of time consuming and expensive real-life experiments (like car crash tests), HPC scientists model and simulate experiments within the computer system which provides a well-defined environment. Scientific models from weather systems to protein folding and nanotechnology are built and run leading to new observations and understanding of phenomena which are too fast or too expensive to grasp in vitro [MMK+12, KS92]. By increasing computing performance, the model granularity can be increased. This is desirable for almost all conducted experiments because new and more detailed results can be achieved which are transferred to knowledge gain. One metric for computing performance is to measure the performed *Floating Point Operations per Second* (FLOPS). Today's supercomputers are in the range of several Petaflops, which corresponds to 10^{15} floating point operations per second. However, since larger scientific problems ask for more computing power, the next three orders of magnitude, *Exascale-Computing* (10^{18} floating point operations per second) is targeted for 2019. Recently, the European Union decided to double its investments in high performance computing[1].

As performance of these supercomputers is the crucial factor, there are several methods to speed up systems [MMK+12]. The processing speed of a single processor can be increased, or the number of processors can be increased – either by fusing more chips into a single machine or by interconnecting multiple machines into a cluster system.

In the past, the performance of applications was improved by packing more functionality into a single chip and increasing the clock frequency of this processor. However, the processor power consumption is proportional to the square of its clock frequency. Thus, doubling the processing count is more power-efficient than doubling the processing frequency [Sey11][2][RMM+01].

The disadvantage of these multi-processor or multi-core chips is the decreased programmability: to fully exploit the hardware parallelism, the work has to be parallelized, too.

The resulting performance boost by adding N more processing units is called *speedup S*. It is ideally measured with the time T_N using N processing units against the time T_1 using one processing unit. How well the speedup is in regard to the used processing units is measured by the efficiency E.

---

[1] http://www.hpcwire.com/hpcwire/2012-02-15/eurpean_commission_announces_plan_to_double_hpc_investments.html, last checked: March 2, 2013

[2] The bachelor thesis has been supervised in conjunction with this thesis

1. Introduction

$$S = \frac{T_1}{T_N} < N \qquad\qquad E = \frac{S}{N} < 1$$

There are two established laws concerning the prediction of scalability, whereas P is the part of the program that is actually affected by the parallelization, *Amdahl's Law* [Amd67] and *Gustafson's Law* [Gus88]:

Amdahl's Law $S = \frac{1}{(1-P)+\frac{P}{N}}$

Every program has parts which cannot be split onto several processing units or which have to be done by every single processing unit (e.g. initialization and communication phases). This overhead is the reason why E is really smaller than 1. The actual speedup now consists of the overhead $(1-P)$ and the parts which are processed faster $\frac{P}{N}$.

Gustafson takes another approach, because the part of a program causing the overhead is usually not consuming a high percentage of the total runtime. The main purpose costing the most time of the program—the calculation—will be parallel, so P is actually 1 while calculating.

Gustafson's Law $S = N - (1-P) \cdot (N-1)$

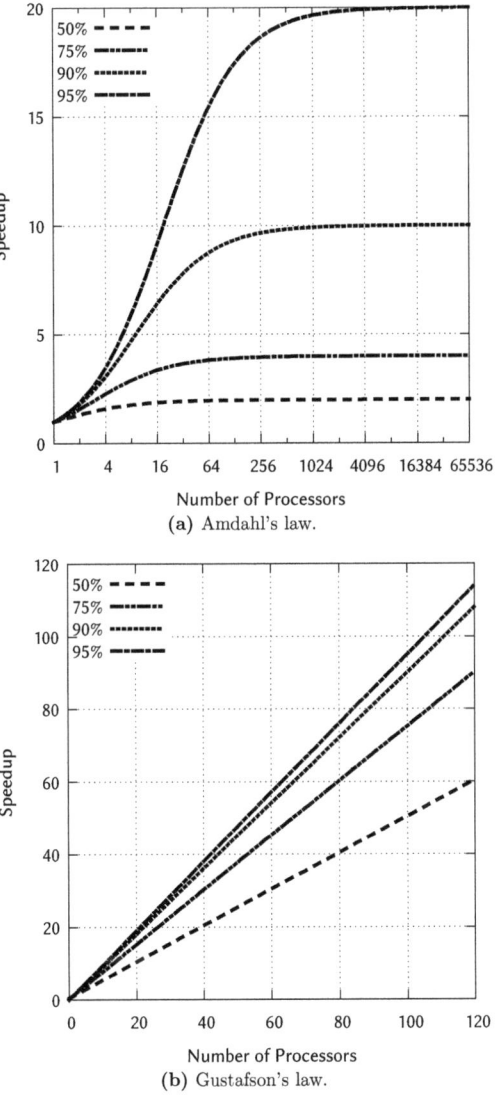

Figure 1.1.: *Amdahl's law and Gustafson's law with different efficiencies [Sey11].*

1. Introduction

As Figure 1.1 shows, Amdahl's law always predicts a possible upper limit, whereas Gustafson's law does not. The reason is the different opinion about the used *problem size*. Problem size actually means the amount of data that has to be processed. Amdahl implies a fixed problem size, so the calculating/communication ratio for every processing unit decreases when more processing units are used.

Gustafson predicts that the users will usually process more data (greater problem size) when they have more machines, mainly for getting more accurate results in the same amount of time. Both laws are valid, as they target slightly different fields under different assumptions. However, significant effort has to be put into the design and implementation of parallel applications to reach a high efficiency.

Consequently, the complexity of designing and implementing parallel applications is even higher than for their sequential versions. Scientific applications intended to run on supercomputers already use multiple programming concepts to get the most performance out of the hardware. Today, in the era of multi-core and multi-socket processors, the challenge is almost the same for developers of desktop and server applications because the independent processors and/or cores must exchange intermediate results by means of communication. This communication process incurs additional latency and might cause idle processors waiting for new data to process. Consequently, careful attention must be given to balance the work evenly among the resources.

There are several programming concepts worth mentioning in this context [MMK+12]. These can be roughly separated into concepts for shared and distributed memory computer architectures. On shared memory architectures (all parts of the parallel program can access the same memory), programs are usually implemented using lightweight processes, so called threads. POSIX and other standardized interfaces – like Boost Threads – provide ways to use threads manually. These usually involve programming on a very low abstraction level. Additionally, more abstract concepts are available. The *Open Multi-Processing* (OpenMP) standard provides semi-automatic parallelization using compiler pragmas and library functions. The GNU Compiler Collection provides full OpenMP support as of version 4.4. More advanced approaches include the Intel's Threading Building Blocks and Microsoft's Parallel Patterns Library. On distributed memory architectures the de-facto standard is to use some kind of message passing, most prominently via the Message Passing Interface (MPI). MPI provides a standardized interface which enables parallel programs to send messages over the network in an efficient manner. Obviously, depending on the network technology used, this introduces even more latency. For this reason, supercomputing vendors often provide implementations tuned for their specific architecture. MPICH and OpenMPI provide open source implementations of the MPI standard. Additionally, version 2 of the MPI standard provides an interface for efficient parallel I/O.

Using these concepts, some numerical algorithms are capable to utilize computing resources on a parallel computer to a high degree. But unfortunately, most applications exploit only a few percent of peak performance [OCC+07]. A highly optimized and parallel algorithm that can saturate the theoretical peak performance to about 60% is the LINPACK benchmark [DLP03], which solves a system of linear equations.

With increasing supercomputer sizes, low efficiencies of applications increase the wasted energy in terms of unused or not fully utilized processing units.

This leads to the observation that energy costs are more and more becoming a limiting factor to supercomputing-based science and engineering. The increase in energy consumption in modern supercomputers is driven by the increasing density of the hardware components and the decrease of the price for hardware [Mud00]. Compared with these factors, the improvement in energy efficiency thus the reduction of energy consumption in an HPC system develops with a slower pace. As a consequence, steadily increasing costs for energy in HPC systems can be noticed due to constantly increasing absolute power consumption. This phenomenon is also referred to as *Jevons' paradox*, as the English economist William Stanley Jevons observed in 1865 that technological improvements that increased the efficiency of coal use led to increased consumption of coal in a wide range of industries [Jev66]. Thus, in economics, the *Jevons' paradox* is *the proposition that technological progress that increases the efficiency with which a resource is used tends to increase (rather than decrease) the rate of consumption of that resource* [Alc05]. In high performance computing, this paradox increases the *Total Costs of Ownership* (TCO) and shifts the relation between the TCO and the acquisition costs into the direction of the TCO. Consequently, operating a supercomputer becomes more expensive than buying it.

This has direct implications on the way research will be conducted in the near future. With the increasing price per experiment[3] it is reasonable to ask: Is the knowledge gain worth the financial investment in terms of electricity costs? And, if the answer is yes: How can this trend be slowed down without affecting the scientific value of the experiments?

These questions recently opened a new field of science – *Green High Performance Computing*. The additional raising political and social awareness of *green* topics attracted many scientists motivated to reduce the ecological footprint of typical supercomputing. Nowadays, individual approaches on different abstraction levels in the complex HPC environments are evaluated. However, there is no integrated approach yet that presents how to operate an HPC environment in an energy-efficient way.

Taking a look at the currently top-ranked system from the TOP500 List[4] of supercomputers, it has a peak power consumption of more than 8 megawatts. This power consumption results in electricity costs of several millions of euros (based on European electricity costs about 8 million Euro per year).

To understand this trend, the following paragraph exemplary analyzes the development of the compute infrastructure of the German climate computing center (DKRZ). The DKRZ was established in Germany as a central service facility to meet the rapidly growing computational demands of the climate research community in 1987[5]. Major investment for the facility were provided by the Federal Ministry of Education and Research (BMBF). The operations were funded jointly by BMBF and the company's shareholders, the Max-Planck-Society for the Advancement of Sciences, the University

---

[3] system power of multiple MW multiplied with the experiment runtime multiplied with the electricity price
[4] http://www.top500.org/, last checked: March 2, 2013
[5] http://www.dkrz.de/about-en/aufgaben/dkrz-geschichte/, last checked: March 2, 2013

1. Introduction

of Hamburg, the GKSS Research Centre and the Alfred-Wegener-Institute for Polar and Marine Research.

Table 1.1.: *DKRZ supercomputer history from 1988 to 2012.*

Installation	Operating time From	To	CPUs	Performance GFlops	Memory GB
CDC Cyber 205	01/88	03/89	1	0.2	0.032
CRAY 2S	11/88	05/94	4	2	1
CRAY YMP	05/91	05/95	3	1	0.512
CRAY C916	04/94	06/01	16	16	6
CRAY T3D	09/94	09/95	32	4.8	2
CRAY T3D	04/97	06/00	128	19.2	8
NEC SX 4	10/01	03/02	16	32	32
NEC SX 6 (1st stage)	03/02	10/02	64	512	512
NEC SX 6 (2nd stage)	11/02	03/03	128	1,024	1,024
NEC SX 6 (3rd stage)	04/03	05/09	192	1,536	1,536
IBM Power6	04/09	04/14	8,448	158,000	20,000

Table 1.1 gives an overview of the DKRZ's computer history from 1988 to 2012. Some of the acquisitions are split (NEC SX 6 supercomputer), which means that the supercomputer was upgraded during its operating time. In detail, the NEC machine was upgraded twice and operated in total from 2002 until 2009. Additionally, some of the installations ran in parallel to minimize non-operational times.

The development in terms of peak performance, main memory and number of CPUs is visualized in Figure 1.2. Naturally, the peaks in all graphs result from new installations starting operation.

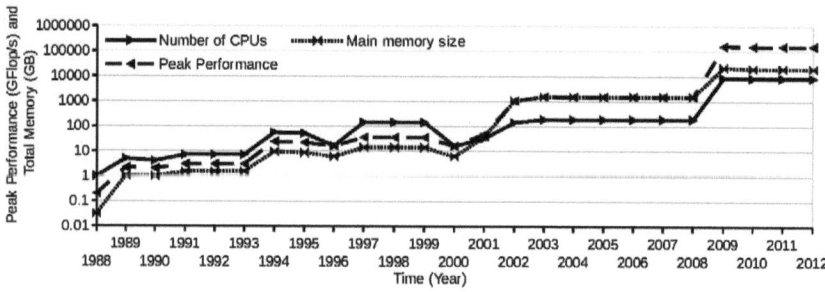

Figure 1.2.: *DKRZ supercomputer history in terms of peak performance, main memory and total number of CPUs.*

But the drawback of this fast increase in calculation power is the increase of the annual center electricity costs as visualized in Figure 1.3. Even though the efficiency in terms of performance per annual electricity costs (Flops/Euro) is increasing, the evolution cannot outweigh the total increase of the electricity costs. Of course, the annual center electricity cost do not solely consists of the supercomputer electricity cost, several small-sized cluster, workstations and desktop computers are included as well as costs for compute room cooling, building heating, lights, etc.. However, these costs are not significant and can be considered as indirect operating costs.

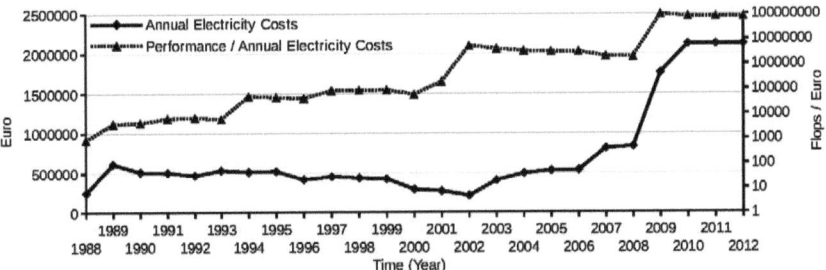

Figure 1.3.: *Increasing efficiency (Flops per Euro annual electricity costs) and electricity costs at the DKRZ from 1988 to 2012.*

Based on the average previous industry electricity prices[6] and the electricity costs, the average computing center power consumption is calculated in Figure 1.4. Thus, the increasing electricity costs are not only due to the electricity price, but also due to the increase of the power needs by high performance installations.

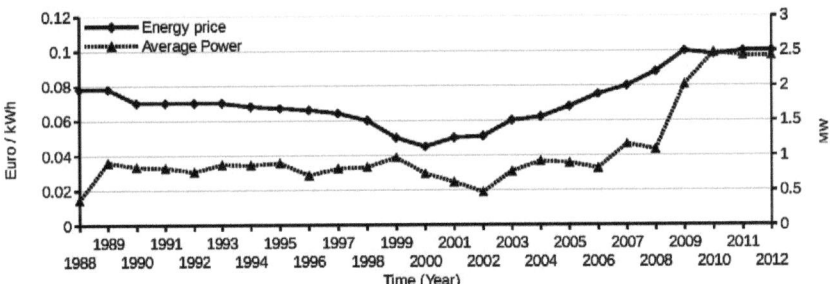

Figure 1.4.: *Increasing power consumption of the DKRZ from 1988 to 2012.*

Several components in an HPC environment contribute here. Starting with the power consumption of the processing unit (which is usually the lion's share), additional energy

---
[6]provided by the Federal Ministry of Economics and Technology

1. Introduction

is needed to operate memory, network and I/O system in a computing node. Furthermore, the generated heat by the electrical components has to be exchanged, which results in further costs for cooling. The whole infrastructure of larger supercomputing centers consumes a considerable amount of energy: In addition to the cooling, power has to be converted, distributed, and sometimes even buffered, which all introduces further power losses.

The efficiency problem of the infrastructure is not restricted to HPC centers, also bigger datacenter or smaller computing centers are confronted with these problems. This problem resulted in broad initiatives like the *GreenGrid*[7] which tries to consolidate knowledge in this area. One first outcome of this initiative is the Power Usage Effectiveness (PUE) metric, which divides the total power by the IT power to evaluate infrastructure effectiveness.

Especially large HPC- and datacenter focus on decreasing the PUE since this approach is an engineering approach and does not affect the performance of the scientific application itself.

One further approach to reduce the power consumption and costs is the change of the computing architecture [Bar05]. Nowadays, special accelerator hardware, like General-Purpose Graphic Processing Units (GPGPUs) or Field Programmable Gate Array (FPGA)-based designs are commonly used in high performance systems [ARH10, AHA+11, AHR+11]. Additionally, the move to low-power (and low-cost) processing devices is considered in various projects – the advantageous performance per cost ratio over x86 based processors motivates this step. For instance, *wimpy nodes* (slower, but efficient nodes) have been analyzed in the FAWN project for data-intensive computing [AFK+09, VFA+09]. The *Green Flash* project also builds a supercomputer with low-power embedded microprocessors [WOS08], the *Mont-Blanc* project[8] uses the ARM architecture. However, the mechanisms cannot easily be used efficiently since the different hardware architecture needs a special adaptation of the application software which often requires a complete rewrite of the application to exploit the full possible performance. The co-development of software and hardware is referred to as *Co-design* and goal of the *CoDEX* (Co-design for Exascale) project[9].

Besides to the cost factor, all approaches try to exploit either the Time-to-Solution (TTS) or Energy-to-Solution (ETS). The relation between Time-to-Solution and Energy-to-Solution is visualized in Figure 1.5 on Page 15. The application needs time t_1 with a power consumption of P_2 on platform A and time t_2 with a much lower power consumption P_1 on platform B. For both cases, the total energy (time multiplied with power, thus the rectangle area) is the same. Thus energy optimization is possible in both ways: Either decrease the runtime and increase power, or increase the runtime and decrease power.

This approach can take place at each step of the design of the scientific application:

---

[7] http://www.thegreengrid.org/, last checked: March 2, 2013
[8] http://www.montblanc-project.eu/, last checked: March 2, 2013
[9] http://www.nersc.gov/research-and-development/exascale-computing/codex-project/, last checked: March 2, 2013

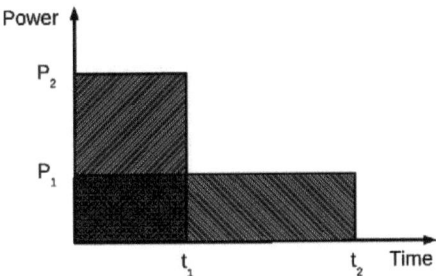

Figure 1.5.: *Relation between Time-to-Solution and Energy-to-Solution.*

- Different mathematical or numerical description of the same problem can result in different runtime and energy behavior on different hardware platforms.
- Design and implementation of the algorithm itself.
- Selection of the appropriate hardware platform for the algorithm.
- Adaptation of the software implementation to the underlying hardware.

Due to hardware power saving mechanisms like Dynamic Voltage and Frequency Scaling (DVFS) of the traditional x86 processor[10], the application can be modified to take advantage of different speed and power settings, too. For example, single processing threads can be slowed down or accelerated to minimize waiting times due to scheduling. This approach can take place fine-granularly (on process level for each processing core) or coarse-granularly (on job level for each computing node). The fine-granular approach is summarized by the term *Application Optimization* or *Application Tuning*, while the coarse-granular approach is classified under the term *Scheduling*. This thesis focuses on the fine granular approach, which is described in the following section as individual approach.

1.1. Individual Approach

Exploiting hardware power saving mechanisms on traditional x86 high performance computing architectures has a strong motivation from the software side. Most software utilizes only a low percentage of the available hardware resources – either the software does not need the resources to perform the task or the software does not handle the resources in an efficient manner [MMK+12]. This is the case for server applications [BH07] as well as for desktop applications [KHLK09]. The problem is exemplarily demonstrated in Figure 1.6a, which plots the processor utilization against the measured relative node power usage. The processor has the highest power consumption when under full load. If the

---
[10] originally developed for mobile computing

load decreases, the hardware still consumes a considerable amount of power. Thus, low utilization is problematic because the utilization and power consumption of the hardware are not proportional. The additional graph visualizes the power efficiency, which is defined as the utilization divided by the relative power usage. Correspondingly, the node is most power efficient if under full load. If the load decreases, the efficiency also decreases.

To deal with unneeded resources the hardware vendors implement low-power idle states, which can be activated when the hardware is idle, meaning zero utilization. But this solves the problem only partially, because low and inefficiently utilized hardware still consumes a high percentage of the maximum power. Additionally, few components (e.g. the processor and the network interface card) support different performance states. The performance can be decreased, and thus can the power consumption. Figure 1.6b visualizes the relative node power usage with disabled and enabled performance states of the processor.

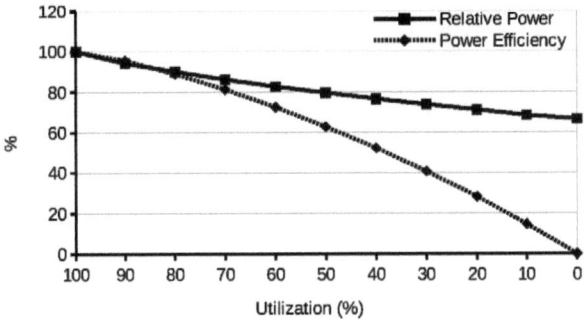

(a) Relative power usage and power efficiency for different utilization levels.

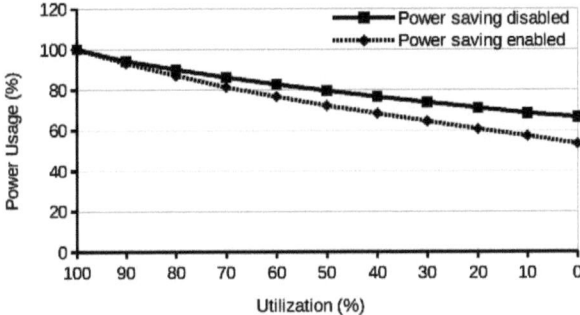

(b) Relative power usage corresponding to performance state settings.

Figure 1.6.: *Relative power measurements for different utilization levels on an Intel Xeon X5560 dual-socket node.*

The relative power consumption decreases more with enabled power saving mechanisms and thus the power efficiency is increased. Unfortunately, there is no power proportional hardware available yet [MKL10]. But with every new processor generation, the power efficiency usually increases compared to the the predecessor.

The low-utilization problem may be disregarded in single personal desktop computers, but as the number of computers vastly increases the energy wastage increases too. This is the case for larger offices using various numbers of desktop computers, and even more important for data centers housing larger numbers of servers or centers built to operate supercomputers.

Supercomputing centers deal with large energy bills, thus there is a bunch of tools available to measure the performance and power consumption of individual components. However, these tools can also be used to investigate the efficiency of server and desktop systems.

1. Introduction

Hardware power consumption depends heavily on the utilization which means the utilization has to be improved to increase the efficiency. But near-optimal utilization of all resources provided on one single chip (or processor) is already a challenging task to developers, compilers and middle-ware. This list includes the operating system as well, which manages the low-level hardware and schedules tasks to the available resources.

For real applications, the efficiency is usually in the range of 1-10 % of the peak performance of a given system. Therefore, tuning and optimization of applications to exploit more of the available resources is an important task to improve performance and efficiency of the facility. It is important to optimize from the most promising performance or energy boosting bottleneck to the least.

Often, performance and energy are directly correlated: more efficient and high performance codes finish earlier, causing less energy consumption. In many cases, using less resources with a higher efficiency is more energy efficient. However, a fast execution is mandatory for the scientist to deliver results. Therefore, the focus is on the execution time. If reducing the executing time by one minute, several Euros[11] can be saved. Runtimes of hours, days and even months are common – correspondingly, huge monetary savings can be reached by application improvements (often referred to as *performance engineering*).

To evaluate not only the performance, but also the energy efficiency of applications, the application contribution to the total power consumption has to be analyzed to quantify improving potential.

As scientific programs usually require a huge amount of resources, one could expect these are especially designed for performance. However, in most cases the performance optimization is performed after the program output is validated. At this late stage a version of the code exists which is tested to some extend. A complete redesign is usually out of reach.

A schematic view of the typical iterative optimization process is shown in Figure 1.7.

In general, the *closed loop of optimization* is not limited to source code, the loop can be applied to any system. To measure performance and power consumption, hardware and software configurations must be selected including the appropriate input in terms of problem statements. It might happen that optimizations made for a particular configuration degrade performance or increase energy consumption on a different setup. Therefore, multiple experimental setups should be measured to increase the validity. Often, the measurement itself influences the system by degrading performance, which must be kept in mind. Picking the appropriate measurement tools helps to reveal the real behavior of the system and applications.

In the next step, obtained empirical data is analyzed to identify optimization potential in the source code and on the system. As execution of each instruction requires some resources, the code areas must be rated. First, code regions requiring a significant portion of the run-time (or system resources and resulting energy consumption) are identified. Once the issues are identified, alternative realizations are developed which tend to mitigate the problems. Then, tuning potential of those hot spots is assessed

---

[11] Assuming annual costs of 2,000,000 €, one minute uptime costs about 3.80 € for the whole system.

1.1. Individual Approach

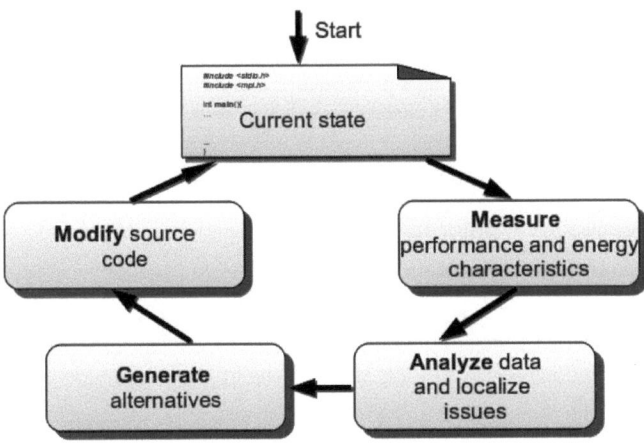

Figure 1.7.: *Closed loop of optimization and tuning [MMK⁺12].*

based on possible performance gains/power reductions considering the time to modify the application code. Changing a few code lines of the main execution base to improve performance is more efficient than to recode whole processes which might be active for only a small percentage of the total runtime. From the viewpoint of the computing facility, already optimizing a program by 1 % increases the benefit of the hardware (because it runs 24 hours a day for months).

At the end of a loop the current source code gets modified to verify the improvement of the new design. The systems gets re-evaluated in the next cycle until potential gains are either too small because the results are already near-optimal, or the time to change the source code outweighs the improvements.

During the optimization process, several points have to be addressed:

- the improvement of algorithmic and/or programming inefficiencies,
- the quality of system or third-party software libraries,
- the match of the software environment and the hardware system itself to maximize the efficiency.

Therefore, the analysis process is often complex and requires a sophisticated set of methodologies and tools.

The goal of this thesis is to design and evaluate tool extensions for power and energy analysis in addition to the already existing performance engineering approaches in parallel systems. The tool extensions must be able to measure the impact of different algorithms or implementation choices in terms of power. According to Figure 1.6b, the node power consumption is highly dependent on the utilization of the different devices. Thus, the first step is to classify different hardware usage pattern and their impact on the power consumption. Most high performance computing applications utilize different devices in phases due to the parallelization scheme. In general, phases can be classified as

- compute intensive, mainly the processing unit is utilized
- communication intensive, mainly the interconnection is utilized
- and I/O intensive, mainly the I/O subsystem is utilized.

Typically, the application phase intensity does not result in the utilization of only one device type. Consider *Ethernet* as interconnection type: The TCP/IP packages have to be packed and unpacked, which is usually done by the main processing unit. Additionally, compute phases can be further classified as *memory-bound*, if the calculation has to move large amounts of data from or to the main memory. The memory speed is normally slower than the processor speed, thus it is possible that the processing unit has to wait for the memory subsystem.

The different phases result in different utilization of the devices – usually not all devices are utilized at the same time. This motivates the investigation of hardware power saving modes as known from mobile or desktop computing. In detail, application phases have to be identified where the usage of hardware power saving modes reduces the power consumption without significant impacts on the application runtime. Otherwise, it is possible that the total energy for the application increases due to the definition of energy (see equation 1.1): If the runtime increase outweighs the power decrease, the total energy increases.

$$E = P * t \tag{1.1}$$

This tradeoff is known as *Energy-Performance-Tradeoff* and has to be considered carefully for every optimization. In addition to the application slow-down by lowering the operating speed, the transition between the power saving modes itself has to be considered, too. Depending on the specific device and mode, the transition induces costs in terms of time (the device may become unavailable) and energy (disk platters have to be spun up, which needs a non-negligible amount of energy). Out of this, mode requirements from different application processes have to be consolidated to avoid fast transitions between power saving modes of (shared) resources. Additionally, it is not possible to switch the hardware power saving modes from within the application without running the application itself in root context. Due to these issues, the design and implementation of a framework for switching hardware power saving modes from within parallel applications is necessary.

Analyzing the tradeoff between energy and performance requires correlation of the application details, the hardware usage, the power saving modes and the power consumption. This correlation promises significant knowledge improvement about the tradeoff through

all software layers. There already exist several tools for performance engineering which cover at least the performance aspects. Thus, for these tools extensions will be designed and implemented for the correlation of additional, energy-related, metrics.
The resulting tool set enables us to measure performance and energy-related characteristics to localize performance and power issues in parallel applications. Additionally, the framework allows us to increase the energy efficiency of parallel applications with manual code instrumentation. This is, in particular, interesting for widely used applications, libraries and operating system middleware.

The rest of this thesis is structured as follows.
Chapter 2 researches fundamental power saving modes of high performance hardware. The component breakdown includes the Central Processing Unit, the General Purpose Graphic Processing Unit, the main memory, the Input/Output system and the interconnect system between the computing nodes. To adjust the power saving modes of these components, available interfaces including the Advanced Configuration and Power Interface are discussed in detail. Additionally, durability issues due to the fast transitions between the power saving modes are briefly discussed.
Using hardware supporting several power saving mechanisms a test infrastructure which consists of five AMD and five Intel nodes is described in Chapter 3. Each of these nodes is connected to power measurement equipment which makes it possible to investigate the power saving potential of the specific test hardware. For this investigation, several idle and load measurements are performed for the two different architectures in different power saving modes. The impact of operating system mechanisms like processor governors or processor idle states are analyzed with the SPECPower benchmark[12]. Additionally, different types of load are evaluated in terms of power and energy consumption dependent on different power saving modes of all different hardware devices.
Based on the demonstrated potential for energy saving, Chapter 4 introduces dynamic switching strategies for reducing parallel application power consumption. Since statically switching the power saving mechanisms usually increases the application runtime, dynamic switching strategies are required. Appropriate application phases that result in idle or partly utilized hardware components are classified in this chapter. These software patterns resulting in these phases are used to describe the hardware-centric and the application-centric strategy, respectively, for exploiting the power saving mechanisms. For the first strategy, the decisions are based on sampled hardware characteristics like the component utilization or processor performance counters. This enables automatic phase detection using various heuristics as implemented in the Linux *ondemand* governor based on the utilization. The second strategy takes advantage of the specific application phases resulting in characteristic hardware utilization to switch the power modes. Following this approach, the different phases can be executed in different power modes via application instrumentation with the advantage of knowing the future utilization of the component.
To provide a software interface to instrument application phases, Chapter 5 describes

---

[12]http://www.spec.org/power_ssj2008/, last checked: March 2, 2013

1. Introduction

the design of the *eeDaemon* software. This software consists of an application interface which can be linked to the scientific application. The phase information is communicated to a server daemon, which runs on each computing node and performs the mode switches. This is necessary for two reasons. On the one hand, the power mode for shared resources has to be negotiated by the different processes. On the other hand, the adjustment of the power modes requires more administrative privileges – thus only the *eeDaemon* server has to run in root context.

Chapter 6 describes tool extensions to correlate the scientific application with energy-related metrics. This includes metrics like hardware utilization or processor performance counters to identify and classify application phases of interest, but also the hardware power saving modes to evaluate the application instrumentation and the result on the device performance. Additionally, the power consumption is correlated with the application since the power consumption is essential for the identification as well as for the evaluation. Furthermore, the chapter describes the chosen tracing approach followed by the exemplary post-mortem visualization of the traced metrics. In detail, the *HD-Trace* and *VampirTrace* tracing environments are extended to provide these kinds of measurements. For visualization of the trace files, *Sunshot* and *Vampir* are used.

Exploiting the developed extensions, several scientific applications are analyzed in Chapter 7 to evaluate the whole approach of this thesis. Using an energy-efficiency benchmark, typical hardware usage patterns are identified to characterize the workload and the impact on the power consumption. Furthermore, the tradeoff between energy and performance is evaluated in detail. Based on this analysis, four parallel applications are examined using the developed tool extensions:

- *partdiff-par*, a partial differential equation solver,
- *swim*, a Shallow Water modeling for weather prediction,
- MPIOM, the Max-Planck-Institute Ocean Model,
- and GETM, the General Estuarine Transport Model.

Appropriate application phases are instrumented using the *eeDaemon* interface to reduce the power consumption with the final goal to save energy for the whole application run on the test cluster.

Finally, Chapter 8 summarizes related work in the field of *Green HPC* while Chapter 9 concludes this thesis, including the description of future work.

2. Hardware Mechanism

High performance computing hardware supports multiple power saving mechanisms comparable to mobile devices which can be exploited if not fully utilized. This chapter breaks a typical high performance computing cluster down into its components and discusses the power saving mechanisms for each manageable device. Components with a low power consumption and/or no manageable power saving mode are only briefly discussed. Furthermore, only components on node level are discussed, additional infrastructure like cooling environment is out of the scope of this chapter. The main goal is to introduce all power consuming components of a high performance computing system including their interfaces to existing power saving mechanisms for future exploitation.

The highly parallel infrastructure of high performance computing environments works well for highly scalable applications with a high degree of parallelism. Unfortunately, the higher the count of processing units or the less efficient the resource usage, the data transfer between the different resources increases. Data needs to be transferred between different processing cores, between a processing core and the main memory or, in the worst case, between two computing nodes. This data transfer is expensive in terms of waiting times – corresponding resources have to wait for the completion of each data transfer.

Additionally, typical high performance applications do not need all hardware devices at the same time: Most applications operate in phases utilizing only a subset of devices.

This issue is originally addressed by the *Advanced Configuration and Power Interface*[1] (ACPI) specification. The ACPI specification describes the structures and mechanisms necessary to design directed power management and to make advanced configuration architectures possible. In other words, the device performance and power consumption is adjusted to the current device utilization.

2.1. Component Overview

To adjust the device performance and power consumption, most hardware devices in a high performance computing system support various power saving states. This section provides a brief overview of the mechanisms, more details of design techniques for system-level dynamic power management can be found here [BBDM00].

---

[1] http://www.acpi.info/spec50.htm/, last checked: March 2, 2013

2.1.1. Central Processing Unit

The central processing unit (CPU) usually consumes the lion's share of the power consumption in a high performance computing system. Correspondingly, the processor has the most hardware mechanisms for reducing the power consumption on the one hand, on the other hand most research focuses on the efficient exploration of these modes. Before studying the hardware mechanisms in detail, Equation 2.1 breaks down the total power consumption (P_{total}) of a multi-core processor into its components [Sey11].

$$P_{total} = \#cores \left(P_{dyn} + P_{leak} + P_{short} \right) + uncore \qquad (2.1)$$

P_{short} is the power caused by a short-circuit current which flows from the supply to the ground during a transition period of input signals. [HOT96]. However, P_{short} only occurs during signal transitions and is negligible for the total chip power consumption [MFMB02]. P_{leak} on the other hand is the gradual loss of energy from charged capacitors or when current leaks out of the intended circuit. It is possible that leakage power drains up to 20 % of P_{total} [BAEP08]. Even if this is a high percentage, P_{leak} can be considered as constant and can thus be disregarded for dynamic power saving modes. On the contrary, P_{dyn} is the power used to actually charge and discharge the capacitance, composed of gate and interconnect capacitance. The higher this dynamic switching current is, the faster capacitive loads can be charged and discharged, enabling a better performing circuit [Sey11]. Additionally, recent processors include more and more components being formerly part of the mainboard. Those components moved to the *uncore* area of the chip next to the computing cores. The main reasons are latency reduction (integration of the memory controller), power efficiency (separate power control unit) and better scalability with many cores. The uncore area can include the memory-controller, the L3 cache or several interconnection links. Based on the concrete architecture (especially the number of cores), the uncore components can consume a considerable amount of the total power consumption.

However, nowadays P_{dyn} dominates the processor power consumption, but it is possible that P_{leak} will grow strongly in the future due to further miniaturization [LHL05]. P_{dyn} consists of several factors: The frequency f, the voltage V, the level of chip activity α and a factor C dependent on the capacitance of the chip as stated in Equation 2.2 [MKL10].

$$P_{dyn} = \alpha \, C \, V^2 \, f \qquad (2.2)$$

To reduce P_{dyn}, two approaches are feasible: Reducing the frequency and reducing the voltage. The minimum voltage is dependent on the frequency – high frequencies require higher voltages and low frequencies lower voltages. Correspondingly, for a fixed frequency the definition of the voltage is crucial for power consumption, because the voltage goes quadratically into the equation. The needed voltage depends on several circumstances like chip design and temperature. The reduction of the voltage to the minimum threshold is also known as *Near-Threshold Computing* (NTC).

Besides to these design principles, there exist two main power saving mechanisms. The first mechanism introduces a set of frequencies for different performance requirements, thus these states are named processor performance states. Each frequency is associated with a voltage requirement resulting in several operating states with the goal to reduce the power loss through leakage. On the processor side, this mechanism is named Dynamic Frequency and Voltage Scaling (DVFS) and is explained in the following section. The second mechanism disables the clock (clock gating) or interrupts the power consumption (power gating) which results in sleep states named processor power states.

Processor Performance States

Coming originally from the mobile area with varying processing workload and increased focus on power consumption, DVFS is now implemented in almost all desktop and server processors. Because the lower frequency also decreases the performance, these frequency states are named *Processor Performance States* (*P-States*) by the ACPI standard [HIM+11]. The maximum performance state is labeled P0, the next lower one P1 and so on. Intel named this mechanism *Enhanced Intel SpeedStep® Technology* (EIST), while AMD named it *Power NOW*. According to Intel [Int09b], the key features of the technology is to provide multiple voltage and frequency operating points for optimal performance at the lowest power. The voltage and frequency selection is software controlled by writing to processor *Machine Specific Registers* (MSRs): If the target frequency is higher than the current frequency, the voltage is ramped up in steps and the *Phase Lock Loop* (PLL) then locks to the new frequency. If the target frequency is lower than the current frequency, the PLL locks to the new frequency and the voltage is changed. Software transitions are accepted at any time. If a previous transition is in progress, the new transition is deferred until the previous transition completes. The processor controls voltage ramp rates internally to ensure smooth transitions. Low transition latency and large number of transitions possible per second, the processor core (including shared cache) is unavailable for less than $2\,\mu s$ during the frequency transition. In conclusion, it takes time (and energy) to switch to another operating point. Consequently, wrong decisions can either harm performance or power consumption. In addition to the reduction of the nominal frequency, it is also possible to increase the frequency, which is named *Turbo Boost* (for Intel [Int08], introduced with the Nehalem architecture) and *Turbo CORE* (for AMD, introduced with the Bulldozer architecture), respectively. The implementation varies with each processor generation, in general a temporarily frequency increase is possible if electrical and thermal conditions are met. This is usually only possible for a subgroup of cores – providing higher performance for one group and reducing performance for the rest which results in performance benefits for some workloads. As exemplarily shown in figure 2.1, due to the processor architecture voltage and frequency can not always be chosen freely for each single core. It is possible that cores share frequency and voltage (Figure 2.1a), frequency but not voltage (Figure 2.1b) or do not share either frequency or voltage (Figure 2.1c). Thus, it is not always possible to use different frequencies for different cores – the concrete implementation is heavily processor and architecture dependent.

2. Hardware Mechanism

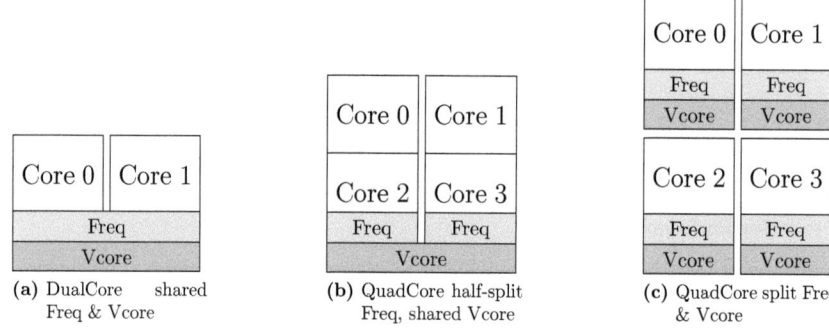

Figure 2.1.: *DVFS architectures in multicore-processors [Sey11]*

Processor Power States

ACPI defines the power state of system processors as being either active (executing) or sleeping (not executing) [HIM+11]. *Processor Power States (C-States)* are named C0, C1, C2, C3, ... Cn. The C0 power state is an active power state where the processor executes instructions. The higher the number, the lower the power consumption and the higher the latency to reach the active power state C0 again. For deeper sleep states, the latency can reach the range of 3 to 245 nanoseconds for the Intel Xeon X5560 series [Int11, Int09b]. The C1 state defines a sleeping state entered when all threads within a core execute a HLT instruction [MMK+12]. The processor transits to the C0 state upon occurrence of an interrupt. While in C1 state, the clock of the core is gated and is thus able to maintain the context of the system caches. The following states offers each improved power savings over the predecessor. Based on the current implementation of the processor architecture, specific processor power states influence also the caching behavior. If the state is deeper than C2, it is possible that the memory cache (level 3) is turned off or flushed, level 1 and 2 might be invalidated, too. Invalidation results in further performance decrease since the caches have to be repopulated. Table 2.1 on Page 27 gives a short overview over the implementation on the hardware side. Depending on the architecture and the concrete power state, power states can be applied per core or per socket.

Processor Throttling States

Besides to the already mentioned states, the processor supports *Processor Throttling States (T-States)* [HIM+11]. The throttling state is one of the three execution states that processors execute code in, the processors execution speed is reduced [MMK+12]. The purpose of the throttling states is to prevent the processor from overheating by lowering its temperature. This is done by introducing idle cycles in the processor which

Table 2.1.: *Processor power states overview based on [Tor08]. It is possible that different processor vendors implement the processor power states slightly different.*

State	Name	CPU implementation
C0	Operating State	CPU fully turned on
C1	Halt	Stops main internal clocks via software
C1E	Enhanced Halt	Stops main internal clocks via software and reduces voltage
C2	Stop Grant	Stops main internal clocks via hardware
C2	Stop Clock	Stops internal and external clocks via hardware
C2E	Extended Stop Grant	Stops main internal clocks via hardware and reduces voltage
C3	Sleep	Stops all internal clocks
C3	Deep Sleep	Stops all internal and external clocks
C3	AltVID	Stops all internal clocks and reduces voltage
C4	Deeper Sleep	Reduces voltage further
C5	Enhanced Deep Sleep	Reduces voltage even more and turns off the memory cache
C6	Deep Power Down	Reduces the internal voltage to any value, including 0 V

results in a reduced performance and temperature. Depending on the processor handling of the idle cycles, no power saving is associated with the throttling states. If no power saving can be reached with the throttling states, the states should be avoided if possible.

2.1.2. General Purpose Graphic Processing Unit

The *General Purpose Graphic Processing Unit* (GPGPU) is commonly used in today's HPC systems as accelerator. Similar to the central processing unit, the GPGPU has clock scaling, voltage scaling and clock gating mechanisms implemented. Common GPGPUs automatically reduces clock speed when running less demanding applications. This allows the GPU to switch to different voltage levels in addition to throttling clocks. Aggressive dynamic clock gating turns off unused blocks of the GPU to achieve the lowest operating power when (at least partially) idle. For the NVIDIA GPU, the corresponding power saving framework is named *PowerMizer* [NVI08]. This framework also include *On-Chip Thermal Management* and *PCI Express Bus Power Management*, the latter will be explained in Section 2.1.5.

2.1.3. Main Memory

For some HPC systems, main memory is a large contributor to the total power consumption. This is mainly based on the system architecture in terms of memory amount per processor core. The main memory power consumption is also dependent on the frequency and the voltage. D(V)FS can also be applied for the main memory, but this is usually not adaptable during the runtime. Supported operating points of frequency and voltage can be only selected before the system startup (via BIOS settings). However, depending on the hardware architecture, the memory controller frequency (and thus the memory frequency) is reduced when the processor adjust its frequency. Consequently, this reduces also the performance (in terms of memory bandwidth) and power consumption of the main memory.

In general, the server memory modules – usually *Registered Dual In-line Memory Modules* (RDIMMs) – support multiple electrical current levels (IDDs[2]) for different operations on the module. Multiplying this current with the voltage results in the DIMM power consumption. However, these states are exploited by the memory controller. Thus it is possible, to use only a subset of the memory ranks in a ready state, while the rest goes to a sleep mode (but still refreshing the memory cells). Disabling the refreshing of main memory (*Partial Array Self Refresh*, PASR) is only possible for mobile DRAM which is used in power sensitive environments, e.g. mobile phones. In this environment, the utilization is usually much lower and thus great power savings can be reached.

2.1.4. Input/Output System

Hard Disk Drives

Hard Disk Drives (HDDs) usually consume a lower percentage of the total power consumption. But in storage system HDDs can consume a considerable amount of power due to the increased number [CPB03]. Most expensive in terms of power consumption is the movement of the plattern around the spindle, but also the electronic components like the device cache consume a considerable amount of energy [HSRJ08]. However, the angular velocity ω of the motor has a quadratic effect on the power consumption (see Equation 2.3). K_e is the motor voltage constant and R is the motor resistance [GSKF03].

$$P_{\text{disk}} = \frac{K_e^2\, \omega^2}{R} \qquad (2.3)$$

Additional contributors to the power consumption are the tracking of the read/write head and the cache buffer of the disk.

Table 2.2.: *Hard disk power saving modes overview [Tec09]. Active and idle mode do not differ in terms of power saving modes (heads, spindle and buffer are in the same state).*

Power mode	Heads	Spindle	Buffer
Active	Tracking	Rotating	Enabled
Idle	Tracking	Rotating	Enabled
Standby	Parked	Stopped	Enabled
Sleep	Parked	Stopped	Disabled

---

[2] defined by the JEDEC consortium, http://www.jedec.org/, last checked: March 2, 2013

2.1. Component Overview

Typical hard disk drives provide programmable power management to provide greater energy efficiency as summarized in Table 2.2. The active (reading, writing or seeking) and idle mode do not differentiate in terms of power management. The first power saving mode (standby) stops the spindle from rotating, thus the heads have to be parked. It is also possible that the spindle just lowers its *Revolutions per Minute* (RPM). In both, idle and standby mode, the drive accepts all commands and returns to active mode when disc access is necessary. In the deeper sleep mode, the disk cache is also disabled. The drive leaves the sleep mode after it receives a hard or soft reset from the host. Each step reduces the power consumption, but also increases the wakeup latency of the device. In addition to these sleep modes, it is also possible to optimize the access pattern to the disk via *Native Command Queuing* (NCQ). This reduces the movement of the head which results in a decreased power consumption since less accelerating and decelerating is necessary in active mode.

Solid State Drives

Additional to traditional hard disks, *Solid State Drive* (SSD) usage increases in datacenters. A Solid State Drive is a flash-based semiconductor memory device. Comparable to main memory, an electrical cell stores the information. In opposition to typical main memory, which is volatile and needs to be refreshed, flash cells are non-volatile. Based on the organization of the flash's transistors, the differentiation in NAND and NOR flash is possible. Today, NAND flash is commonly used for storing large data amounts. Due to the random access to the memory cells organized by the drive's controller, SSDs can achieve a multiple of the performance of traditional HDDs for reading operations. Furthermore, since no moving parts are needed, the latency is much slower and the power consumption is decreased. If no access to memory cells occur, the power consumed by the flash memory is negligible (for almost all flash types). Hence, in today's SSDs no additional power saving mechanisms are implemented.

2.1.5. Interconnection Systems

Device Interconnection

For multi-socket systems, the interconnection between different processor sockets is crucial for the total system performance. Thus, the interconnection type changes with almost each new processor architecture. In the following, two interconnection types are introduced used by Intel and AMD, respectively, the *Quick Path Interconnect* (QPI) and *HyperTransport* (HT). HyperTransport also facilitates power management as it is ACPI compliant. Changes in processor sleep states can signal changes in device states, e.g. powering off disks when the processor goes to sleep. HyperTransport 3.0 added further capabilities to allow a centralized power management controller to implement power management policies. QPI on the other hand is a point-to-point interconnection, usually including the processor sockets, the memory controller and the chipset. Several QPI *Link Power States* (*L-States*) are available: L0, L0s and L1 [Int09a]. The power states disable a subset of data channels – thus the (bi)directional transmission speed is decreased. The further connection of peripheral components (like GPGPUs) to the main processor is usually implemented via *Peripheral Component Interconnect Express* (PCIe). PCIe supports the same power states named *Active State Power Management* (ASPM) [Int02], but only L0s and L1 are used during active state power management, at least by Intel. The power saving opportunities during the very low latency power state L0s include most of the transceiver circuitry as well as the clock gating of at least the link layer logic. For the low latency power state L1, the power saving opportunities include the shutdown of most of the transceiver circuitry, clock gating of most PCI Express architecture logic, and finally the shutdown of the PLL. Configuration of attached devices into *Device States* (D-States) will automatically cause the PCIe links to transition to the appropriate L-States. *Serial Advanced Technology Attachment* (SATA) is one of the possible interconnection of hard drives and the mainboard chipset. SATA *Link Power Management* (LPM) switches the physical layer (PHY) of the connection into one out of two energy saving states. These states are independent of possible power saving mechanisms of the attached devices. The SATA-controller and the attached device negotiate the appropriate power saving mode, if no further transfer data is in the corresponding queues. Usually, the usage of the LPM modes of the interconnect are followed by the switching of the device power mode by the device itself – if no data is ready to be transfered, both the link and the device can be switched to a power saving mode.

Node-to-Node

In high performance computing systems, a broad variety of node interconnection types exist. Most common types include Infiniband (fibre channel) and 10/40 Gbit Ethernet. The best interconnection type is usually the most expensive one. This subsection focuses only on Ethernet, since Ethernet will be used for all following experiments.
Ethernet devices can usually adjust the speed of the transmission of network packets. Originally, this is a backward compatibility issue – to communicate at the least common denominator. This speed decrease reduces also the power consumption slightly. In addition to the general slowdown of the network processing, the internal network processor can be slowed down (e.g. in phases with less network activity) to reduce the power consumption. If the device is idle, it is further possible to use power gating for several components (e.g. power gating the processor disables the (de-)coding of the signals). This mechanism is in particular interesting if the device is unused (no cable connected) and is replicated at switch side. The switch automatically detects which network ports are connected to an active system (e.g. a computer that's switched on compared to a computer that's switched off or in standby), and only provides power to the ports that are active. Additionally, the switch can vary the amperage (signal intensity) depending on the length of wire between the switch and another device on the network[3]. Unfortunately, none if these power saving modes is applied in today's server network cards

---

[3]D-Link named this technology *Green Technology*

except for the network speed reduction for compatibility reasons.

2.2. Interfaces

The exploitation of the aforementioned power saving modes of the different hardware components requires a software interface which allows the programmer to interact with the hardware power saving modes. In the following, the interface of each hardware device is discussed briefly to allow manual interaction with the hardware. For the Linux operating system the /proc and /sys interfaces, respectively, can monitor and manage most of the hardware states. For the processor, the P-States, C-States and the T-States are the main power saving mechanisms. All mechanisms can be disabled in the *Basic Input/Output System* (BIOS) before the *Operating System* (OS) is loaded. Most systems support the fine-granular adjustment of the modes such as disabling all C-States deeper than C3 or disabling the turbo mode (as specific P-State). This is in particular interesting for system administrators, who can control the global system behavior and eliminate additional sources for defects. Since the decision about the specific C- and T-States is based on load and temperature measurements of the processor chip itself, no further management interface to the operating system exists. The decision about the concrete P-State is software-based (e.g. user-specific decision to reduce the processor power consumption on a mobile device to increase battery lifetime) and thus manageable by the OS. To manage these processor states, the corresponding Linux kernel module has to be loaded. In case of Intel processors, this is the cpufreq module, for AMD processors the powernow module is needed. Using this interface, the operating system can manage the states using multiple strategies. With the Linux commands cpufreq-info and cpufreq-set the strategy and the frequencies can be monitored and changed for each logical processor, respectively.

```
$ cpufreq-set -c 0-4 -f 2800000
```

The above example requests the frequency of processor cores 0,1,2,3 and 4 to be at 2,800,000 kHz. The turbo mode is referred to a special frequency +1 MHz: if 2,800 MHz is the maximum frequency, 2,801 MHz indicates the turbo mode. Due to further hardware constraints (e.g. shared frequency and voltage between cores, see Figure 2.1) it might not be possible for the hardware to realize the request. The hardware always picks the least common denominator out of all requests. The usage of the C- and T-States is also reported to the operating system. But the C-States reported by the OS are not necessarily the same as available at the hardware level – usually all hardware states deeper or equal than the C3 state are summarized by the operating system.

Furthermore, both AMD/ATI and NVIDIA provide frameworks that allow the upper limit on the frequency and voltage of the GPGPU to be scaled by the user.

The main memory voltage can be adjusted in the BIOS to reduce the power consumption, but unfortunately no further interface (especially to the operating system) is available. Furthermore, for some hardware architectures, the memory controller frequency (and thus the memory frequency) is reduced when the processor adjust its frequency.

2. Hardware Mechanism

The hard disk power saving modes of the spinning drives can be adjusted via `hdparm` which reads and writes the ATA parameters of the drive. The program allows to check the drive state and to change to sleep and standby mode, respectively. Additionally, it is possible to adjust the internal idle timeouts of the device – if no requests arrives for a specified threshold, the devices transits to the next deeper power saving mode.

```
$ hdparm -C /dev/sda

/dev/sda:
 drive state is:   active/idle

$ hdparm -y /dev/sda

$ hdparm -Y /dev/sda
```

In the above example, the first command checks the drive state, while the second and third command forces the drive to standby and sleep mode, respectively. `hdparm` is available via SourceForge[4].

The power saving modes for QPI, HT, PCIe and SATA as device interconnections are only manageable via the BIOS and can be disabled or enabled, respectively.

The Ethernet power saving modes (speed and duplex mode) can be modified with the `ethtool` program. Usually, the auto-negotiation mode decides about the network speed and duplex mode.

```
$ ethtool -s eth0 speed 100 duplex full autoneg off
```

The above command disables the auto-negotiation mode on the one hand, on the other hand the card speed is set to 100 Mbit and full duplex mode. `ethtool` is also available via SourceForge[5].

Each of the described commands needs administrator privileges.

2.3. Durability Issues

Besides to the positive impact on the power consumption, the power saving mechanisms might also impact the durability of each device type. Reducing the processing frequency and corresponding voltage also reduces the chip's temperature, which should have positive impact on the durability since the chip is designed for higher temperatures. The only possible influence might be the diverse temperature gradient when some cores run at high temperature and others at low temperature. Furthermore, too frequent switching might harm the voltage regulator located on the mainboard – but this component is designed for exactly this task. However, controlled switching of the P-States should not harm the hardware at all.

The usage of the disk sleep and standby mode results into frequent decelerating and accelerating of the spindle, which could result into a increased failure rate over a longer

---
[4]http://sourceforge.net/projects/hdparm/, last checked: March 2, 2013
[5]http://sourceforge.net/projects/gkernel/, last checked: March 2, 2013

time frame. In a recent study realized by Google[6], the impact after three years of frequent switching was a increased failure rate of 2 %. After two years, no impact was measurable. Thus, the impact of controlled switching should be negligible for the disk's lifetime.

Switching the network speed is the most critical issue, since the switching itself can take several seconds. If the task is interrupted, the network card might stay in an undefined state, which can only be resolved by (re-)setting the device parameters. No additional implications on the network card's durability occurred during this study.

High performance computing hardware – despite its name – supports a broad variety of performance and sleep modes to be exploited by the system or the user. In detail, the CPU, the hard disk and the interconnect provide several power saving mechanisms and interfaces, mainly based on the ACPI standard. Furthermore, the impact of the power saving mechanisms on the device durability is negligible if wisely used. Unfortunately, the mechanisms for the power management of network devices are very limited in the server space, even if promising research is conducted [NPI+08, GS07b, AHC+09, GS07a] and will possible be available in the future. Additionally, the main memory has significant potential for power saving as evaluated by several simulations [DGMB07, DFG+11].

---

[6] http://static.googleusercontent.com/external_content/untrusted_dlcp/research.google.com/en//archive/disk_failures.pdf, last checked: March 2, 2013

3. Power and Energy Saving Potential

The last chapter described available hardware mechanisms to reduce the power consumption. In this chapter, the focus is on the exploitation of these mechanisms to measure the real power saving potential for various hardware devices. A research cluster is designed using energy-efficient components supporting a broad range of the power saving mechanisms. This cluster is attached to a sophisticated measurement infrastructure to provide power measurements on node level. Using this infrastructure, the power saving potential of different hardware components is evaluated under different load scenarios.

3.1. Test Infrastructure

The test infrastructure *eeClust* (energy-efficient Cluster Computing)[1] consists of a small HPC cluster and additional power measurement devices. The concrete test setup is shown in Figure 3.1.

The HPC cluster consists of 10 compute nodes, 2 I/O nodes and one head node. The nodes are connected via 1,000 Mbit Ethernet to exchange data between the nodes. In addition to the communication and storage network, the nodes are connected via a 100 Mbit *Intelligent Platform Management Interface* (IPMI)[2] network for administration of the nodes. This network can also be used for reading out sensors connected to the *Baseboard Management Controller* (BMC) of the node's mainboard without interaction of additional hardware components like the processor or the main network. Figure 3.2 visualizes the cluster in a physical view.

The compute node architecture itself is as follows: The 10 node compute part of the cluster is split into 5 Intel Nehalem nodes (Xeon X5560) and 5 AMD Magny-Cours nodes (Opteron 6168) with the goal to analyze the architecture dependent energy-saving mechanisms. The Xeon nodes have 2 sockets, each with 4 cores and a processing frequency of 2.8 GHz. In addition to various C-States and P-States ranging from 1,600 MHz to 2,800 MHz, the X5560 processor also supports Turbo Boost in two steps, each with 133 MHz. Further, it is possible to enable throttling of the cores or to disable whole subgroups of cores in the system BIOS. Additionally, the Xeon nodes support *Symmetric Multithreading* (SMT) which results in 16 logical cores per node.

The Opteron nodes do not support SMP, but have a higher physical core count of 12 cores per socket with a frequency of 1.9 GHz. The AMD nodes support also a various

---
[1]Founded by the german ministry of education and reasearch (BMBF) under grant number 01IH08008E
[2]http://www.intel.com/design/servers/ipmi/, last checked: March 2, 2013

3. Power and Energy Saving Potential

Figure 3.1.: *Picture of test infrastructure eeClust with 10 computing nodes and 3 power measurement devices highlighted with a red rectangle.*

range of P-States, but no C-States except for the enhanced C1 mode (C1E). The P-States range from 800 MHz to 1,900 MHz, no Turbo CORE mode is supported. Also for the Opteron architecture, disabling of core groups in the system BIOS is possible.

To sum up, the cluster has a total compute capability of 120 processing cores split over 10 nodes and 2 architectures supporting various power saving modes.

Furthermore, the Intel and AMD nodes have a different memory setup. The Intel nodes have a total memory of 12 GByte and 3 memory channels per socket, which results in 2 GByte per memory channel and 1.5 GByte per core (with disabled SMT). The AMD nodes have 1.3 GByte of memory per core, which results in a total memory capacity of 32 GByte. Each of the four channels per socket is populated with 4 GBytes. The memory type is for both architectures DDR3 with 1,333 MHz. The additional hardware is similar for both architectures: Both use a Seagate Barracuda 7200 hard disk and

3.1. Test Infrastructure

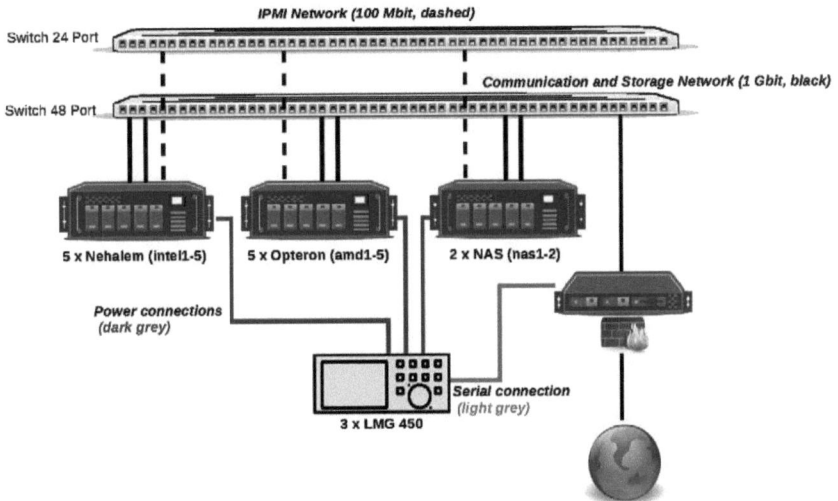

Figure 3.2.: *Physical view on the eeClust infrastructure.*

Gigabit Ethernet provided by the Intel chipset. Both device types support various power saving modes: The disk can be put into sleep and deep sleep mode, while the network card can reduce its speed and change the duplex mode. The existing power saving modes of the concrete hardware are only partially exploited by the operating system or the hardware itself. In our test environment, each of the cluster nodes is installed with openSUSE 11.2 using the *2.6.37-default* kernel. Usually, the P-States of the processor are adjusted to the system load, while the disk goes to sleep mode if idle for a defined threshold. The network power saving modes are not exploited at all.

Additionally, power measurement devices are connected to the research cluster. In general, two types of measurements are possible for measuring the power consumption: primary and secondary measurement [MMK+12]. Primary measurement means capturing the power consumption of nodes or servers as a whole. For this purpose, usually power measurement devices such as power meters are looped through between the *Power Distribution Unit* (PDU) and the power supply of the node. There exist a bunch of different power meters, which mainly differ in the count of measurement channels, the accuracy of the measurement, the interface to read the measurement values and, of course, the price. Table 3.1 gives an short overview about some device types.

The costs per measurement channel for each device type scales with the accuracy and the available interface types. While the external devices in general have a higher accuracy, in most cases a further software API is needed to extract the measurement values from the hardware interface. If the device supports some higher level protocols, like the *Simple Network Management Protocol* (SNMP), the fetching of the measurement data is in most

3. Power and Energy Saving Potential

Table 3.1.: *Example power measurement devices overview by type, internal accuracy, measurement interval, measurement channels and data interface [MMK+12].*

Device	ZES LMG [ZES]	WattsUp [Ele]	PX-5528 [Rar10]
Type	external	external	integrated
Accuracy	High	Low	Mid-Range
	(+/- 0.1%)	(+/- 1.5%)	(+/- 1.0%)
Interval	10 ms	1 s	1 s
Channels	1-8	1	24
Interface	Serial/Firewire	USB/LAN	Serial/LAN/SNMP

cases easier, but it is possible that the fetching interval and the measurement interval are different. If using integrated measurement devices in the PDU or the power supply, the advantage is the simple installation – the disadvantage the low measurement interval.

From a computer scientist's point of view, the power meters work all the same way: Every fixed timestep a measurement takes place, which results in discrete measurement values (in general, an interpolation of device internal measurements). These measurement values can be read from the device and can be further analyzed. The general problem when interpreting the data is the problem of buffers, conversion losses and load-dependency.

The relation of the input and the output power of the power supply (*efficiency*) of the computing nodes ranges from 60% up to over 95% for a *Switched-Mode Power Supply* (SMPS) [AH03]. However, the power supply efficiency depends on the concrete load. Usually, the efficiency is better for low and high utilization than for medium utilization. Additionally, the power supply has capacitive buffers to compensate for short term variation. Thus a short increase of the power consumption of the node devices may be unrecognized by a primary measurement device. Further the measurement device itself may have a buffer for the measurement values, so the correlation of the measurement data and the resources utilization has to be validated. In most cases, this is possible with timestamps provided by the measurement device on the one hand and the node on the other hand, potential communication delays have to be deducted. However, the breakdown to the component power consumption is in most cases difficult.

With secondary measurement, each outlet of the power supply can be measured separately. The simplest method are power supplies with integrated measurement devices which distribute the data for example via the *Power System Management Protocol* (PM-Bus)[3] or the IPMI interface. Unfortunately, only few power supply vendors integrate such capabilities.

Another approach is to use direct current sensor clamps and connect them to each outlet of the power supply [MMK+12]. These sensors use the *Hall Effect* to measure the power

---
[3] http://pmbus.org/, last checked: March 2, 2013

consumption contact-less. Each of these clamps has to be connected to further devices like a power meter or oscilloscope. There are two main problems: On the one hand, the general acceptable accuracy of about 2 % can not be guaranteed for low direct currents. On the other hand, this results in a large number of measurement devices, which is less practical for large-scale installations. Additionally, it is comparatively simple to measure the power consumption of a disk, because each disk has its own power connection – for the processors it is more difficult to determine the device power consumption. Some connections are shared with other devices (like the ATX connector) and each processor could be supplied by multiple connections. A possible solution are special system main boards that provide interfaces to measure the power consumption of each device.

However, in this test infrastructure, the node power consumption is measured, since the energy consumed between the power supply and the outlet is the energy which is charged by the electricity company. Thus, the setup measures the *real* power and includes potential inefficiencies in power conversion.

To measure the node power consumption to evaluate the potential of the power saving mechanisms each node (except for the head node) is connected to a power measurement channel. In detail, LMG 450 power meters are used with a measurement accuracy over 99.9 %. In Figure 3.1, the LMG 450 devices are highlighted with the red rectangle. The maximum frequency of the measurement devices is 20 Hz, which means 20 measurements per second (one measurement every 50 ms). Each LMG 450 has 4 measurement channels, thus 3 devices can measure the power of 12 cluster nodes. The power meters are connected to the head node via the serial interface, a developed software component called *PowerTracer* reads out the measurement values and saves them into a *postgresql* database. The software interface is described in Section 6.2.1.

3.2. Evaluation of Hardware Power Saving Modes

Each of the mentioned hardware components contributes to the node power consumption. For different system designs, the component breakdown might look very different [MGW09]. In datacenters, the most power consuming component is usually the main memory, because the nodes are used as virtualization hosts and need a large amount of memory per processing core. On the contrary, for high performance computing the focus is in almost every case on the processing power – thus the most energy is spend on the processor. Due to the processor consuming usually the lion's share of the power, the focus is clearly on this component. However, the power consumption varies based on the current load and the power saving mode of the specific component. In this section, each power saving mode of each component will be analyzed under different load scenarios.

Table 3.2 shows the measured AMD node power consumption for different P-States using the measurement infrastructure described in the last section. Additionally, the average socket voltage is measured via IPMI. All measurements are performed for the idle processor and the processor under load. For generating the load on all processing cores, a parallel partial differential equation solver is used which is further described in Section 7.2.1. If the P-State is increased, the processing frequency is decreased corresponding to

39

the ACPI specification. Correspondingly, the socket voltage as well as the node power consumption decreases. Interestingly, the socket voltage for the idle scenario is higher than under load – this can only be explained with an additional voltage supply which is not covered by the IPMI measurement. However, for the load scenario, the power consumption can be decreased from about 312 Watt to about 219 Watt (about 30 %) while the power saving for the idle processor is only about 7 %.

Table 3.2.: *Measured node power consumption and average socket voltage for AMD Opteron 6168 series.*

P-State	Frequency (MHz)	Socket Voltage (V)		Node power (W)	
		Load	Idle	Load	Idle
P0	1,900	1.07	1.12	314.3	113.4
P1	1,500	1.03	1.07	278.7	111.2
P2	1,300	1.00	1.04	257.5	109.6
P3	1,000	0.98	1.02	235.8	105.9
P4	800	0.97	0.99	219.4	105.2

For the Intel nodes (see Table 3.3 on Page 41), the power consumption under load can be decreased by almost 27 % if decreasing the frequency from 2,800 MHz to 1,600 MHz. In opposition to the Opteron nodes, the Xeon nodes have a constant power consumption if idle, the processing frequency seems to be disregarded. The reasons are the additional C-States of the processor.

Table 3.4 refers to the corresponding manual of the processor and shows the difference in processor power consumption for power gating as published by Intel. If the processor transits into C6 state, the processor power consumption can be decreased by almost 90 %. But power gating has also disadvantages: The state is only possible if the processor is completely idle. Furthermore, the L3 cache of the processor is flushed which might result in performance loss since the processor has to repopulate the caches again. To better evaluate the DVFS mechanisms Table 3.5 visualizes the same measurements with disabled C-States.

Now, the measured difference in power consumption is about 6 % and comparable to the Opteron measurements. Under full load, the C-States do not influence the power consumption (as expected). To sum up: If the processor is idle, power gating comes into place and reduces the power consumption even more as DVFS.

3.2. Evaluation of Hardware Power Saving Modes

Table 3.3.: *Measured node power consumption and average socket voltage for Intel Xeon X5560 series. The processor C-States are enabled in the system BIOS.*

P-State	Frequency (MHz)	Socket Voltage (V) Load	Idle	Node power (W) Load	Idle
P0 (Turbo)	2,800-3,066	1.18	0.94	340.4	133.1
P0	2,800	1.06	0.94	288.5	133.1
P1	2,667	1.05	0.94	270.6	133.1
P2	2,533	1.03	0.94	257.7	133.0
P3	2,400	1.02	0.94	246.3	133.0
P4	2,267	1.00	0.94	237.2	132.9
P5	2,133	0.98	0.94	228.2	133.0
P6	2,000	0.97	0.94	219.3	133.0
P7	1,867	0.96	0.94	211.3	133.1
P8	1,733	0.94	0.93	203.7	133.1
P9	1,600	0.93	0.93	196.7	133.0

Table 3.4.: *Processor package C-State power specifications for the Intel Xeon X5560 series [Int09b].*

C-State	Power (W)
C0	95
C1E	30
C3	26
C6	10

3. Power and Energy Saving Potential

Table 3.5.: *Measured node power consumption and average socket voltage for Intel Xeon X5560 series. The processor C-States are disabled in the system BIOS.*

P-State	Frequency (MHz)	Socket Voltage (V) Load	Idle	Node power (W) Load	Idle
P0 (Turbo)	2,800-3,066	1.18	1.19	338.8	178.9
P0	2,800	1.06	1.08	285.4	166.5
P1	2,667	1.05	1.06	270.5	159.8
P2	2,533	1.03	1.05	257.9	158.2
P3	2,400	1.02	1.03	246.1	156.3
P4	2,267	1.00	1.02	236.5	154.9
P5	2,133	0.98	1.00	227.7	153.4
P6	2,000	0.97	0.99	219.0	152.1
P7	1,867	0.96	0.97	211.2	150.6
P8	1,733	0.94	0.96	203.3	149.6
P9	1,600	0.93	0.94	196.5	148.6

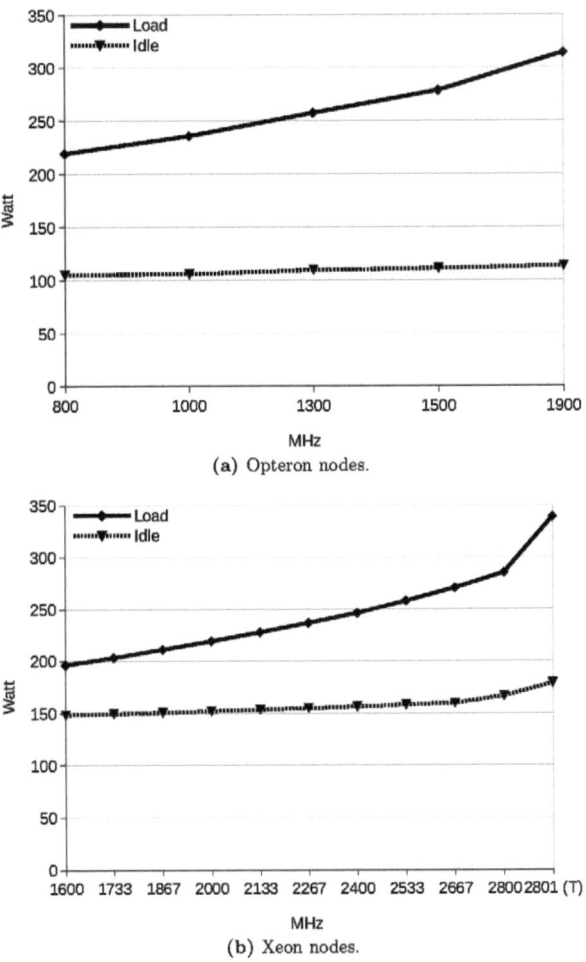

Figure 3.3.: *Power consumption for Opteron and Xeon nodes depending on P-State and utilization. The Intel Xeon C-States are disabled in the system BIOS.*

3. Power and Energy Saving Potential

Figures 3.3a and 3.3b on Page 43 visualize the measurements for the Opteron and Xeon nodes, respectively. For both architectures, the DVFS power saving potential under full load is much higher than without load. Of course this potential is highly dependent on the kind of load (e.g. floating point or integer operations, divide or multiply operations, ...), but also on the concrete utilization level. One benchmark addressing several utilization levels of a server workload is the SPECPower benchmark[4] set up by the *Standard Performance Evaluation Corporation* (SPEC). This benchmark consists of only one subset of server workloads: the performance of server side Java. However, the SPECPower benchmark is an industry-standard power-performance benchmark and thus also used in high performance computing environments to measure the power efficiency of computing nodes. Figures 3.4 and 3.5 on Page 46 show the benchmark results with and without DVFS for different load levels, the utilization of the processor is decreased in 10 % steps. The load is measured in ssj_ops, the power consumption in Watt and the power efficiency in ssj_ops per Watt for each level.

---

[4]http://www.spec.org/power_ssj2008/, last checked: March 2, 2013

3.2. Evaluation of Hardware Power Saving Modes

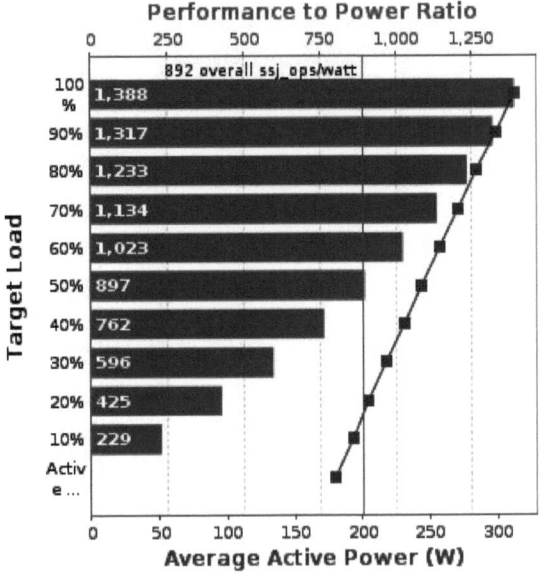

(a) P-States disabled.

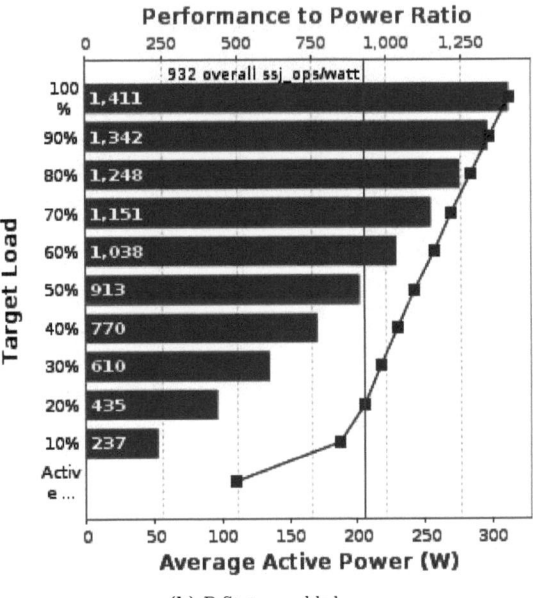

(b) P-States enabled.

Figure 3.4.: *SPECPower Measurements for AMD Opteron nodes with and without P-States [Min09].*

3. Power and Energy Saving Potential

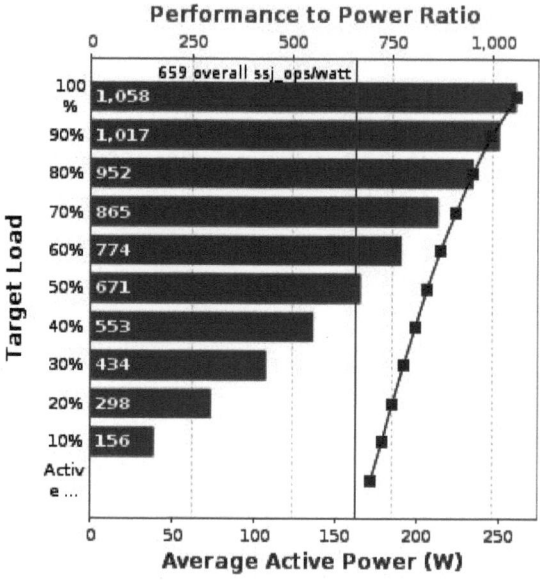

(a) P-States disabled.

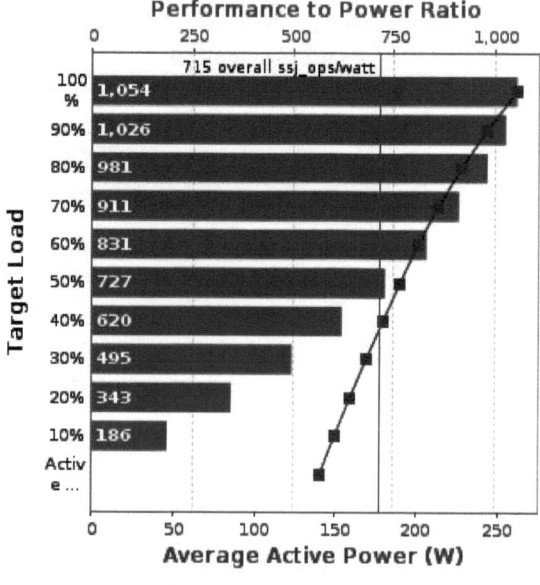

(b) P-States enabled.

Figure 3.5.: *SPECPower Measurements for Intel Xeon nodes with and without P-States. The Intel Xeon C-States are disabled in the system BIOS [Min09].*

For both architectures, enabling DVFS increases the power efficiency without any recognizable decreases in performance. Additionally, the C1E state of the Opteron node reduces the power consumption further if idle (referring to *Active [Idle]* in the corresponding figure).

Unfortunately, the SPECPower workload does not really reflect a typical high performance computing workload. For HPC, especially the ratio between compute-intensive and memory-intensive operations is interesting. This ratio can be measured in processor operations per byte transferred from the memory (operations per Byte, OPB). If the ratio is small, the workload is considered *memory-bound* (the processor waits for data from the memory). Correspondingly, a high ratio is considered *cpu-bound* (less interaction with the main memory).

In Figure 3.6, the energy is measured which is needed to perform workloads with different OPB values for the multiplication of two double values with different processing frequencies.

3. Power and Energy Saving Potential

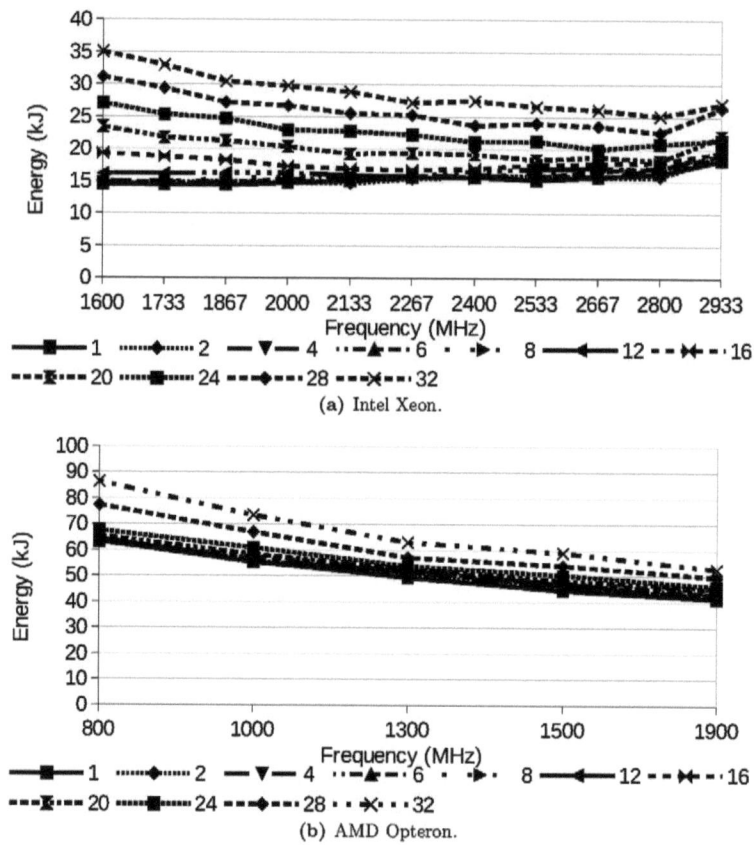

Figure 3.6.: *Energy consumption of the Intel Xeon and AMD Opteron nodes for different workloads. Each workload is executed with different processor frequencies (X-axis). The workloads differ in terms of OPB values (memory-boundness) for the multiplication of two double values. Each specific workload is represented by one line in the plot [MMKK12].*

For the Intel nodes, increasing the processing frequency results in lower energy measurements for high OPB values. Due to the higher processing frequency, more multiplications can be processed in a smaller amount of time – thus the energy decreases. For lower OPB values, the energy remains constant or even increases with the frequency. The benefit of increasing the processing frequency is negligible – the processor has to wait for the memory most of the time and thus the increased power consumption affects the total energy in a negative way. Interestingly, the AMD nodes show a different behavior: Independent of the operation per Byte, the energy decreases with increasing the frequency. In terms of energy efficiency, it only makes sense to reduce the core frequency where the memory bandwidth remains high. Of course, this is only possible if the memory bandwidth is independent from the socket voltage – the memory subsystem has to have its own voltage regulator which does not seems to be the case for the AMD nodes. More in detail, Figure 3.7 displays the memory scaling with different processor frequencies for both architectures.

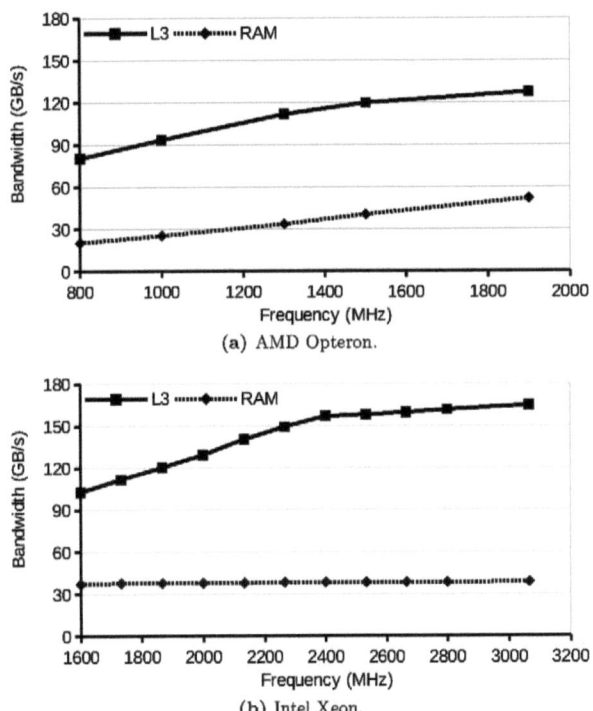

Figure 3.7.: *Memory and L3 cache scaling with different processor frequencies for the Intel Xeon and AMD Opteron nodes [MMKK12].*

These measurements clearly show the different hardware implementation for the two architectures. For the concrete Opteron architecture, reducing the processing frequency for memory-bound workloads does not improve the energy efficiency, while it does for the Xeon architecture.

In addition to pure computation, the processor can also be utilized in communication or I/O phases. In general, the distinction between the type of I/O (local or distributed) and

3. Power and Energy Saving Potential

communication (intra- oder inter-node) is necessary to assess the power saving potential. For the test infrastructure, distributed I/O results in inter-node communication, because all data is sent via the standard network interface card to the NFS server.

In the following, the DVFS potential for point-to-point and collective communication is analyzed in addition to local file input and output.

Figures 3.8a and 3.8b visualize the power saving potential for point-to-point communication using MPI_Send/MPI_Recv. Plotted are the relative values for runtime, power and energy for the minimum frequency setup using the maximum frequency setup as baseline. Further, different data sizes resulting in a different durations of measurements are plotted. The shortest setup with a data size of 4 MB has a absolute runtime for the maximum frequency setup of 0.8 s on the AMD nodes and 0.3 s on the Intel nodes. Doubling the data size means also doubling the runtime.

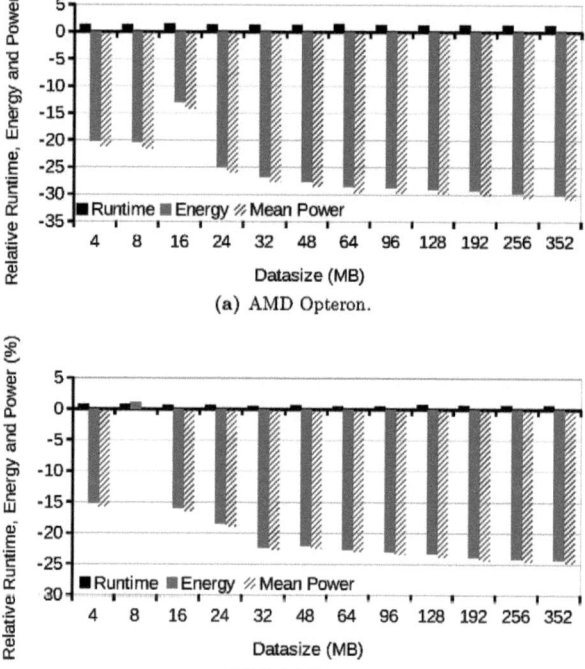

Figure 3.8.: *Relative runtime, energy and power for point-to-point communication using MPI_Send/MPI_Recv of the Intel Xeon and AMD Opteron nodes with varying data sizes. The baseline is the highest frequency setup for each architecture.*

3.2. Evaluation of Hardware Power Saving Modes

For both architectures, the power decrease is significant (up to 25 % for Intel and 30 % for AMD). In general, the longer the communication phase, the higher the power saving potential. The impact on the benchmark runtime is not significant (below 2 %), thus the energy-saving potential increases, too.

For the collective case visualized in Figure 3.9, the power decreases with the increase of the data size, but the runtime and thus the energy decreases slower. A data size of 16 MB results for the maximum frequency setup in an absolute runtime of 0.5 s and 0.3 s on the AMD and Intel nodes, respectively. For the Intel nodes, energy saving can be reached with a data size greater or equal 128 MB (2 s), while a data size of 256 MB (8 s) is still not big enough to reach savings on the AMD nodes. But for both architectures, the general trend is comparable. The explanation for the slower development on the AMD nodes might be the higher core count resulting in more processes.

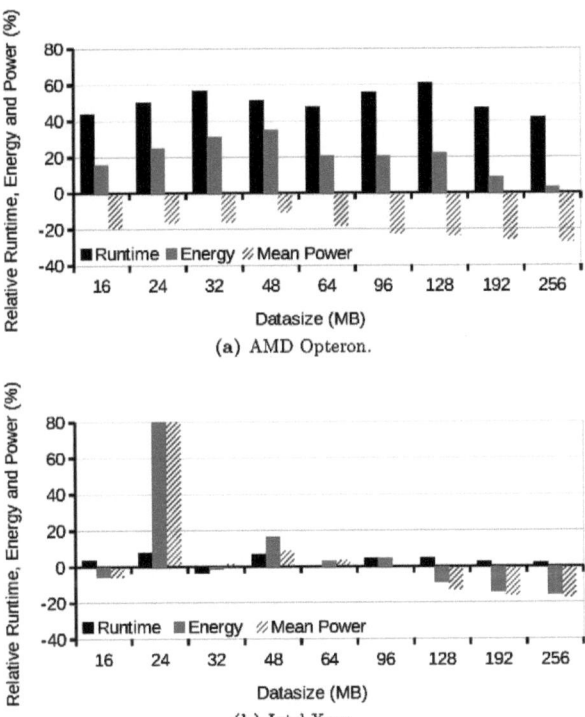

Figure 3.9.: *Relative runtime, energy and power for collective communication using MPI_Allreduce on the Intel Xeon and AMD Opteron nodes with varying data sizes. The baseline is the highest frequency setup for each architecture.*

3. Power and Energy Saving Potential

In addition to the communication behavior, file input and output power saving potential is analyzed. For the local I/O test cases, data is read or written from/to the local file system by each process. The amount of data is chosen to fill the main memory to avoid caching mechanisms during the measurements (700 MB and 650 MB for AMD and Intel, respectively). The granularity value decides about the amount of operations generated by the benchmark: Each operation has the size of granularity and is repeated until the data size is reached. Unfortunately, the results are not really trustworthy due to the complex structure of the I/O stack and the simplicity of the tests. However, Figures 3.10 and 3.11 on Page 54 indicate clear power and also energy-saving potential for read and write operations, respectively. Only the write measurements for AMD with a granularity of 700 MB do not show any energy-saving potential, indeed the energy is increased by almost 200 %. Anyway, a clear power saving potential is indicated by these first measurements and will be further analyzed in the following chapters.

3.2. Evaluation of Hardware Power Saving Modes

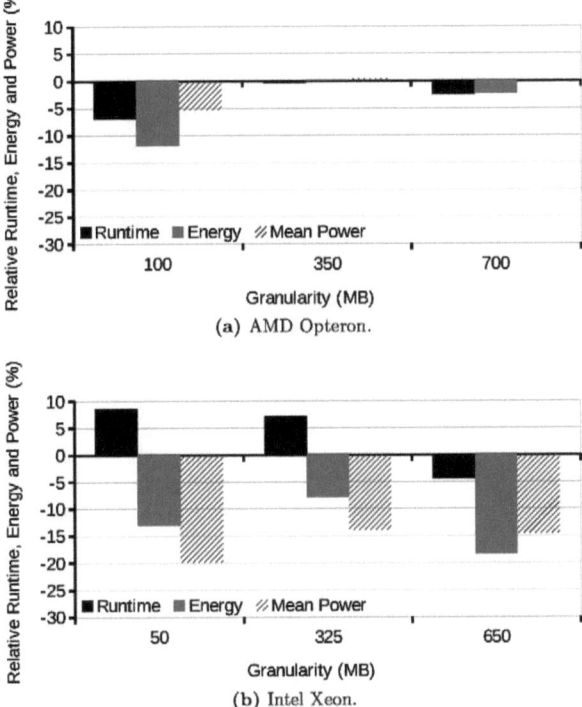

Figure 3.10.: *Relative runtime, energy and power for disk read operations of the Intel Xeon and AMD Opteron nodes with varying granularities. The baseline is the highest frequency setup for each architecture.*

3. Power and Energy Saving Potential

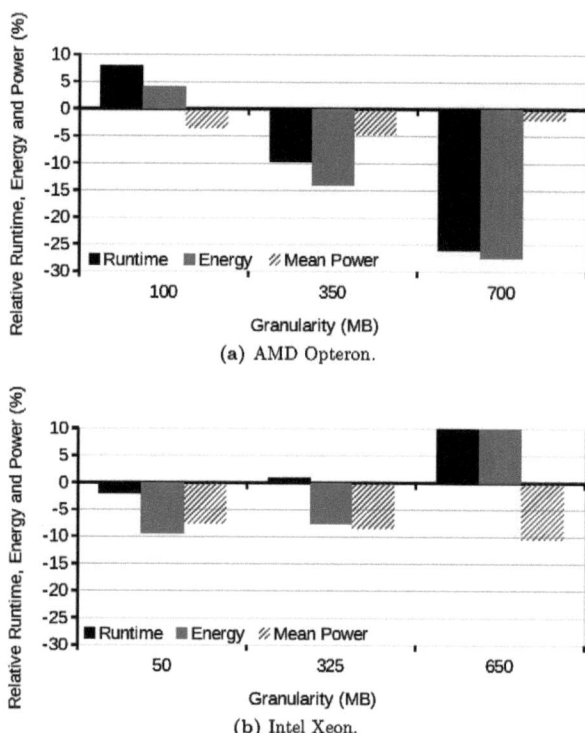

Figure 3.11.: *Relative runtime, energy and power for disk write operations of the Intel Xeon and AMD Opteron nodes with varying granularities. The baseline is the highest frequency setup for each architecture.*

Furthermore, the Xeon nodes of our cluster are equipped with Intel 82574 Gigabit Ethernet adapters[5], while the Opteron nodes are equipped with the 82576 adapters[6]. The power consumption for the various network speeds is displayed in Table 3.6 on Page 55(only the 82574 adapter, the values for the 82576 adapter are similar).

Table 3.6.: *Network interface card power consumption of the Intel 82574 Gigabit Ethernet controller family.*

Speed (Mbit/s)	Power active (mW)	Power idle (mW)
1,000	878	642
100	351	190
10	416	167
no link	-	44

Unfortunately, varying the speed and the duplex mode of the network card under load does not result into any energy saving at all due to the significantly increased runtime. Table A.4 on Page VIII in the appendix summarizes several measurements on the Intel nodes, AMD measurements are comparable due to the similar network card.

However, power saving can be reached by exploiting the disk's power saving mechanisms. Table 3.7 on Page 55 shows the corresponding power saving potential.

Table 3.7.: *Hard disk power consumption of the Seagate Barracuda ST3500418AS [Tec09].*

Mode	Power (W)
Idle	5.00
Operating	6.57
Standby	0.79
Sleep	0.79

Interesting is the decrease in power consumption when switching from idle to standby or sleep of about 83 %. This potential can only be exploited if the disk is idle, the disk has no power saving mechanism when under load. Figure 3.12 summarizes the different modes of the devices and their impact on the power consumption.

This chapter described the used infrastructure for all following power and energy measurements. Besides to the description of the test setup including hardware components

---

[5]http://download.intel.com/design/network/datashts/82574.pdf, last checked: March 2, 2013
[6]http://download.intel.com/design/network/datashts/82576_Datasheet.pdf, last checked: March 2, 2013

3. Power and Energy Saving Potential

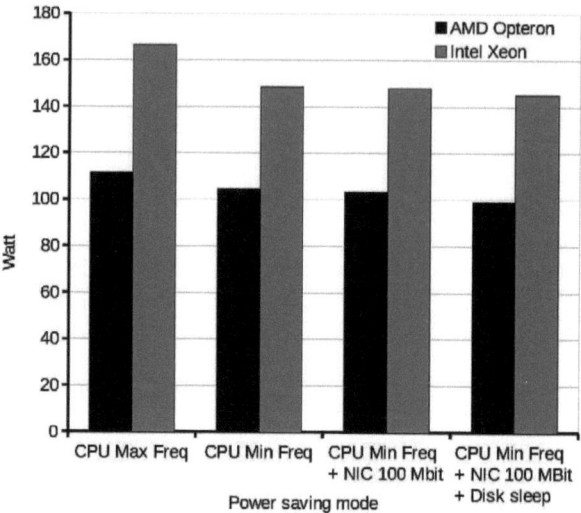

Figure 3.12.: *Idle power consumption for Opteron and Xeon nodes depending on the increasing count of device power saving modes. The Intel Xeon C-States are disabled in the system BIOS.*

and measurement devices, the power saving potential of various power saving mechanisms is evaluated. In detail, processor DVFS measurements are performed for different strong memory-bound computation, communication and I/O. Remarkable is the architecture difference between the Intel Xeon and Opteron AMD nodes: While the Opteron processors scale the memory bandwidth with the core frequency, the Xeon processors do not. Thus the energy-saving potential for the Opteron processors is negligible for memory-bound phases. However, a significant power and energy-saving potential could be measured for longer communication and I/O phases. Also in these phases, the behavior of the two processor architectures is slightly different, but mainly due to the different core count and memory setup. Unfortunately, the energy-saving potential of the network card under load is negligible, too. But the power saving potential of disk and network card in idle phases are significant.

4. Strategies for Reducing Parallel Application Power Consumption

After evaluating the power saving potential of single devices, this chapter introduces strategies for reducing parallel application power consumption. As static switching of power saving mechanisms for the whole application run usually increases the runtime, specific application phases have to be defined. In these phases, several dynamic switching strategies can be applied to reduce the power consumption. The strategies can roughly be divided into hardware-centric approaches and application-centric approaches. Hardware-centric approaches make the decision about the concrete hardware power state dependent on the hardware usage. Operating systems usually implement several heuristics for exploiting these approaches. On the other hand, the application-centric approach starts the analysis at the application layer which allows considering future behavior.

4.1. Application Phases of Interest

Application phases of interest from a power saving perspective are application phases, where hardware components

- are only partially utilized or even completely idle,
- are utilized, but not directly contributing to problem solution.

Figure 4.1 exemplary visualizes application phases and resulting hardware component utilization. In this schematic sketch, two application processes first enter a compute phase, followed by a communication phase where Process 1 sends data to Process 0. The data is than written to disk by Process 0. Process 0 runs on Core 0 while Process 1 runs on Core 1.

The compute phase means moving data from main memory to the processor core, operating on data and moving data from processor core to main memory. This phase utilizes processor and main memory, disk and network are for now unused. In general, more complex setups involve e.g. the network card during memory operations, as it is the case for a distributed memory system with global address space. However, corresponding to the measurements in the last chapter, the power saving potential varies with the concrete workload. A further differentiation in memory-bound and cpu-bound workloads is necessary. From a utilization point of view, no differentiation is possible. In both cases,

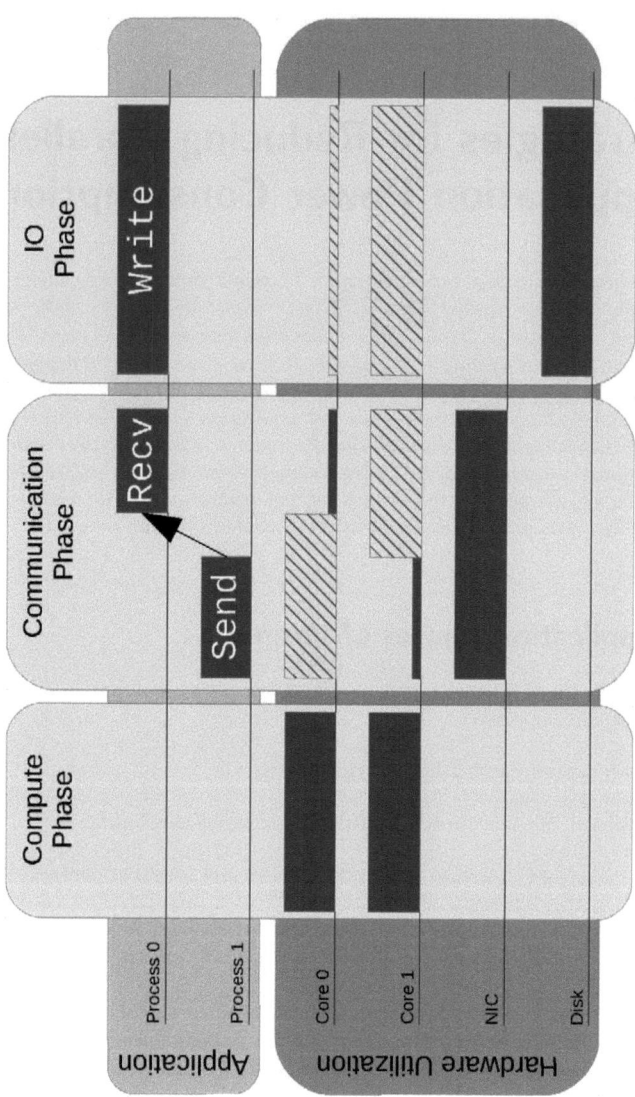

Figure 4.1.: *Schematic application phases and resulting hardware utilization.*

the processor cores are fully utilized, but for the memory-bound workload a higher percentage of processor wait cycles occur, e.g. due to memory bandwidth limitation or cache misses.

The communication phase is a term for the inter-process communication (sending and receiving data between processes). The component utilization in this phase is very dependent on the concrete communication library implementation. Process 0 could be sent to sleep or also busy-waiting for the data to be sent from Process 1, this is indicated by the hatched utilization. Clearly, sending and receiving involves the corresponding core, at least for TCP/IP, since the network packets have to be (un)packed. This usually results in a lower processor load. Nevertheless, Process 1 might be busy-waiting until Process 0 fully received the data – depending on the the type of communication (blocking/non-blocking) and again the implementation. If the network card is involved depends also on the type of communication: If the processes are running on different nodes (inter-node communication), the network card has to take care of sending the data over the network. Otherwise, for intra-node communication, it again depends on the communication library implementation which could use *Direct Memory Access* (DMA) here for inter-process communication on the same node.

The *File Input/Output* (I/O) phase consists of data write of Process 0 to the I/O subsystem. I/O can be differentiated in local (POSIX, MPI with local file system) and distributed (global file system with distributed server and clients) I/O. Therefore, local I/O only involves the local I/O subsystem and does not require additional network communication as it might be required in the distributed case. Figure 4.1 visualizes the local case, the network is not utilized. The corresponding Process 0 might be slightly utilized (depends on the usage of DMA). Again, based on the implementation of the parallel I/O library, Process 1 might be actively waiting for Process 0 to finish the I/O activity.

In summary, the classification of different phases in terms of compute phase, communication phase and I/O phase is straight forward. More difficult is the concrete classification of the resulting hardware workload and utilization which is specific for each environment. However, the greater the overlap of the different phases on the hardware side, the better is also the performance. Considering again the example in Figure 4.1: If there is no data dependency (different data calculated than exchanged than written) all phases could overlap theoretically and thus significantly decrease the application runtime. Nevertheless, in the majority of cases the specific problem or the parallelization schema introduces data dependency and thus overlapping phases is not possible even if it would be also the best solution in terms of energy efficiency. The resulting hardware utilization pattern introduces a clear potential for reducing the power consumption of parallel applications:

- The processor frequency can be reduced if idle, busy-waiting or memory-bound,
- the disk can be sent to sleep if unused,
- and the network card can reduce its speed if unused.

4.2. Hardware-centric Approach

The hardware-centric approach as strategy for reducing parallel application power consumption does not include any application knowledge in the decision-making. Consequently, the decision-making is independent of any user interaction and thus predestined for implementation in the background, e.g. by the *Operating System* (OS). Usually, the hardware-centric approach is fully automatic, only manual calibration and/or disabling is possible. Furthermore, the decisions are made online – thus while the application is running. In the following, two different sampling-based approaches are discussed in detail.

4.2.1. Sampling Utilization

The most common approach to detect device idle times is utilization sampling. A device is considered idle if the utilization is lower as a specified threshold for a specified time. Based on this historic knowledge, the device is considered idle for the near future and its hardware state is changed. Thus, the power consumption can decrease significantly in idle times.

Utilization sampling is commonly used for the main processor and the hard disk. While the strategy for the hard disk is quite simple (if idle for a specified time, go to sleep), the main processor offers more operating points and thus different strategies. These different strategies are named *governors* in the Linux operating system and implemented in the cpufreq module. Governors are the power management policies that decide when/if to change the processor frequency.

The following governors are merged into the kernel and offer two policies to chose from [Sey11, PS06, PLB07]:

- The *ondemand* governor aggressively sets the processor speed depending on the current utilization, it mainly switches to the highest frequency in order to complete the task and then switches stepwise to the lowest available frequency. This strategy is also called *race-to-idle*. The ondemand governor is the standard governor (see Algorithm 1) which further adds tunables (UP_THRESHOLD and DOWN_THRESHOLD) to the strategy.

- The *conservative* governor, much like the ondemand governor, sets the processor depending on the current usage, but it also increases the processor speed step-wise.

For the sake of completeness: three more governors exist, but these essentially disable dynamic strategies by locking the frequency:

- The *performance* governor sets the processor statically to the highest frequency scaling_max_freq.

- The *powersave* governor sets the processor statically to the lowest frequency scaling_min_freq.

Algorithm 1 Original Ondemand algorithm [PS06]
for for every CPU in the system **do**
  get utilization since last check
  if utilization > UP_THRESHOLD **then**
    increase frequency to MAX
  else if utilization < DOWN_THRESHOLD **then**
    decrease frequency by 20 %
  end if
end for

- The *userspace* governor allows the user, or any userspace program running with administrative privileges, to set the processor to a specific supported frequency by making a `sysfs` file `scaling_setspeed` available.

The performance and powersave governor, respectively, are more suitable for mobile devices to switch the strategy due to further environment changes. For example, if a mobile device plugged into wall switch to the performance governor with the highest frequency, otherwise use the powersave governor for power capping. The userspace governor is especially interesting for manual instrumentation and will be further explored in the following chapter.

As the `cpufreq` module exploits the processor performance states, the `cpuidle` module is the generic kernel subsystem managing the processor power states reported by ACPI. The following governor are merged into the kernel [Sey11, PLB07]:

- The *ladder* governor works fine with periodic tick-based kernels. It checks every tick if it can go in a deeper idle state or not. This step-wise model works not very well with tick-less kernels, because without a periodic timer tick it may not get a chance to use a deeper idle state whenever it goes idle.

- The *menu* governor on the other hand looks at different parameters like what the expected sleep time is (as provided by the tick-less kernel), latency requirements, previous C-state residency and maximum C-State requirement and then picks the deepest possible idle state straight away.

Figure 4.2 gives a simple overview over the two frameworks, pointing out the general similarity. Up to now, these two frameworks are working absolutely independent from each other [PS07].
More details of the implementation and the tunables can be found in [Sey11].
The advantages of utilization sampling is the low overhead in terms of system performance and also user interaction. Additionally, no special kinds of sensors are needed, the statistics can be collected by the operating system itself.
However, the usage of the aforementioned power saving strategies can decrease the system performance due to wake-up latencies. Especially for frequent behavior changes, this

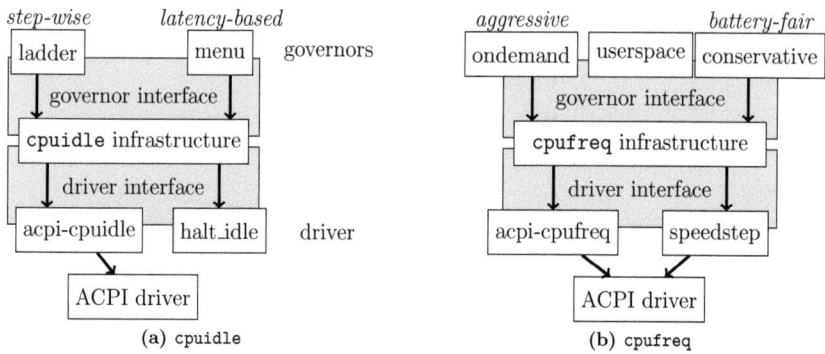

Figure 4.2.: *Design overview* cpuidle *and* cpufreq *[Sey11].*

approach introduces significant performance drawbacks. Furthermore, the utilization itself is not classified – it is thus not possible to detect busy-waiting or memory-bound application phases. As a result, the processor performance states, the processor power states and the device power states are usually disabled on high performance computing systems.

4.2.2. Sampling Performance Counters

In addition to the pure utilization of the device, some devices offer further information about their usage, named *Performance Counters*. Nowadays, almost all processor vendors implement performance counters in their devices. These are special purpose registers on the hardware, which count hardware-related events in terms of floating point operations or cache misses. This sophisticated set of metrics allows to classify the processor utilization in more detail. Using the provided interface via the *Machine Specific Registers* (MSRs) of the operating system, these values can be exploited for usage analysis. This information is currently only available for processors.

However, performance counters can be sampled as base for processor performance states decisions. This approach can also be used to detect idle phases, but performance counters are widely used to detect memory-bound application phases. If the underlying architecture does not scale down the memory bandwidth with the processor frequency, the processor frequency can be reduced in phases where the memory bandwidth is a bottleneck. In addition to the ondemand governor, the performance counter approach allows a better categorization of utilization. This significantly increases the power saving potential, since the power saving mechanism is not only dependent on device idle times. Nevertheless, both hardware-centric approaches have the high potential for wrong decisions resulting from changing hardware usage pattern. To avoid wrong decisions, it is common to predict the future pattern using machine learning or additional statistics (see

Chapter 8 for more details). However, in worst-case scenarios the switching overhead and wrong decisions result in an energy-efficiency decrease.

4.3. Application-centric Approach

Instead of using the hardware usage as base for decision-making, the application-centric approach focusses on the application, or better the application code phases. As visualized in Figure 4.1, different application phases result in different hardware usage patterns. Corresponding to the previous sections, the following classification of application phases will be used:

- Compute phases with high load on the processor and/or main memory, further distinction in
  - Cpu-bound, mainly processor load and
  - Memory-bound, mainly operating on main memory, processor has high number of waiting cycles.
- Communication phases due to inter-process communication, further distinction in
  - Intra-node, communicating processes are on the same node and
  - Inter-node, communication processes are on different nodes.
- I/O phases with high load on the I/O subsystem, further distinction in
  - Local I/O, subsystem is in the same node and
  - Distributed I/O, subsystem is (at least partially) on different nodes.

The advantage of this approach is the application knowledge about the future behavior of application phases. For the hardware-centric approach, the hardware state can only be changed after the usage pattern has already changed. Consider the following pseudo code in Listing 2 as simple example.

The nested loops simply update a $1,000 \times 1,000$ matrix, followed by a checkpoint (write the whole matrix to disk) and update the matrix again. The matrix update only utilizes the processor and the main memory, while the checkpointing utilizes mainly the disk. If the power saving mechanisms are disabled (e.g. for performance reasons), all devices are active independent of the hardware utilization. If the operating system takes care of the power saving modes, the processor is, independent of the application phase, active, even if the processor utilization is low during the checkpointing phase. The disk is in sleep mode during the matrix update if the duration of the matrix update is higher than the specified disk idle threshold. Unfortunately, this results into a delay for checkpointing, since the disk has to wake up and reach the ready state again. To avoid this delay, the disk can be enabled before it is used again by inserting corresponding calls in the application code. Furthermore, the processor can reduce its frequency during the checkpointing phase, which only introduces a small delay due to the low transition time for P-States.

4. Strategies for Reducing Parallel Application Power Consumption

Algorithm 2 Example pseudo code of a simple matrix update followed by writing a checkpoint.

for i=0; i < 1000; ++i **do**
  for j=0; j < 1000; ++j **do**
    update matrix cell [i][j]
  end for
end for
write matrix to disk
for i=0; i < 1000; ++i **do**
  for j=0; j < 1000; ++j **do**
    update matrix cell [i][j]
  end for
end for
write matrix to disk

Algorithm 3 Instrumented pseudo code of a simple matrix update followed by writing a checkpoint.

for i=0; i < 1000; ++i **do**
  for j=0; j < 1000; ++j **do**
    update matrix cell [i][j]
  end for
  if i = 900 **then**
    wake up disk
  end if
end for
Reduce processor frequency
write matrix to disk
Increase processor frequency
for i=0; i < 1000; ++i **do**
  for j=0; j < 1000; ++j **do**
    update matrix cell [i][j]
  end for
  if i = 900 **then**
    wake up disk
  end if
end for
Reduce processor frequency
write matrix to disk

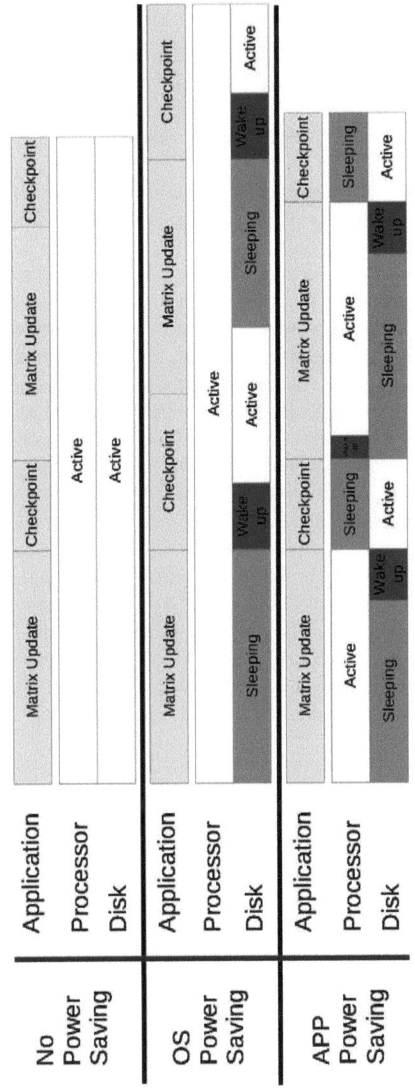

Figure 4.3.: *Schematic application and device phases for different power saving scenarios.*

4. Strategies for Reducing Parallel Application Power Consumption

Figure 4.3 gives a schematic overview of all three scenarios.

While the OS power saving scenario decrease the application runtime significantly (two times the disk wake-up time), in the application-centric scenario the runtime increase is negligible. Of course, the impact on the total consumed energy (and thus the saving potential) varies based on the concrete device power consumption, wake-up latencies and phase durations.

However, several options are possible for the information flow from the application to the hardware. All of the options require a processing of the application code at different stages of compiling, linking and running. These different kinds of instrumentation are distinguished in offline instrumentation (before running the application) and online instrumentation (while running the application). The simplest and native way of offline instrumentation is the manual instrumentation of the application itself. Inserting calls to switch the hardware power saving modes can be done statically or also conditionally, latter requires preprocessing of the application code. Using already existing interfaces for phase annotations, the complexity of manual instrumentation can be decreased. Furthermore, additional libraries (like the message passing library) can be instrumented to automatically switch the hardware power saving modes during specific operations, e.g. collective communication. Additionally, the compiler can detect phases in the assembler code and insert calls to switch the hardware power saving mode correspondingly. The online instrumentation concept works similar: The automatic pattern detection during the application run can trigger the hardware power saving mode changes.

Nevertheless, to optimize each of the approaches a *post-mortem* (after the application run) analysis of the application is helpful to evaluate the result and to tune the instrumentation further. Especially due to phase overlapping the classification of application phases is not always straight forward. Additionally, the compiler may reorganize code instructions which results in different, for the application developer unexpected, hardware utilization.

Comparing the hardware-centric approach with the application-centric approach, the hardware-centric approach is much easier to realize without user interaction. But also the energy-saving potential due to the higher risk of wrong decisions and resulting wake-up latencies is lower. Consequently, in the following the application-centric approach will be explored using manual code instrumentation in combination with hardware-centric metrics. Even if manual code instrumentation requires a high degree of user interaction, the further analysis of the approach and especially the development of the tools paves the road for future work in terms of automatic offline or online instrumentation.

Dynamic switching strategies considering the hardware usage in application phases allow to adjust the power consumption in a fine-granular way. It is for example possible, to reduce the processing frequency and thus the power consumption for memory-bound application phases. Automatic detection of appropriate phases using heuristics as already exploited by the operating system has a high potential for wrong decisions due frequent changing hardware usage pattern. The application-centric approach seems to be better suitable, since the analysis starts at the application layer and allows to consider future hardware usage pattern. However, for a well-founded decision a correlation of the application, the power saving modes and the power consumption is necessary for both approaches.

5. Management of Power Saving Modes

This chapter focuses on the efficient management of the power saving modes on a per node base. Each of the nodes has a fixed set of resources (processor cores, hard disks and network interface cards) and each of the resources various power saving modes with different performance and power characteristics which have to be managed efficiently. The requirements, the design and the implementation of the management daemon are discussed in the following sections.

Usually, the operating system manages the device states based on historical knowledge about the corresponding device utilization. If a device is not utilized for a defined threshold, the device switches to a deeper ACPI mode and consumes less power. From the performance point of view, this procedure is critical due to the fact that the future utilization is unknown. Thus if a device just switched to a deeper sleep mode and is immediately used, the calling process has to wait until the device is in the ready state again. This is very critical in high performance computing clusters, typically all power saving modes are disabled by the system administrator. On the contrary, user processes have detailed knowledge about the future utilization, but no privileges to change the power saving modes.

In the following, the idea of forwarding this usage information from the application running in user space to a server daemon in root context is explored. Based on this knowledge, the server daemon is able to switch the power saving modes efficiently. This concept is visualized in Figure 5.1: A user library called *eeClient* is linked to each parallel application running on a computing node and forwards the usage information to the *eeDaemon* (single instance per node).

The daemon has to take care of selecting the right mode for each resource, based on the different requirements from the running applications. This is especially necessary for shared resources: Hard disk and network interface card. But also the processor sockets, if the core frequency is only manageable per socket. If the core frequency is only manageable per socket, each core requirement has to be considered. For all shared resources, the least common denominator is selected (the highest, most performant mode wins). If a device is considered unused by the application for a specified timespan, the daemon has to take care to bring it up in time to be ready again after the considered timespan. For this approach, the different device transition times have to be known by the daemon. This guarantees minimal impact on the application performance.

Correspondingly, the key design of the *eeDaemon* is to split the management process into a node server process and a client library. The client library is linked to the application,

5. Management of Power Saving Modes

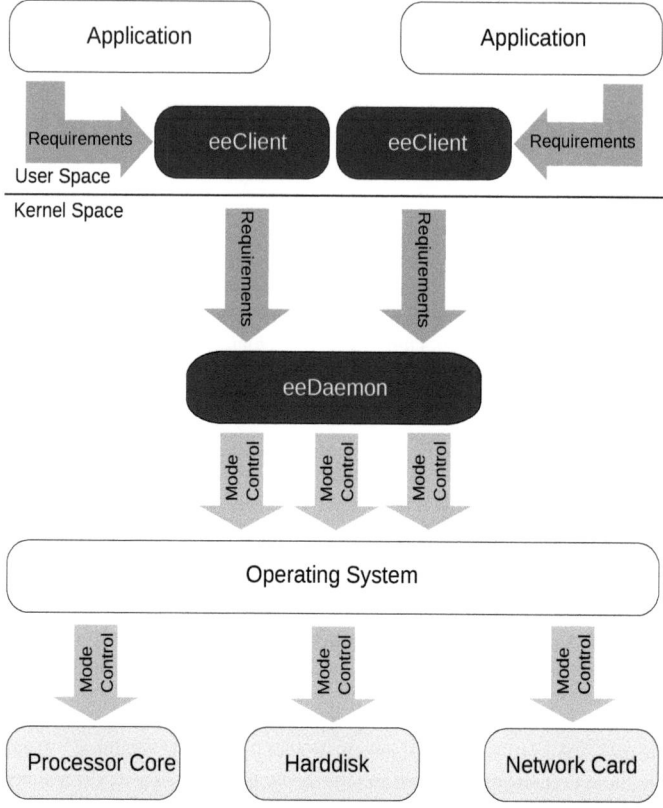

Figure 5.1.: *eeDaemon mode control based on [MMK+11].*

forwards the usage information via Unix sockets to the node-local server which allows an immediate return to the application itself. Furthermore, the server saves the application requests in a queue and updates the device states considering all requests for each device.

5.1. Server Design

This section focuses on the server design, while the following sections focus on the application interface and the concrete implementation.

5.1. Server Design

5.1.1. Map Processes to Hardware Devices

To allocate the corresponding resources on the server, each application client process has to register itself at the server. The server registers a new user process for each shared resource. A resource is considered shared, if multiple processes use it. For the eeDaemon devices, the network interface card and the hard disk are considered shared (each process on a node can send/receive and read/write data using the shared resource). Because the server communicates only with the client located on the same node, the allocation of the shared devices is trivial. Only the assignment of processor cores to the processes has to be coordinated. Due to the scheduling of the operating system, each process can migrate between different cores. This migration can be stopped using a pinning mechanism (which pins each application process to a processing core), which is available at different levels. Pinning can be exploited programmatically (that means each application is tuned for itself), but a more common use case is to let the execution environment (e.g. mpiexec as part of the MPICH2 environment) pin the processes after spawning them. Usually, high performance application codes are pinned anyway, since pinning avoids cache misses and increases the performance. However, pinning of the application in the eeDaemon library destroys the application or system process mapping and results in performance decrease. Consequently, the application is assumed to be already pinned. To avoid a fixed pattern for pinning (e.g. linear: Process 0 pinned to Core 0, Process 1 pinned to Core 1, ...), the client library destines the current core ID and forwards it to the server process at the registration. Afterwards, the application process is registered as a user of the core with the transmitted id. This straight-forward mapping of the application processes makes it possible to switch the hardware device states under consideration of possible interferences due to different process requirements.

5.1.2. Switching Hardware Device States

Even if the future hardware device usage is known for each application process, the daemon has to find the optimal operating policy out of all requests for a shared resource. To enable this decision, the usage patterns are abstracted to the internal modes MODE_UNUSED, MODE_MIN, MODE_MED, MODE_MAX and MODE_TURBO. Based on the different modes requested for a specific hardware device by different processes, the highest mode (with the least impact on the application performance) is selected. Table 5.1 gives an overview over the implementation on device side.

Two different types of requests are supported by the daemon: Time and mode request. The former request should be submitted if the application process starts an activity with a defined duration. After the duration, the resource has to be in the requested mode. The latter initiates an immediate resource switch (corresponding to setting the duration in the time request to zero). The following example motivates the two different types: If a communication phase has a duration of 10 s and all devices except for the network card should be switched to a low-power mode for this duration, there are two scenarios. First, the cores and hard disks can be switched to MODE_UNUSED with a mode request. After the phase, the devices have to be switched back again to MODE_MAX – this should

5. Management of Power Saving Modes

Table 5.1.: *eeDaemon modes and corresponding device mode.*

Mode	Processor core		Hard disk	Network card	
	Frequency	Turbo mode		Speed	Duplex mode
TURBO	Highest	Enabled	Active	Highest	Full
MAX	Highest	Disabled	Active	Highest	Full
MED	Medium	Disabled	Active	Medium	Full
MIN	Lowest	Disabled	Powersave	Lowest	Full
UNUSED	Lowest	Disabled	Sleep	Lowest	Half

be done before the communication phase ends to avoid performance decrease. Thus, a second request has to be added within the communication phase. More practical is the use of the time request with a duration of e.g. 9 s (considering a switch time of 1 s), afterwards the devices are up again without the need for a second call. Of course, the server needs for this operation the mode switch durations for each device – but these can be measured once by the daemon itself and stored in a configuration file. Additionally, the server process needs to check when to wake up which device, which is implemented using a fixed interval. The main algorithm is described in Algorithm 4. This algorithm is especially necessary to understand how to use the application interface to achieve the desired behavior of the hardware devices.

5.1.3. Runtime Overhead

Switching the hardware device states using the eeDaemon results in some overhead: On the one hand, the state switch itself results in a timespan, where the device is unusable. On the other hand, the daemon design (especially the interval checking for requests) results in overheads. Since the device switching overhead is constant, the focus is on the daemon overhead itself.

Figure 5.2 compares the runtime of an application instrumented using the eeDaemon interface with different resource update intervals. An interval of zero corresponds to no instrumentation (all requests are ignored), for all other values the value defines the update cycle of the resource mode in microseconds. For small values (< 200 microseconds), the duration is increased by about 5 seconds which corresponds to about 7 % performance overhead. However, very fast mode switches usually do not improve the energy efficiency due to the costs for the transition (see Chapter 3). For this reason, the resource update interval should be set to higher values. For larger values, the software switching overhead is negligible. All following measurements use a interval time of 100,000 microseconds (= 100 ms).

Algorithm 4 Pseudo code for updating the eeDaemon server device mode

if no user registered for this resource **then**
   return MODE_UNUSED
end if
if no requests submitted **then**
   return MODE_MAX
end if
for iterate over all requests **do**
   if is time request **then**
     update the time
     if request has to wake up now due to time request **then**
       update request type to mode request
       update consent mode to requested mode
     end if
   else
     increase the mode occurrence array for the requested mode
   end if
end for
if consent mode is MODE_MAX **then**
   return MODE_MAX
end if
for iterate over the mode occurrence array **do**
   determine minimal possible consent
end for
return consent mode

5. Management of Power Saving Modes

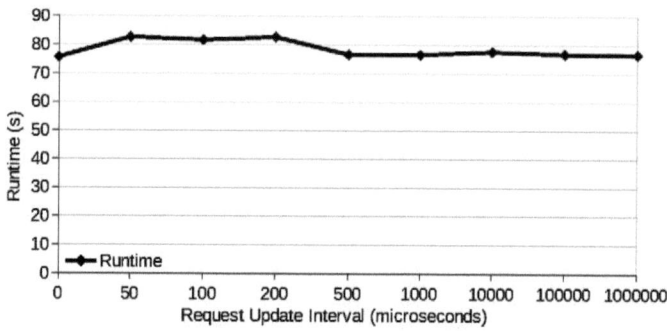

Figure 5.2.: *Instrumented application runtime dependent on eeDaemon interval time.*

5.1.4. Resource Management

One important requirement of the eeDaemon server design is to avoid undesired influences of the cluster system. This could happen due to the invalid usage of the instrumentation (e.g. missing ee_finalize) or due to application crashes. In this case, it is possible that not all devices are in the active mode again after the unclean application exit. This case can be handled by interaction with the resource management system. The resource management system, which takes care of the allocation of jobs to nodes and the execution of the jobs itself provides a powerful environment. Amongst others, scripts are provided which are executed before (*prologue*) and after (*epilogue*) execution of the job.

Using this script environment, it is possible to avoid a undefined hardware state after the execution of the application. The environment can be extended to switch all devices into operating modes before executing the job itself and back into power saving mode (independent of job exit state) afterwards. This procedure has the advantage, that the devices are in power saving mode if no job is running – which saves further energy. The disadvantage is the switching overhead before each job for a larger number of short jobs which might decrease the performance. One alternative is to use the *epilogue.precancel* script which is called in case of job errors to manually unregister all devices at the server in the case the application does exit with an error code.

But still, the interaction of instrumented and uninstrumented application for power saving modes is undefined. In general, it is possible that several applications are started (some instrumented, some not) and running in parallel on the computing nodes as visualized in Figure 5.3.

Because uninstrumented jobs do not indicate their device usage, the eeDaemon server process cannot take these applications into account. For shared resources (hard disk and network card) the solution is trivial – the *prologue* script can register the shared resources and request the maximum mode for the whole application run to avoid performance impact. But to get the exclusive resources (processor cores) per job, the resource

5.1. Server Design

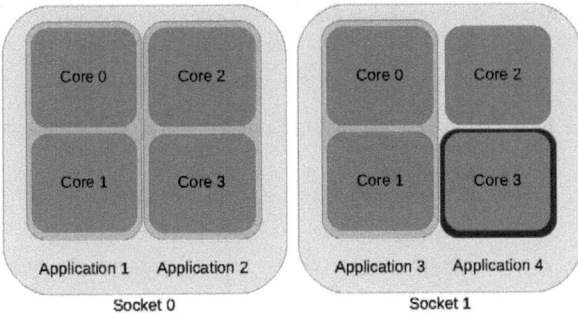

Figure 5.3.: *Scheduling of applications on processor cores: Instrumented applications are light grey and uninstrumented applications are dark grey.*

management system has to collaborate with the MPI library to provide this information. Otherwise, the unregistered resources are considered to be idle. This collaboration is not implemented yet – for the moment, the parallel running of instrumented and uninstrumented applications on the same node is not supported.

5.1.5. Server configuration

As discussed in the last subsections, several settings for the eeClust server process influence the application logic on the one hand and the performance on the other hand. To provide easy access to these settings, a configuration file is read once at the server startup. This configuration file includes mainly the hardware specifications (e.g. the core number) as well as device names to be associated with the internal IDs. The configuration should be encapsulated from the application programmer, thus the configuration is only accessible to the admin user. In detail, the file contains the following entries as exemplary specified in Listing 5.1.

Listing 5.1: *Example eeDaemon server configuration file for the Intel Xeon nodes.*

```
1  # Configuration for eeClust Intel nodes
2
3  # Processor group, in each line represents a core list for a socket
4  [Processor]
5  # List with cores located on Socket0 (e.g. 0;[1;...])
6  Socket0=0;1;2;3;
7  # List with cores located on Socket1 (e.g. 0;[1;...])
8  Socket1=4;5;6;7;
9
10 # Devices group, each line represents a device list for each type (
      NIC and Disk)
11 [Devices]
12 # List with all network devices (e.g. eth0;[eth1;...])
13 NIC=eth0;
```

5. Management of Power Saving Modes

```
14 # List with all harddrives (e.g. /dev/sda;[/dev/sdb;...])
15 Disk=/dev/sda;
16
17 # Settings for devices, needed for decision process
18 [Settings]
19 # Time in microseconds needed for a core to be in MODE_MAX (e.g.
      100)
20 Processor State Change=53
21 # Time in microseconds needed for a network device to be in MODE_MAX
      (e.g. 100)
22 NIC State Change=2587366
23 # Time in microseconds needed for a harddisk to be in MODE_MAX (e.g.
      100)
24 Disk State Change=20000000
25 # If all cores on a socket can only have the same frequency (true/
      false)
26 Core Shared Voltage Regulator=true
27 # Interval in microseconds for mode updates of the request per
      device (e.g. 100)
28 Resource Update Interval=100000
```

This file can be generated by the daemon itself and adjusted afterwards. For this generation, all interesting devices of the operating system are included. Furthermore, the power mode transition duration for each of these device change is measured. The only setting which cannot be determined by the process itself is the one about cores sharing a voltage regulator or not. For this setting, the power consumption has to be measured for various processor frequency settings.

Providing all these information to the server process encapsulates the hardware setting from the application programmer who just uses the provided application interface of the daemon.

5.2. Application interface

From the perspective of the application, the eeDaemon interface is very simple. Listing 5.2 shows the concrete application interface for instrumentation of parallel applications written in the C programming language. An similar wrapper interface is provided in the Fortran programming language [Ehm12][1].

Listing 5.2: *eeDaemon application interface* eed.c

```
1 /**
2  * Registers the process at the Daemon.
3  *
4  * @param argc Pointer to count of commandline args
5  * @param argv Pointer to commandline args
6  * @param tag Tag for this process
7  * @param rank Rank for this process
8  */
```

---

[1]The bachelor thesis has been supervised in conjunction with this thesis

5.2. Application interface

```
 9 void ee_init(int * argc, char *** argv, int tag, int rank);
10
11 /**
12  * Request Mode for device
13  *
14  * @param device_id Id for this device
15  * @param mode_id Id for the desired mode
16  */
17 void ee_dev_mode(int device_id, int mode_id);
18
19 /**
20  * The device has to be in the specified mode in secs seconds
21  *
22  * @param device_id Id for this device
23  * @param mode_id Id for the desired mode
24  * @param secs Seconds afterwards this device should be in mode
25  */
26 void ee_dev_mode_in(int device_id, int mode_id, int secs);
27
28 /**
29  * Unregisters the process at the Daemon.
30  * Unregistering possibly triggers a mode change.
31  */
32 void ee_finalize();
33
34 /**
35  * Unregisters all processes with tag (all processes within a job)
36  * Unregistering possibly triggers a mode change.
37  */
38 void ee_finalize_all(int tag);
```

First, each (MPI) process has to call the `ee_init` function to register itself at the eeDaemon server. For the unique identification, each process submits a specific tag to identify the application (e.g. the job ID of the workload manager) in addition to the MPI rank or thread id. This function should be called immediately after the `MPI_Init` function. The name of the application (included in `argv`), is not necessary for the identification of the process, but allows to generate more meaningful debugging and information messages.

To register the right set of resources for each process, the current core ID is destined via the `sched_getcpu` function. This is especially necessary for the processor, since the eeDaemon server decisions are dependent on the process core. However, this requires the process to not migrate between processor cores – thus the application itself has to be pinned to the processor core.

To communicate the usage pattern of each resource from the application to the eeDaemon server, the two functions `ee_dev_mode_in` and `ee_dev_mode` are available to the application developer. The first function declares a specific device to be in a specific mode in at least *secs* seconds. The corresponding device and mode IDs are specified in the header file. To simplify the access, the environment variables `MY_CORE_IDS`, `MY_DISK_IDS` and `MY_NIC_IDS` identify the corresponding set of resources for each process. The second function behaves like the first function with a timespan of zero seconds – thus immediate

77

changes are required by the server process. To unregister a process from the eeDaemon, the function ee_finalize has to be called. This function releases all allocated resources and this process is not considered anymore for mode decisions and possible existing requests are discarded which might result in mode changes. The ee_finalize_all function unregisters all processes with a specified tag and should be called either by the application itself or by the resource management system in case of application crashes.

5.3. Software package

The eeDaemon software is implemented in the C programming language and released under the BSD open source license[2]. As well the server as the client are designed in object-oriented, parallel data structures using the *glib 2.0* library. The communication and synchronization between server and client is done via g_async_queues. Using the *glib* test environment, extensive unit tests, integration tests and system tests ensure the software usability and functionality. The software package itself is documented using *Doxygen*. To build, install and run the software including the test cases, the *waf* build system is used. Additionally, *init* scripts are provided to integrate the eeDaemon server process in Linux systems as well as *epilogue* and *prologue* scripts for the resource management system.

In this chapter, the eeDaemon is designed to efficiently manage the device power saving modes on a per node base without significant runtime overhead. The key design of the eeDaemon is to split the management process into a node server process and an application client library. The client library is linked to the application and forwards the usage information via sockets to the node-local server. The server saves the application requests and updates the device states considering all requests for each device. The design of the daemon guarantees low additional software overhead.

---

[2]http://www.eeclust.de/software/eeDaemon-1.0.tar.gz, last checked: March 2, 2013

6. Correlating Applications and Energy-Related Metrics

The correlation of the application and energy-related metrics is essential to identify hot spots in the application. This chapter covers the collection and evaluation of the specific application and hardware characteristics via the tracing approach. After introducing the chosen tracing approach, the concrete extensions for recording energy-related metrics are discussed. In detail, extensions are developed to correlate the parallel application with the classified device utilization, the power saving mode and the node power consumption with the final goal to identify application hot shots in terms of energy and performance. The visual identification process is exemplarily illustrated with two tool environments, originally developed for performance analysis of parallel applications.

6.1. Tracing Approach

The goal of this chapter is to collect and analyze data which characterizes the application run and the system. This data can be generated by hardware devices or within software, either the operating system, the application itself or additional tools [MMK+12].

One way of keeping the information is to store *statistics*, e.g. absolute values like the number of function invocations, the average execution time of a function, or the performed floating point operations. Application statistics represent the *profile* during the application run. In contrast to a profile, a *trace* records states and events of a program together with their timestamps. Traces allow to analyze temporal dependencies and event specific information like the communication pattern between processes. Events can be traced synchronously by tracing the entry and exit point or asynchronously by checking in defined intervals which event is active.

For each way of aggregation, the data has to be correlated to the investigated application. There are several approaches to measure the characteristics of a given application. In general, a *monitor* is a system which collects data about the program execution. Monitors mostly rely on software to measure the state of the system. Additionally, data from available hardware sensors can be queried if possible and necessary. Popular methods are different kind of instrumentations: Either alter source code, relink object files with patched functions (library instrumentation) or modify machine code directly (binary instrumentation) [SMAb01].

It is desirable to be able to learn about the relationship of certain events which happen at different levels of the system. Thus, it may be useful to be able to tell which specific processor activity on the computing node was triggered by which application code sequence. Usually, this is impossible using a system tool, because of concurrent operations and complex optimizations on each level of the system. A common way for tracing approaches to correlate different events with each other is to use timestamps. In some cases for specific groups of events like data from external devices (e.g. a power meter) it might be necessary to use timestamps. However, timestamps establish an implicit relationship between events. The usage of timestamps can introduce additional need for post-processing after the application itself finishes. For example, it may be necessary to merge the different traces into one unified trace, which can then be used by trace analysis tools.

However, users analyze the data recorded by the monitoring system to localize optimization potential. The data is recorded during program execution and assessed after the application finishes. This approach of post-mortem analysis is referred to as *offline* analysis. The main advantage of this methodology is that data can be analyzed multiple times and compared with older results.

Another approach is to gather and assess data *online* – while the application is running. This way feedback is provided immediately to the user, who can adjust the application code and the monitor environment based on the results.

Due to the vast amount of data, sophisticated tools are required to localize performance and power issues of the system and correlate them with application behavior and finally source code. Tools operate either manually, i.e. the user must inspect the data himself or the tools try to assess data automatically. The tools could also give hints to the user where abnormalities or inefficiencies are found (semi-automatic tools).

Tool environments, which localize and tune code automatically, without user interaction, are on the wish list of all programmers. However, because of the system and application complexity automatic tools are only applicable for a very small set of problems.

In this section, two offline tracing tools, namely VampirTrace and HDTrace, are introduced with the focus on the capability of further integration of additional tracing sources related to energy-efficiency analysis. In general, the scope of operations of VampirTrace and HDTrace is similar for this purpose. However, a detailed comparison of the tools is out of the scope of this work, both tool environments are used in this thesis to reach a greater community on the one hand and to demonstrate the portability of the approach on the other hand.

6.1.1. HDTrace

The *HDTrace* environment is a tracing environment developed under the GPL [MKL12, MMK+12] at the University of Hamburg. HDTrace concentrates on the evaluation of new ideas and thus new modifications are considered to be experimental. Figure 6.1 shows the components of the environment.

The application code itself has not to be modified. To generate the trace files, a wrapper library for the MPI library (*MPI-Wrapper*) has to be linked to the application. Events (like MPI function calls) are stored in XML trace files using the *TraceWriting-C Library*. Additionally, statistics are periodically recorded and stored in a binary format with

6.1. Tracing Approach

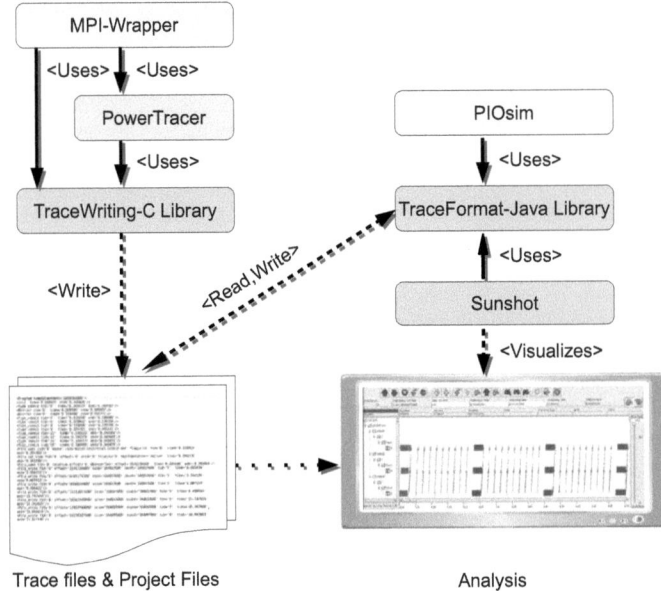

Trace files & Project Files   Analysis

Figure 6.1.: *HDTrace components [MMK+12].*

XML description header. This statistic interface allows to easily add new information sources for performance and energy analysis. The *PowerTracer* is an extension to the trace environment, which periodically traces information about power usage from an external power meter in statistic files [Kre09]. A project file links together all trace and statistic files of multiple sources without conversion. Furthermore, *PIOsim* is a event based simulator which reads the application event traces and allows to run them in virtual cluster environments. The simulation generates trace files of the run and internal components for further inspection, but this is out of the scope of this thesis. Trace files of application or simulation runs are visualized by *Sunshot* (see Subsection 6.3.1).

To generate trace files for an application run the application has to be linked against the HDTrace libraries. Upon execution the application will generate three types of files [Ehm12]. Each MPI rank generates a `trc` file containing the synchronous MPI events in XML format. The `stat` files contain external statistics in a binary format gathered from external libraries or daemons. This data is collected periodically (asynchronously) and upon visualization synchronized with the `trc` files via timestamps. Additionally, `info` files contain structural information such as MPI data types.

After the application run, the python script `project-description-merger.py` has to be called with the `info` files as input. The script creates the `proj` file to be further processed by Sunshot to visualize the trace.

6.1.2. VampirTrace

VampirTrace [MKJ+07, KBD+08] is an open source tracing tool developed by the Center for Information Services and High Performance Computing (ZIH). This subsection is partially based on [MMK+12]. It is used to instrument applications in order to generate trace files in the *Open Trace Format*[1] (OTF) that can be analyzed using several performance tools. Depending on the type of instrumentation, the trace files contain events like function entries end exits, MPI messages send between processes, hardware performance counters, etc. All events are stored with a timestamp, thus events of different processes can be visualized with the correct timing behavior. To include additional information about the hardware. the VampirTrace's plugin counter interface [STHI10] can be used.

Figure 6.2 shows the possible data sources that can be accessed using VampirTrace.

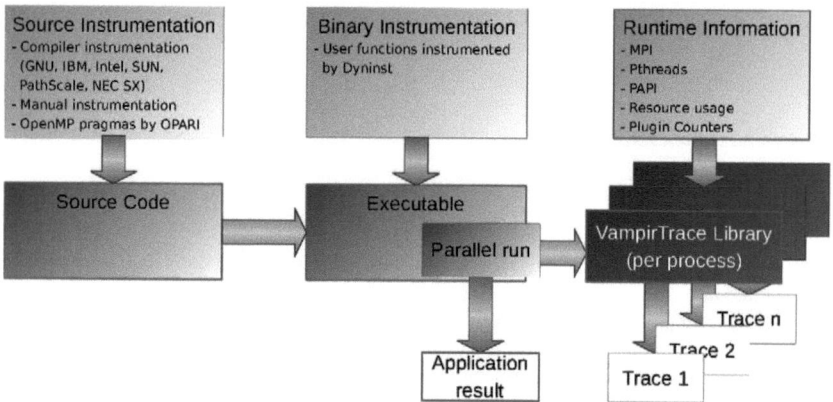

Figure 6.2.: *VampirTrace data sources [MMK+12].*

In order to generate a trace file using VampirTrace the application has to be recompiled using the provided wrappers. Afterwards the application generates trace files when it is executed. Per process, a uctl and a z file is generated. After the trace unification, a otf file is generated out of all uctl files to be visualized by Vampir. Additionally, during the trace unification, the plugin counter interface integrates all post-mortem information.

6.1.3. Intrinsic Tracing Tool Problems

The tracing approach has system inherent problems because the device under test and the measurement device is the same physical device. The influences of the measurement

---
[1] http://www.tu-dresden.de/zih/otf/, last checked: March 2, 2013

on the device under test cannot be fully avoided. Correspondingly, the application performance is usually decreased during measurement. However, to proof the performance or energy improvement of the application, the original application version (without tracing) has to be compared to the modified version (also without tracing).

Furthermore, the tracing approach has some drawbacks inherent to highly parallel applications. The inter-node communication of processes significantly impacts the performance with increasing process count. Additionally, the tracing data to be stored increases, too. This results in high requirements on the system architecture, some systems provide additional tracing infrastructure on the hardware side to reduce influences of the running application. Nevertheless, the more processes the application uses and the longer the application run, the more information has to be stored which results in even larger trace files.

One common way to reduce the size of trace files is to reduce the information to be traced. Typically, filters are used to be defined by the user or also generated automatically by the environment. Additionally, redundant data like periodic events can be automatically detected and stored only once. The usual way for larger applications is to start with automatic instrumentation, then apply more and more filters until the trace file includes just enough information for the analysis, and then instrument the remaining functions manually to reduce the overhead at runtime.

However, saving the trace files to the local hard disk may influence the measurements in several ways [MMK+12]. On the one hand, there may be an impact on the performance, because – depending on the amount of the traced information – the disk may be busy writing out the traces. On the other hand, writing the traces may inhibit the storage system from using a power-saving idle mode. One way to circumvent this problem is to use the main memory instead of the disk. But this solution also has drawbacks, traces can use quite a large amount of space which lowers the total amount of main memory available for other purposes.

Another way to deal with this is to store the traces on some kind of remote storage system, but this requires the use of the network. Again, due to the utilization of the network, this may have an impact on both the performance and the power consumption. Overall, a solution based on the specific environment and problem must be used. For example, if a – possibly slower – service network is available, it may be used for sending the traces to a remote storage system. If most of the main memory is unused, it can be utilized to temporarily store the traces.

Nevertheless, intrinsic tracing tool problems are out of the scope of this work. More details can be found here [TDZ, Ehm12, MMK+12]. The integration of further energy-related metrics to the tracing environments will definitely introduce additional overhead, but it is ensured that this overhead is as low as possible.

6.2. Integration of Energy-Related Metrics

Further energy-related metrics can be integrated into the two tracing environments using HDTrace's statistics [MKL12] and VampirTrace's Plugin Counter [STHI10] interfaces,

6. Correlating Applications and Energy-Related Metrics

respectively. Both interfaces provide the capability of asynchronous tracing of further metrics like the node power consumption. The values are synchronized via timestamps. The Plugin Counter interface supports also synchronous tracing – but to provide a consistent setup, asynchronous tracing is used for both environments.

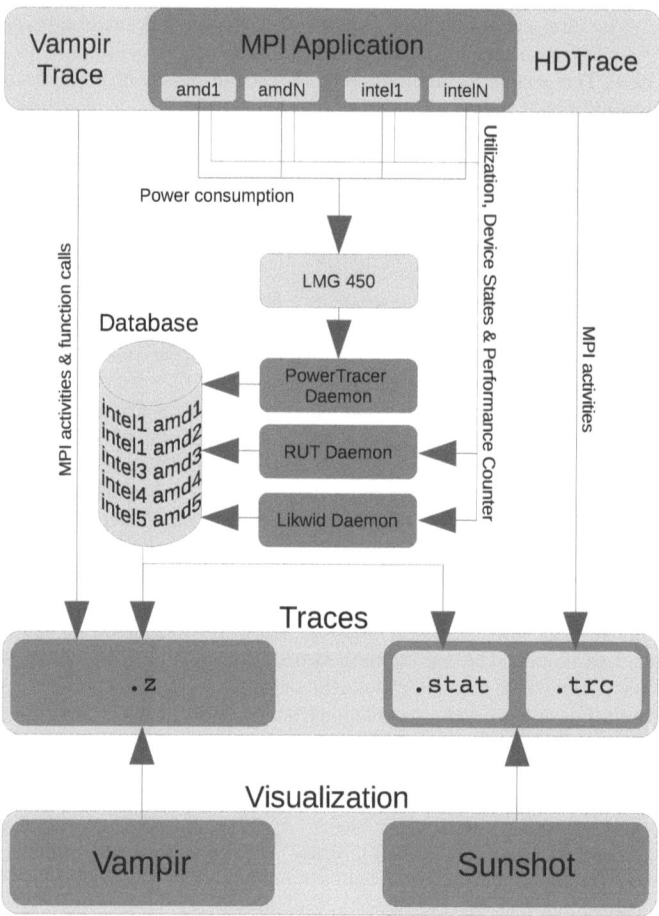

Figure 6.3.: *Trace environment with tool extensions for the integration of additional energy-related metrics.*

Figure 6.3 shows the integration of additional infrastructure in the existing two tracing environments. All additional values are sampled asynchronously using several daemons into a database. The database values are merged post-mortem into the corresponding trace files of each environment. To provide a simple interface to the `postgresql` database[2] for these tasks, the *DBConnector* is implemented in C. Additionally, each tracing environment has to provide an interface for merging the database values into the corresponding trace files. For VampirTrace, a plugin counter interface has been developed for the specific test setup by the Center for Information Services and High Performance Computing (ZIH) in the eeClust framework[3] using the DBConnector which has been adjusted for the daemons [MMK+11]. The corresponding software packages can be found on the eeClust project website[4]. For HDTrace, the additional support is added to the *ResourceUtilizationTracing* library [Kre09] which is further described in Subsection 6.2.2.

The database itself can be stored on a dedicated node, e.g. the master node. This setup requires the data to be sent via the network to the database host, but no further node interaction like writing data directly to the trace files is required. The splitting of the sampling task into several daemons allows to run the daemons on different nodes to further minimize the impact on the running application. Furthermore, each daemon can be tuned for its specific task. In detail, the following daemons and extensions are implemented:

- The *PowerTracer* daemon, sampling the node power consumption,

- the *Resource Utilization Tracing* daemon, sampling the device utilization and hardware power states,

- the *Likwid Tracing* daemon, sampling the processor performance counters,

- and the tracing extension of the eeDaemon to log the decisions about the hardware power states.

In the following subsections, the different requirements, dependencies and designs are discussed for each of the daemons.

6.2.1. Power

The *PowerTracer* daemon samples the node power consumption using the three LMG 450 measurement devices. The daemon is a complete redesign of the corresponding library implemented for HDTrace [Kre09]. Each of the measurement device has 4 channels, thus in total 12 values can be traced in every sampling iteration. As described in Figure 3.2, the power measurement infrastructure is independent of the computing notes.. Hence, the measurement values can be collected by a dedicated node without interferences with the running application. Thus, there is no measurement overhead for collecting the node power consumption in this setup. The serial ports of the power

---

[2]http://www.postgresql.org/, last checked: March 2, 2013
[3]energy-efficient Cluster Computing, http://www.eeclust.de, last checked: March 2, 2013
[4]http://www.eeclust.de/downloads.en.html, last checked: March 2, 2013

measurement devices are connected to the master node, which also hosts the database. To minimize the measurement impact, the daemon is implemented on the master node. The measurement values are collected in a round-robin schema in a freely chosen interval corresponding to the LMG 450 specification. The default interval time is 100 ms (10 Hz), thus 10 values are collected per second per channel.

The daemon creates a database table for each measurement channel. Each table has two columns for the timestamp in microseconds and the value in Watt. Since the timestamp is unique, the column is created as a primary table key with index function. This simple database structure allows to easily insert and select values from the tables. On the one hand, the tables can be selected after each application run and merged into the corresponding trace files. On the other hand the capability of running database operations on the measurement values provides further knowledge (e.g. calculating the average power consumption or the minimum/maximum power consumption).

However, due to this daemon implementation instead of the library implementation, the sampling overhead of the daemon is insignificant since no interaction with the computing nodes and thus the running application is necessary.

For HDTrace, the power tracing is automatically enabled if linked to the ResourceUtilizationTracing library. If values are available in the database, these are included into the trace files. For VampirTrace, the environment variable VT_PLUGIN_CNTR_METRICS has to be set to eeClustPlugin_<host>_power (see Line 14 in Listing A.1 in the appendix).

6.2.2. Device Utilization and Hardware States

On the contrary, tracing the device utilization and the device power states influences the application run. The corresponding *ResourceUtilizationTracing* daemon is based on the *ResourceUtilizationTracing* library [Kre09] implemented for HDTrace. The library traces already the processor utilization (on per core base), the used main memory and network and hard disk activity using libgtop[5]. Originally, the library is linked with the HDTrace environment to the application. Due to the incompatibility with the database tracing environment, the library is partially rewritten to be a stand-alone daemon which traces the measured values into the database. Corresponding to the PowerTracer, a database table is created for each metric and each node, containing a timestamp and a corresponding value.

Additionally, the daemon has been extended to trace the hardware power saving states. The processor performance and sleep states are traced using the cpufreq and sysfs interface, respectively [Sey11]. The cpufreq interface allows to trace the current processor frequency in Kilohertz. The sysfs interface does not allow to trace the current processor C-State, because the state changes are too frequent. But it is possible to trace the interval usage of the different C-States in percent. More details about these two interfaces are summarized in the related work (Chapter 8). However, the hard disk power saving state is traced sending the ATA command CHECKPOWERMODE which returns if the device is in standby, spinning up or down, idle or active. Furthermore, the network

---

[5]http://developer.gnome.org/libgtop/stable/, last checked: March 2, 2013

6.2. Integration of Energy-Related Metrics

interface card speed and duplex mode is checked using the ioctl interface.
The correlation of the current usage and power state decisions is especially interesting to localize waiting times resulting from inefficient power saving mode usages. However, also the localization of device idle times which are not exploited by the operating system is possible.
To reduce the tracing influences to the compute node, it is possible to trace some power data via IPMI. In general, it is possible to trace the socket voltage, the memory voltage and several voltage lines to mainboard via IPMI. Unfortunately, not all mainboards support the same data. Additionally, the interval time is limited (about 200 ms) and the measured values are not always plausible without additional measurements. However, via IPMI the measurement of the socket voltage is possible, which can be correlated to the processor P-States (see Chapter 3). The main advantage is the non-existent tracing overhead, since the IPMI communication is handled over the service network. If starting the IPMI tracing daemon on the master node, no influences on the running application are measurable.
For HDTrace, the device utilization and hardware state tracing is automatically enabled if linked to the ResourceUtilizationTracing library. For VampirTrace, the environment variable VT_PLUGIN_CNTR_METRICS has to be set to eeClustPlugin_<host>_util_<metric>, where metric could be for example mem_free for tracing the free main memory in gigabyte (see Line 16 in Listing A.1 in the appendix).

6.2.3. Performance Counters

In addition to the utilization tracing, it is essential to classify the type of utilization, especially for the processing cores. Processor performance counters provide hardware measurements about the utilization of different function units of the processor on event level. Every time an event (like a floating point operation) occurs, the corresponding event counter is increased.
VampirTrace natively supports performance counters via the *Performance Application Programming Interface* (PAPI) [TJYD09, MMK+12]. According to the project website[6], PAPI provides the tool designer and application engineer with a consistent interface and methodology for use of the performance counter hardware found in most major microprocessors. Synchronous tracing of the hardware performance counters with VampirTrace can be configured using the VT_METRICS environment variable.
HDTrace experimentally supports performance counters via the *likwid* toolset [THW10]. Likwid stands for *Like I knew what I am doing*[7]. Amongst other command line tools for Linux to support programmers in developing high performance multi threaded programs, the *likwid-perfctr* tool allows to measure hardware performance counters on Intel and AMD processors.
In the following, likwid will be used to sample performance counters due to the better usability – no kernel patching is necessary and the program code is well written and

---
[6]http://icl.cs.utk.edu/papi/, last checked: March 2, 2013
[7]http://code.google.com/p/likwid/, last checked: March 2, 2013

6. Correlating Applications and Energy-Related Metrics

documented which allows to easily integrate support for the DBConnector. Likwid samples the performance counters in predefined groups and derivates several performance metrics. For example, the memory group (MEM) provides the local memory bandwidth, the remote memory bandwidth and the processor *Cycles per Instruction* (CPI).

For HDTrace, the performance counter tracing is automatically enabled if linked to the ResourceUtilizationTracing library. For VampirTrace, the environment variable VT_PLUGIN_CNTR_METRICS has to be set to eeClustPlugin_<host>_likwid_<metric>_thread<no>, where metric could be for example l3_miss_rate_thread0 for tracing the L3 cache miss rate of Socket 0 (see Line 26 in Listing A.1 in the appendix). However, for both environment the tracing daemon has to be started manually. The counter group, interval size and the processor cores for the collecting the performance counters have to be specified (see Line 32 in Listing A.1 in the appendix).

6.2.4. eeDaemon Decisions

If suitable application phases for power saving are identified, the eeDaemon enables efficient management of the power saving modes of the hardware. To support tracing of the hardware power saving mode decisions by the eeDaemon, the daemon logs each decision using the DBConnector. This is possible synchronously (each decision is logged when completed) or asynchronously (the current mode is logged in a fixed interval time). This correlation allows to identify application phases, where the provided user instrumentation is inaccurate. In general, the user instrumentation is inaccurate if the energy efficiency in the identified application phase is decreased. This happens if the application slowdown outbalances the power decrease, due to

- decreasing the processor frequency in a cpu-bound phase,
- one processor core keeping the voltage up for the whole processor socket,
- the latency introduced by the state switching significantly impacting the phase duration,
- or the device not being ready when used again.

Depending on the eeDaemon toolset build environment, the daemon automatically generates the database entries or the stat file for the device modes. For HDTrace, the mode tracing is automatically enabled if the corresponding stat file exists. For VampirTrace, the environment variable VT_PLUGIN_CNTR_METRICS has to be set to eeClustPlugin_<host>_eed_<device>_mode, where device could be for example core0 for tracing the mode decisions for processor Core 0 (see Line 38 in Listing A.1 in the appendix).

To exemplarily quantify the additional tracing overhead by the eeDaemon, Figure 6.4 shows the application runtime and the trace file size (stat file) for various trace interval sizes. The eeDaemon internal request update interval is set to one millisecond, the tracing of all metrics is enabled. For a small trace interval time of 1,000 microseconds (=

6.3. Visualization of Trace Files

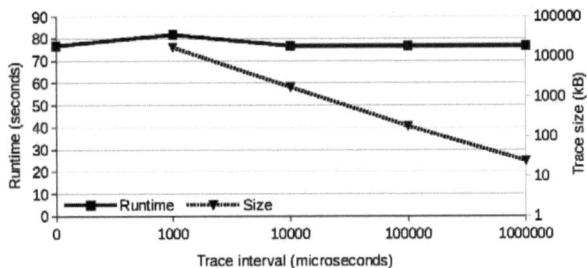

Figure 6.4.: *Application runtime and statistics file size dependent on HDTrace interval.*

1 ms), the application runtime is slightly increased by about 5 %, while for interval times $\geq 10,000$ microseconds the increase is not measurable. For all following measurements, a trace interval of 100 ms corresponding to the power measurement is used. Naturally, the trace file size linearly decreases with the increasing tracing interval.

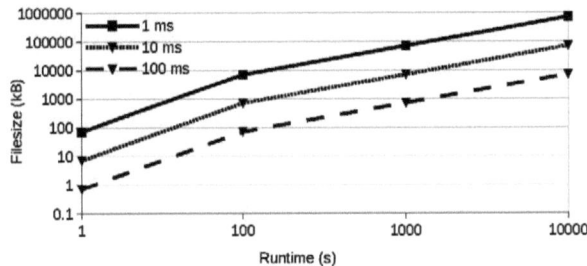

Figure 6.5.: *Statistics file size dependent on HDTrace interval and application runtime.*

Additionally, Figure 6.5 visualizes the statistics file size dependent on the application runtime for different tracing intervals. For a tracing interval of 100 ms, the file size in kilobytes equals the application runtime in seconds. Of course, this correlation depends on the set of enabled metrics.

6.3. Visualization of Trace Files

In this section the visualization tools are introduced that can be used to analyze the traces generated by the tools discussed in the previous sections. Vampir and Sunshot are used to visualize the trace files generated by VampirTrace and HDTrace, respectively. Vampir and Sunshot are timeline-based tools which allow to navigate through the whole sequence of events [MMK+12]. Both tools provide the capability of correlating the parallel application on process level with the energy-related metrics to visually identify the application phases. To demonstrate the phase identification, screenshots of Sunshot and Vampir illustrate various examples.

6.3.1. Sunshot

Sunshot is a Java-Swing application whose original design is based on *Jumpshot*[8] [MKL12, MMK+12]. The Jumpshot viewer is part of the MPI implementation MPICH2, which allows to visualize the *SLOG2* trace format of the *MPI Parallel Environment* (MPE). The timeline-based visualization tool Sunshot provides additional capabilities like trace profiles, histograms and user defined metrics. Sunshot allows the programmer to analyze the chronology of activities in parallel processes or threads. Figure 6.6 on Page 91 shows a typical screenshot of Sunshot to analyze MPI applications. The timelines show the sequence of events for all processes and threads. If function groups where defined during the tracing, these are represented by different colors to quickly identify program phases. Messages between processes can be represented by black lines. A well balanced application usually shows a regular pattern of calculation and communication phases. Load imbalances as well as abnormally behaving processes can quickly be identified in the timelines.

The first 8 timelines represent the activities of the MPI library generated from the trc files. Each process on each node has its own timeline, correspondingly one node with 8 processes is visualized. Below the MPI timelines the external statistics from the stat files are shown. Hardware components like the processor cores, the network interface cards or the hard disk can each have several timelines indicating their utilization or power state at a certain point during the application execution. This example only shows the average processor utilization and frequency, it is however possible to trace and visualize the data for each core individually.

The elements in the MPI timelines offer a context view to show detailed information (see Figure 6.7 on Page 92). Information like the exact duration, the timestamp when the function call was executed, involved ranks and the function name is shown. For functions like MPI_File_write it also shows the amount of data written, the file name and the offset that was used for writing the file.

Figure 6.8 on Page 93 visualizes 8 MPI processes running into a barrier on one node, each rank is pinned to the corresponding core of the processor [MKL12]. The upper three out of eight rows in the figure display each rank over time and the different entry point in the barrier[9]. The corresponding frequency for each core is visualized in the following 4 timelines[9]. The operating system uses the ondemand governor, the corresponding processor frequency is sampled every second. The next row shows the corresponding node power consumption in watts. With each rank entering the barrier, the power consumption is increased because the corresponding processor core increases its utilization. The utilization increase is specific to this MPI implementation – probably the implementation uses busy-waiting to wait for a message to leave the barrier. However, the busy-waiting

---

[8]http://www.mcs.anl.gov/research/projects/perfvis/software/viewers/index.htm, last checked: March 2, 2013

[9]For clearness, five out of the eight rows are omitted

6.3. Visualization of Trace Files

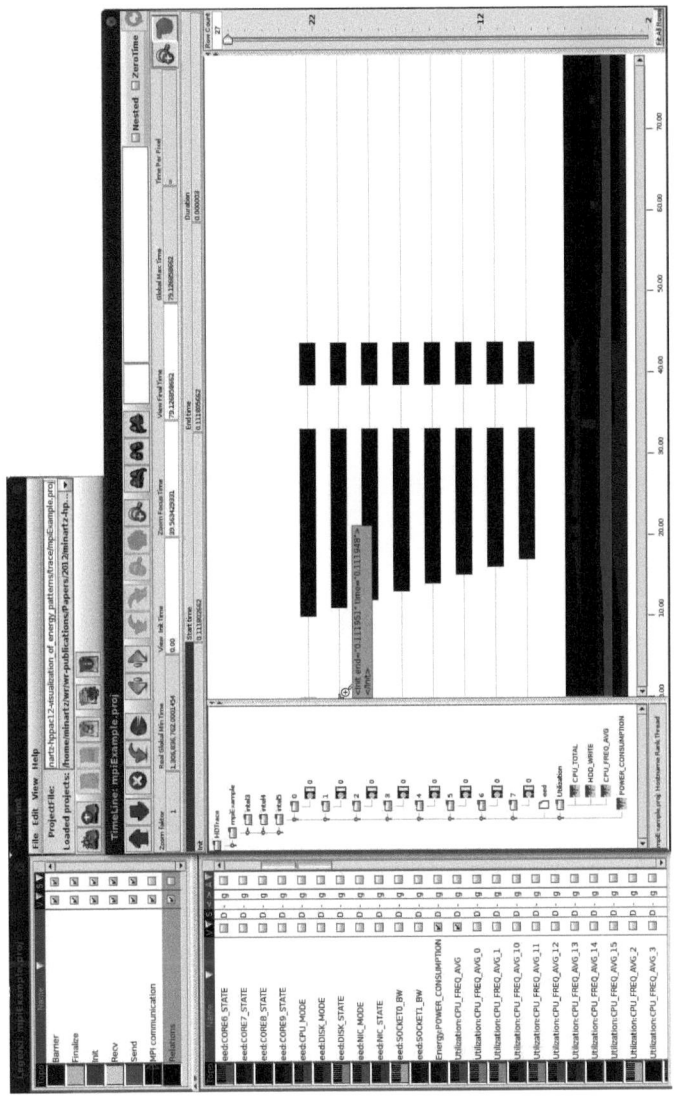

Figure 6.6.: *Main window of Sunshot.*

6. Correlating Applications and Energy-Related Metrics

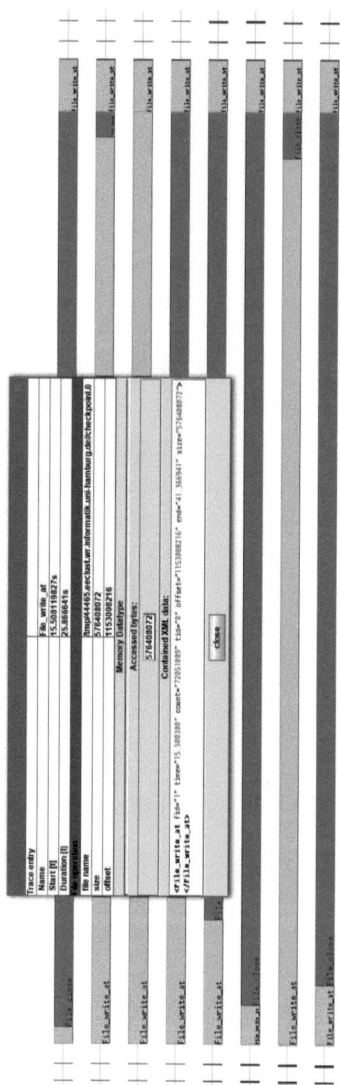

Figure 6.7.: *Context view of HDTrace timeline elements [Ehm12].*

6.3. Visualization of Trace Files

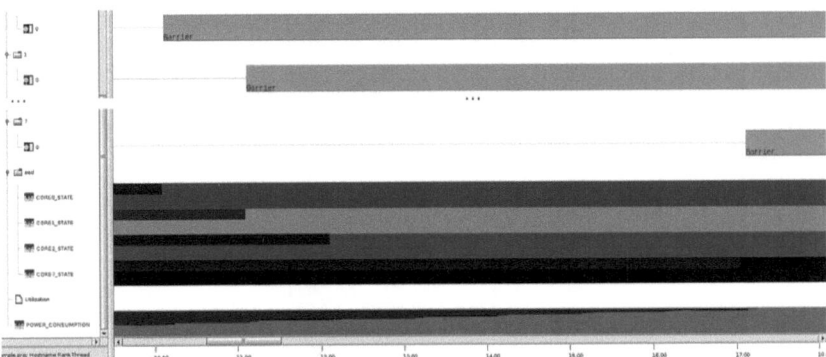

Figure 6.8.: *Sunshot screenshot of* MPI_Barrier *with ondemand governor for all cores [MKL12].*

phase results in an increase of the core frequency because the operating system can not distinguish between the classifications of utilization (see Subsection 4.2.1).

Taking a look at Figure 6.9 on Page 94, the power consumption increase is not based on the increased frequency; instead it is based on the changed C-State of the corresponding cores. Figure 6.9 visualizes the same example with a fixed frequency of 2,800 MHz per socket, but now the C-States are visualized (CPU_IDLE_X_C0) exemplarily for the same ranks. The C-State usage is also sampled per second. Opposed to the P-States in Figure 6.8, the C-States are reported in percent. With each rank entering the barrier, the C0 (active) state usage of the corresponding core increases to 100 % – which explains the increased power consumption.

However, the per device sampling has the advantage of more detailed information; for example, the time delay when switching device states can be visualized. In Figure 6.10 on Page 95, the power saving mode of devices has been manually switched using the eeDaemon displayed as CPU_MODE, DISK_MODE and NIC_MODE. The corresponding state as reported from the hardware is sampled as DISK_STATE and NIC_STATE (see the upper 5 timelines, the CPU_STATE is not shown here in detail as already discussed in Figures 6.8 and 6.9). The four timelines between the power consumption and the device states show the utilization of the disk and the network interface (HDD_READ, HDD_WRITE, NET_IN and NET_OUT). After the first MPI_Barrier, the disk is switched into a sleep state, which is instantly changed by the disk. The reduction of the network interface card from 1,000 Mbit to 10 Mbit is initiated after the second barrier, but it takes about 6 seconds until the device reaches the new operating mode (the darker block in the timeline at the bottom). Further, the utilization of each device could be displayed concurrently to detect performance issues, e.g. a wake-up of the disk by writing to the device.

The insights which can be gained by the visualization of the device switching times are

6. Correlating Applications and Energy-Related Metrics

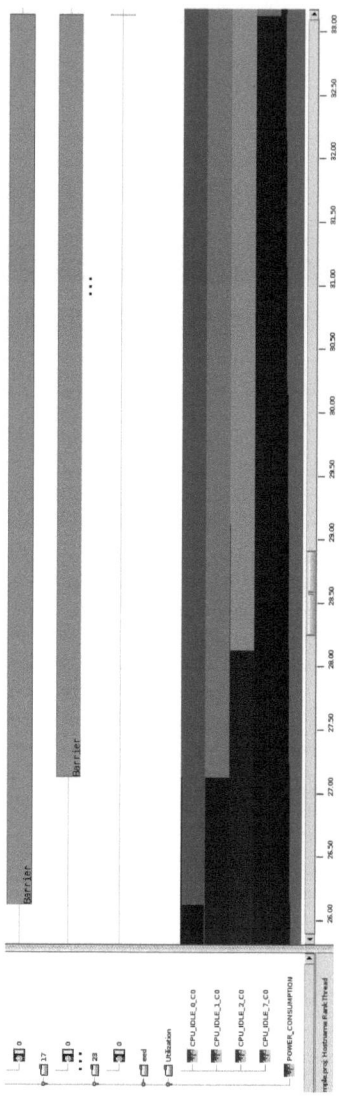

Figure 6.9.: *Sunshot screenshot of* MPI_Barrier *at fixed maximum processing frequency for all cores [MKL12].*

6.3. Visualization of Trace Files

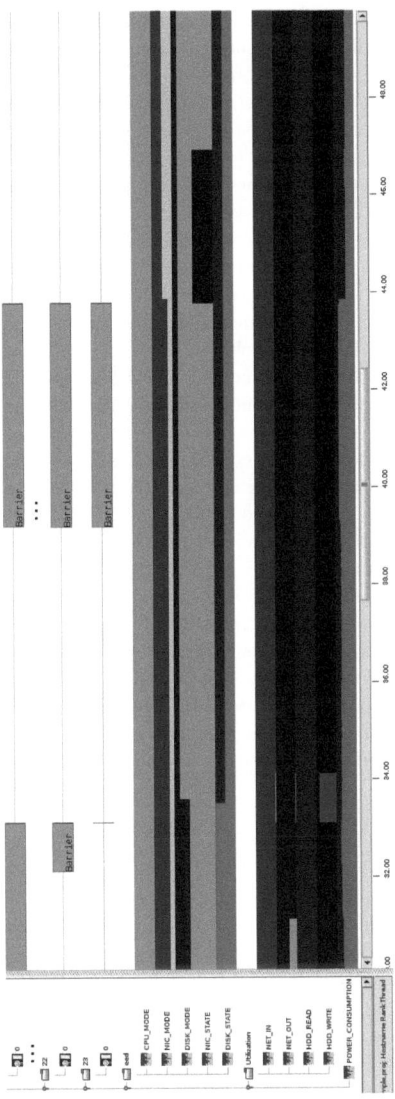

Figure 6.10.: *Sunshot screenshot of MPI_Barrier with manually switched device power states [MKL12].*

valuable to avoid performance decreases when making wrong decisions about the device state. Tracing related information, such as memory bandwidth per socket or the L3 cache misses, for example, is very helpful when deciding about the C-State and P-State of the processor. The higher sleep states can (depending on the implementation) flush the cache and the lower performance states can also reduce the memory bandwidth.

Figure 6.11 on Page 97 visualizes the memory bandwidth of the Intel system. The frequency of all eight cores is switched between the minimum frequency (1,600 MHz) and the maximum frequency (2,800 MHz) sampled as CORE_STATE. Additionally, the corresponding socket voltages are traced via IPMI as SOCKET0_BW and SOCKET1_BW, respectively. The maximum internal measurement frequency of IPMI is about 200 milliseconds, which explains the offset between the socket voltage and the other timelines. As all cores are under full load, reducing the frequency results in reducing the node power consumption and the socket voltage. But it is only reduced if all cores on the socket are switched into the lowest frequency. For the specific hardware, the cores 0-3 and 4-7 are grouped on one socket. Due to this implementation issue (the cores on each socket share the voltage regulator), switching single cores has almost no effect to the power consumption. The node power consumption is only reduced if the socket voltages drops since the highest core frequency dictates the socket voltage (see Chapter 3).

The application itself does not seem to be limited by the speed of the memory accesses, because the reduced frequency also affects the socket bandwidth. In terms of energy efficiency, it only makes sense to reduce the core frequency for phases of the applications where the bandwidth remains high. In this case, slower processing does not increase the duration of the phase at all since the data transfers to or from the memory subsystem are the bottleneck. Of course, this is only true if the memory bandwidth is independent from the socket voltage – the memory subsystem has to have its own voltage regulator as is the case for the underlying architecture. Summing up, reducing the frequency in this phase of the example application does not make sense in terms of energy saving because the energy efficiency decreases due to the cpu boundness.

6.3.2. Vampir

Vampir [MKJ+07, KBD+08, MMK+12] is a performance analysis and optimization tool developed by the Center for Information Services and High Performance Computing (ZIH) of the Technical University of Dresden, Germany. The timeline-based tool visualizes trace files that have been generated with VampirTrace. In comparison to Sunshot, Vampir is a commercial tool containing much more development effort resulting in better distribution and accept in the HPC tool community. In general, the scope of operations of Vampir and Sunshot is similar.

Figure 6.12 on Page 98 shows the main window of Vampir which consists of several displays. The top bar shows the main timeline of the whole application run consolidating all processes. It shows a histogram of the time spent per function group. The *Function Summary* display summarizes the time per function group, in this example 97 seconds are spent in functions of the application, 91 seconds in functions of the MPI library and 41 seconds in the VampirTrace library itself. The four graphs in the top left corner which

6.3. Visualization of Trace Files

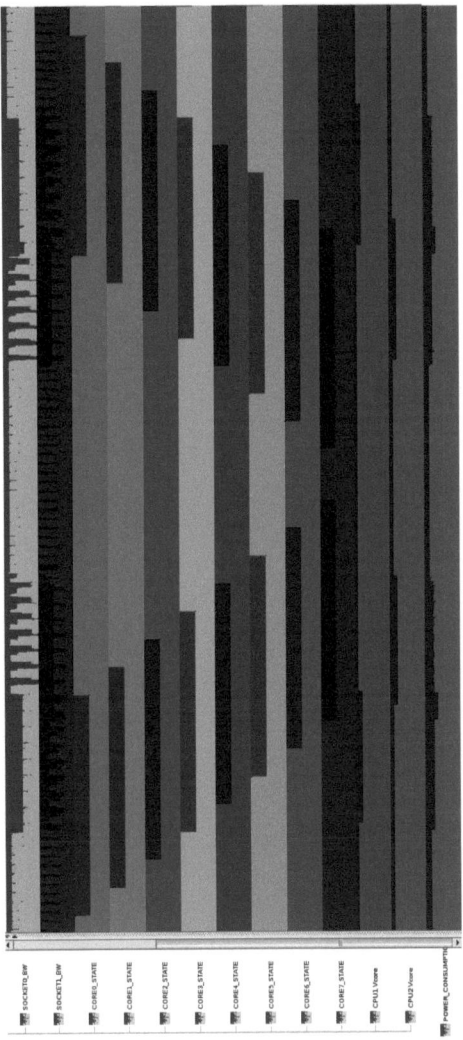

Figure 6.11.: *Sunshot screenshot of correlation of memory bandwidth and processor performance states. In detail, the timelines display the memory bandwidth, the processor performance states, the socket voltage and the node power consumption while the processor cores are under heavy processing load [MKL12].*

6. Correlating Applications and Energy-Related Metrics

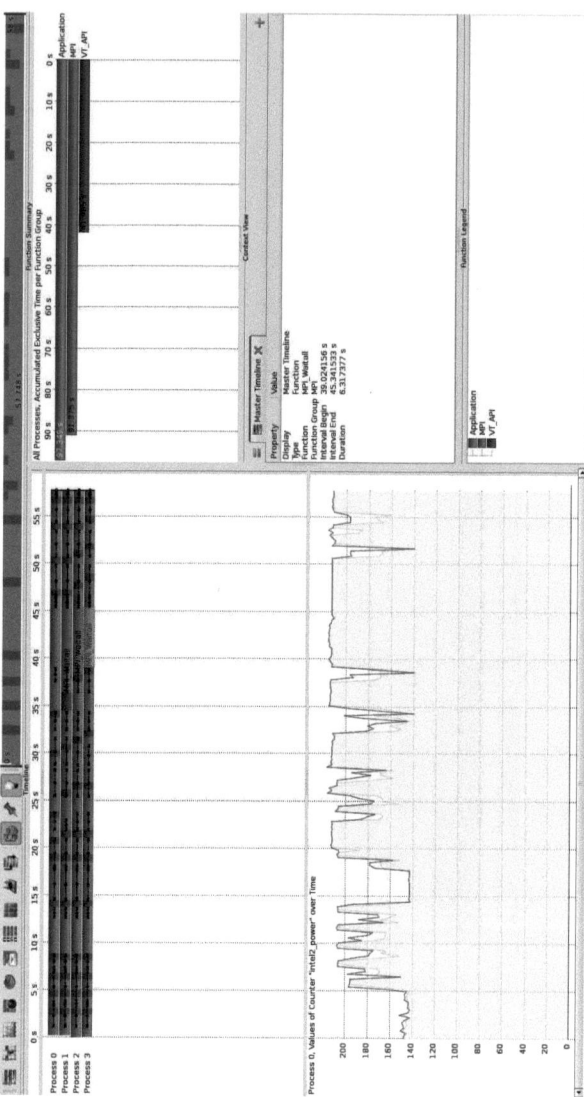

Figure 6.12.: *Main window of Vampir [Ehm12].*

6.3. Visualization of Trace Files

are named *Process 0-3* and show timelines of the function calls of each process spawned by the MPI library. Combining these two displays allows to identify code regions with a high optimization potential (i.e. a significant portion of the runtime combined with low utilization of the hardware). The *Counter Timeline* below is used to display the node power consumption which has been recorded using VampirTrace's plugin interface for external counters.

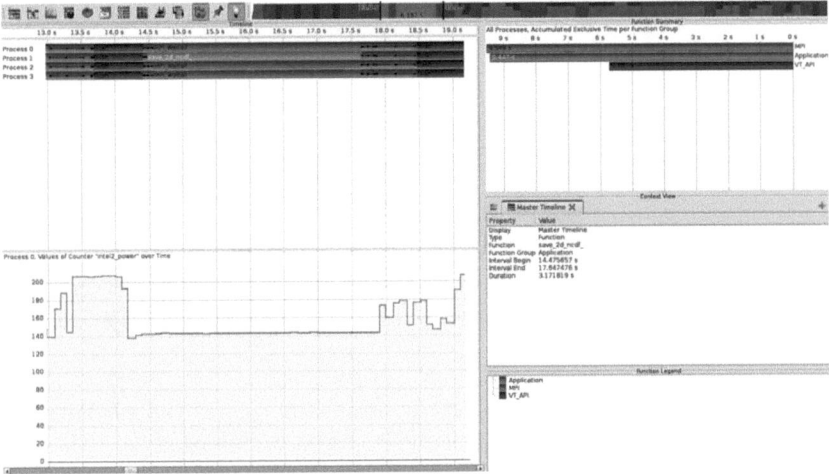

Figure 6.13.: *Vampir screenshot of zoomed-in timeline [Ehm12].*

It is possible to zoom in on an area of the main timeline which affects all other charts. Figure 6.13 displaying the power consumption chart is now more precise and in the process timeline the function names are shown. The areas representing function calls can be clicked and then show information like call duration, interval, name and involved processes in the *Context View* display on the right.

Figure 6.14 on Page 100 exemplarily displays the same example as Figure 6.9 for Sunshot including the processor C-States and the node power consumption in the counter timelines.

To sum up, Vampir with VampirTrace and Sunshot with HDTrace provide similar approaches, at least for the correlation of the parallel application with additional asynchronous metrics. With both tools, it is possible to correlate the application with the energy-related metrics like device utilization, performance and sleep states, performance counters, eeDaemon decisions and finally the node power consumption. This correlation of the application and energy-related metrics is essential to identify performance and energy hot spots in the application. The exemplary illustration of the visual identification process confirms this statement, the complex environment has a need for analyzing

6. Correlating Applications and Energy-Related Metrics

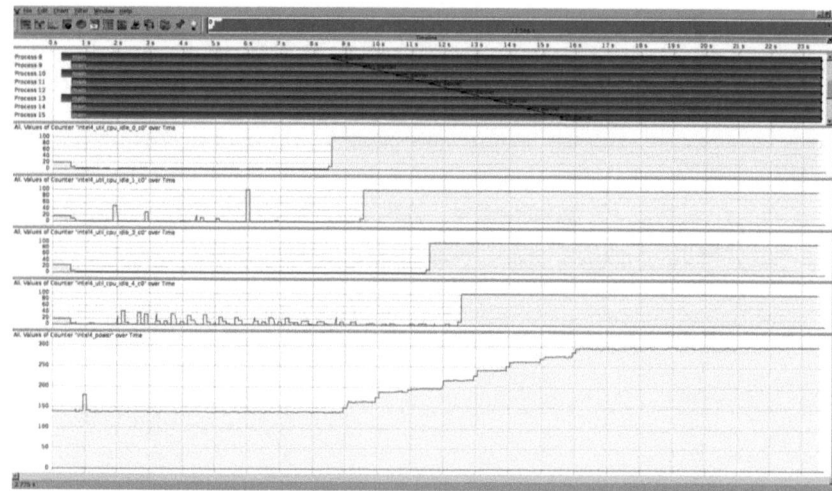

Figure 6.14.: *Vampir screenshot of* `MPI_Barrier` *at fixed maximum processing frequency for all cores.*

temporal dependencies and event specific information to decrease not only the power consumption, but also the energy. However, a deep understanding of the application, the system and especially the device power saving mechanisms is necessary to exploit the approach.

7. Evaluation

This chapter evaluates the strategies and tool extensions for reducing parallel application power consumption. Using eeMark, an energy-efficiency benchmark for HPC clusters, hardware usage patterns in terms of utilization and different performance counter shapings are identified. This includes detailed analysis of memory-bound application phases as well as various resource intensive application phases like communication and I/O phases. Additionally, the tradeoff between energy and performance is evaluated for the benchmark. Based on this analysis, four real parallel applications are examined using the devloped tool extensions. Appropriate application phases are instrumented using the eeDaemon interface to reduce the power consumption with the final goal of saving energy for the whole application run on the test cluster. Finally, the synthetic and application results are summarized and discussed.

7.1. Synthetic Benchmark

In this section *eeMark* – an energy-efficiency benchmark for HPC clusters, is used to correlate different workloads under usage of different power saving mechanisms and the hardware behavior. Large systems are often complex, therefore, application logic may be reduced to the core of the algorithm – the application kernel. The application is then implemented in a benchmark to show potential of system and modifications which reduces complexity. The eeMark benchmark has been developed within the eeClust project[1] by the Center for Information Services and High Performance Computing (ZIH), Technical University of Dresden. The following description of the benchmark and the reference run is partially based on [MHS+11] and [Mol11].

A configurable source code generator is used to create various resource intensive kernels that can be tailored. These kernels are combined with MPI communication and I/O operations to create parallel workloads that provide the necessary scalability to be executed on HPC clusters. Amongst others, the PowerTracer infrastructure (see 3.1) is supported which determines the power usage during the execution of the well-defined workloads.

The performance and power consumption of HPC systems is strongly influenced by the workload. Three classes of benchmarking kernels are available to stress different components [MHS+11]:

- compute kernels that generate a high load on the CPUs and/or memory,

---

[1]Energy-efficient Cluster Computing, http://www.eeclust.de, last checked: March 2, 2013

7. Evaluation

- communication kernels that stress the network between the compute nodes,

- I/O kernels that use the file system.

An in-depth description of all kernel classes can be found in [MHS+11].
The workload is specified in separate benchspec files that are passed to the benchmark as argument. The benchspec defines:

- problem size (**ps**),

- data set sizes,

- number of iterations,

- group definitions and associated kernel sequences.

The problem size determines the amount of data that is processed by each kernel in a single call. The data set size defines the size of the *input* and *output* buffers and has to be a multiple of the problem size. Each rank performs its kernel sequence on the complete data set multiple times as defined by the number of iterations. Within each iteration, the kernel sequence is repeated for every memory block of size **ps** which allows to send results of the first block to other ranks before all data is processed. Start and end of each iteration are synchronized via `MPI_Barrier`. Within the interval there is no synchronization other than through message passing.

The compute kernel perform a variable amount of operations per byte in order to generate a cpu-bound or memory-bound workload. Each kernel defines in the corresponding sequence how many operations are performed. The kernel perform simple vector operations using different arithmetic operations (add, mul, div, sqrt) on various data types (32 and 64 Bit integer, single and double precision floating point). High performance processors typically feature SIMD extensions (like SSE, Altivec, AVX) that increase performance of such data parallel operations. Many compilers support automatic loop vectorization to use such extensions. However, only basic loop forms can be covered by this optimization.

The communication kernel allow to exchange data between ranks within a group and between ranks in different groups. Available kernels are:

- global broadcast, reduce, and allreduce that involves all ranks in all groups,

- global broadcast, reduce, and allreduce that involve only the first rank of every group,

- broadcast, reduce, and allreduce within a group,

- send and receive between groups that exchange data between ranks with the same group rank,

- rotate up and down within a group.

7.1. Synthetic Benchmark

The I/O kernel use POSIX and MPI I/O functions to read and write files.
Especially the communication kernels depend heavily on the work placement on the physical nodes – thus the placement can be influenced with `distribution` parameter. The distribution `compact` results in continuous blocks, `round-robin` in round robin distribution and `fine` in weighted round robin (depending on the group ratio).
The used eeMark configuration for the evaluation can be found in Listing A.2 in the appendix.
The rest of this section includes detailed explanations of the eeMark reference run for detailed analysis of memory-bound and operation-based manual instrumentation and an analysis of the energy-performance-tradeoff.

7.1.1. Reference Run

The eeMark suite contains a reference benchset, which contains a broad set of kernels to cover different applications [Mol11].
Running a `benchset` creates a summary with the individual benchmark results: runtime, average power and total energy. The `reference.benchset` evaluates the efficiency for different classes of applications:

- compute benchmarks,
- communication benchmarks,
- I/O benchmarks and
- combined workloads.

The compute benchmarks perform no or little I/O operations and do not communicate between ranks. The three workloads have different ratios of arithmetic operations and memory accesses. The `compute1` benchspec performs many arithmetic operations with every opperand thus it depends on high utilization of the ALUs or FPUs to achieve high performance. The `compute2` benchspec performs only a few calculations on every operand thus it benefits from high memory bandwidth. The `compute3` benchspec uses a mix of cpu-bound and memory-bound kernels. Each workload is performed for different data types.
The communication benchmarks perform no or little I/O operations. Data is exchanged frequently between ranks which perform only a few calculations on the data. The `comm1` benchspec uses two equally sized groups of ranks that bidirectionally exchange data with `MPI_Send` and `MPI_Recv`. The `comm2` benchspec has a single master rank that distributes and collects data using `MPI_Bcast` and `MPI_Reduce`, respectively. The `comm3` benchspec is a producer-consumer scenario with 3 consumers for every producer. The measurements are repeated for different distributions of ranks where it makes sense.
The I/O benchmarks perform mainly I/O operations on large files. The `io1` benchspec reads files, performs a single arithmetic operation on every element, and writes the result into another file. The `io2` benchspec only reads from files and tests every element for

7. Evaluation

abnormal values (NaN[2] or infinite). The io3 benchspec writes random data to files. Each I/O benchspec is available in an MPI I/O (reference.benchset) and POSIX I/O (reference_nompiio.benchset) variant. The MPI I/O variants use large files that are shared between all ranks in a group, whereas the POSIX I/O versions use smaller files for every rank.

The combined workloads use a mix of operations from the above three categories. The combined1 benchspec uses MPI_Send and MPI_Recv to exchange data between ranks, whereas the combined2 benchspec uses collective MPI operations. Each workload is performed for different data types. The measurements are repeated for different distributions of ranks where it makes sense.

7.1.2. Memory-bound Instrumentation

As analyzed in Chapter 3, memory-bound compute benchmark have a huge potential for increasing the energy efficiency under usage of DVFS. In this subsection, the compute benchspec files of the reference run are instrumented to switch the processor frequency based on the degree of memory-boundness (OPB, processor operations per byte transfered from the main memory). However, due to the outcomes of Section 3.2, the AMD Opteron nodes are disregarded because the memory bandwidth scales with the processor frequency and thus the saving potential in memory-bound phases is negligible. For each combination of arithmetic operation, datatype and OPB, the optimal processor frequency can be identified using exhaustive experiments depending on the hardware architecture. The term *optimal processor frequency* can be interpreted in various ways – optimal in terms of:

- minimal Time-to-Solution (TTS) as metric for performance,
- minimal Energy-to-Solution (ETS) as metric for energy efficiency,
- and minimal Energy-Delay-Product (EDP) as example combined metric, the product of energy and time.

In the following, the focus is on the frequency with the minimal Energy-to-Solution. Since the OPB are well-known when generating the benchmark sources, it is straightforward to automatically instrument the routines using the eeDaemon interface described in Chapter 5) with a predefined set of frequencies.

Due to the structure of the compute reference benchspecs, memory-bound and cpu-bound phases are alternating, which results every time in frequency switches as shown in Figure 7.1 on Page 105. Remarkable is the fact that the power consumption increase in the figure results from the memory-bound phases – these consume more power than the cpu-bound phases (226 Watt compared to 207 Watt).

For the problem- and dataset sizes of the references benchmark specifications, the phase length is in almost all cases sufficient to hide the device latencies. The energy-performance tradeoff is analyzed independently in Subsection 7.1.4.

---

[2]NaN is the abbreviation for *Not a Number*

7.1. Synthetic Benchmark

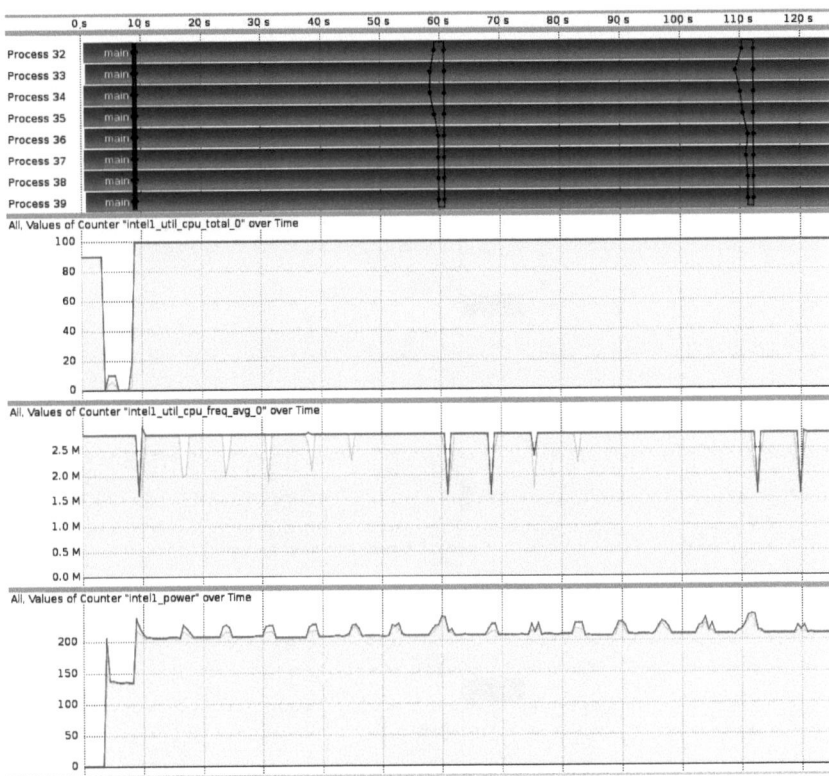

Figure 7.1.: *Vampir screenshot of the instrumented* `compute3` *reference run on one of the Intel Xeon nodes. The first counter timelines display the utilization and average frequency for processor core 0, while the last counter timeline displays the node power consumption. The power consumption increases during the memory-bound phases of the benchmark.*

Figure 3.6 in Chapter 3 already exemplarily explained the correlation between different strong memory-bound setups and the total energy for the test infrastructure. Since only the Nehalem memory bandwidth does not scale with the processor frequency, the Opteron infrastructure is disregarded in the following measurements.

Figures 7.2 and 7.3 on Page 107 visualize the measured relative runtime, energy and power for the different instrumented benchmark specifications, the baseline is the ondemand governor and the static 2,800 MHZ frequency, respectively. Compared to the ondemand governor, the instrumented version improves every compute benchmark in terms of power consumption. Because the influence on the performance is comparable

105

7. Evaluation

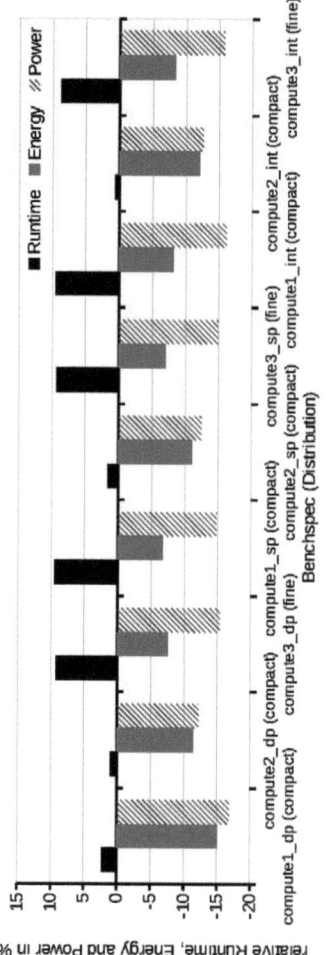

Figure 7.2.: *Relative compute benchmarks of the eeMark reference run on the Intel Xeon nodes. The benchmarks are instrumented for the minimal Energy-to-Solution. The baseline is the non-instrumented run with enabled ondemand governor of the operating system.*

low (the maximum is about 11 %), the total energy is also decreased in every setup. This clearly indicates that the ondemand governor is not the best choice – at least for the cpu-bound setups (compute1 benchmarks) the improvements should be insignificant. The

7.1. Synthetic Benchmark

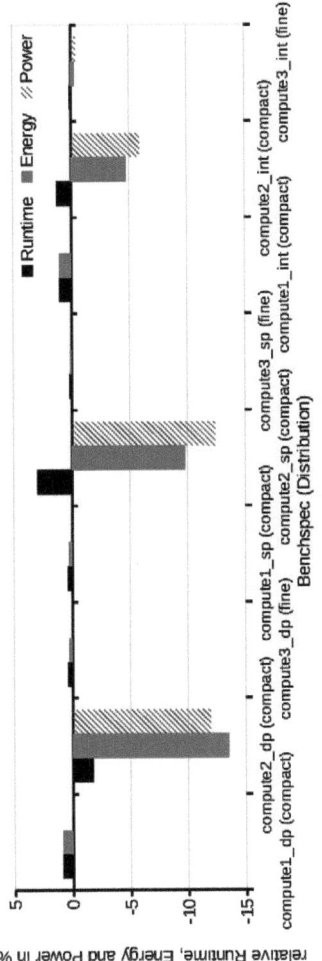

Figure 7.3.: *Relative compute benchmarks of the eeMark reference run on the Intel Xeon nodes. The benchmarks are instrumented for the minimal Energy-to-Solution. The baseline is the non-instrumented run with a fixed processing frequency of 2,800 MHz.*

better choice is the static frequency setup. Only the memory-bound setups (compute2 benchmarks) profit from the instrumentation. Here the improvement in terms of energy is up to 14%. The additional decreases in runtime for compute2_dp can be explained

7. Evaluation

with the usage of the Turbo Boost, which could be enabled by the instrumentation. In contrast, for the mix of cpu-bound and memory-bound kernels (`compute3` benchmarks) the instrumentation does not bring any improvements. The phase transitions are too frequent and the duration is too short to save any energy. Typical phase durations for memory- and cpu-bound phases are 33 ms and 779 ms respectively (see Figure A.1 in Appendix). If both sockets can reduce the frequency, the power consumption is decreased from 286 Watt to 212 Watt. For one socket, the power consumption accounts for 227 Watt. Even if the power consumption savings are significant during the memory-bound phases, the small runtime percentage (6 % of the total runtime) avoids energy savings.

Comparing the benchmark scores in addition to the pure measurement values, the same behavior is reflected: For the memory-bound benchmarks, the performance score remains constant while the efficiency and thus the combined score increases (see Figure 7.4).

Even though the energy savings for the memory-bound benchmarks are significant, for real applications the degree of memory-boundness is usually not known in advance. Although there exist methods to estimate the processor operations based on the source-code, a more convenient and reliable method is the analysis of hardware performance counters.

Performance Counters Analysis

The well-defined workload of the benchmark makes it possible to analyze the effect of different memory-bound or cpu-bound setups on the highly hardware specific processor performance counters. In Figures 7.5, 7.6 and 7.7, different sets of performance counters and metrics are compared for a strict memory-bound (1 Operation per Byte) and a rather cpu-bound (32 Operations per Byte) setup. Each setup is executed at different, meaningful processor frequencies: 2,801 MHz (enabled Turbo Boost), 2,800 Mhz (maximum frequency), 2,267 MHz (medium frequency) and 1,600 MHz (minimum frequency). The relative measurements compared to the maximum frequency setup are plotted.

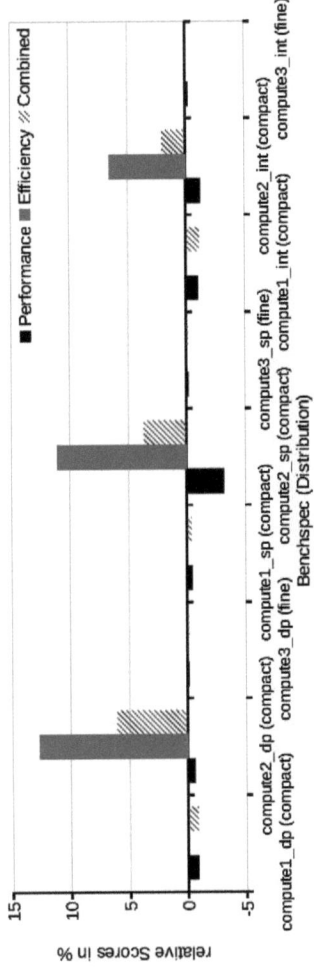

Figure 7.4.: *Relative compute benchmark scores of the eeMark reference run on the Intel Xeon nodes. The benchmarks are instrumented for the minimal Energy-to-Solution. The baseline is the non-instrumented run with a fixed processing frequency of 2,800 MHz.*

7. Evaluation

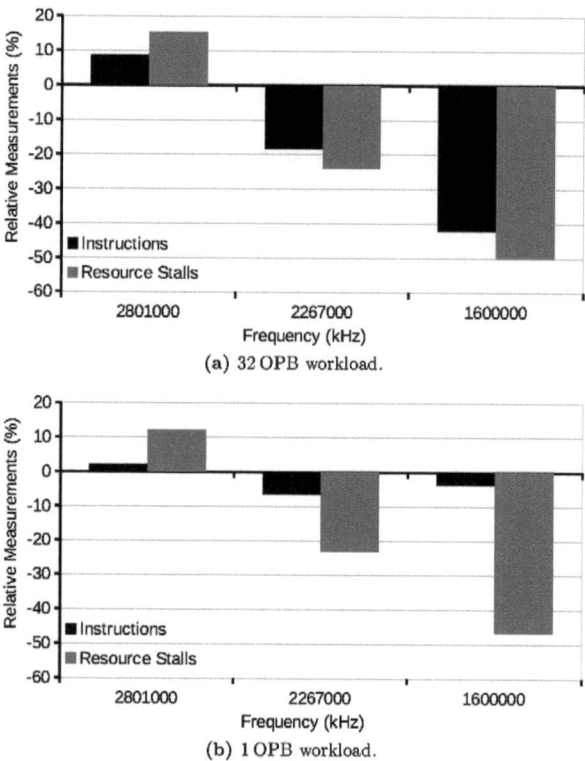

Figure 7.5.: *Instructions and resource stalls performance counters measurements for different processing frequencies of a cpu-bound workload (32 OPB) and a memory-bound workload (1 OPB) on the Intel Xeon nodes. The performance counters are averaged in 10 ms interval steps. The baseline is a run with a fixed processing frequency of 2,800 MHz.*

7.1. Synthetic Benchmark

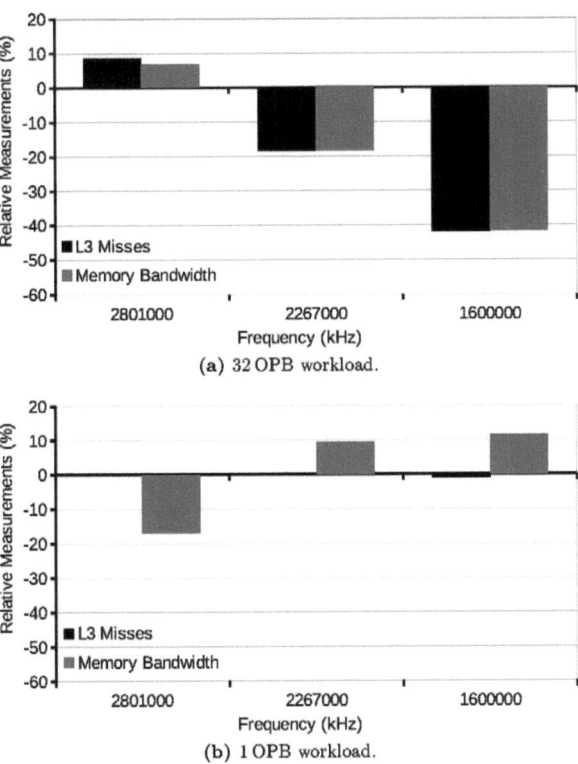

(a) 32 OPB workload.

(b) 1 OPB workload.

Figure 7.6.: *L3 Cache misses and total memory bandwidth performance counters measurements for different processing frequencies of a cpu-bound workload (32 OPB) and a memory-bound workload (1 OPB) on the Intel Xeon nodes. The performance counters are averaged in 10 ms interval steps. The baseline is a run with a fixed processing frequency of 2,800 MHz.*

7. Evaluation

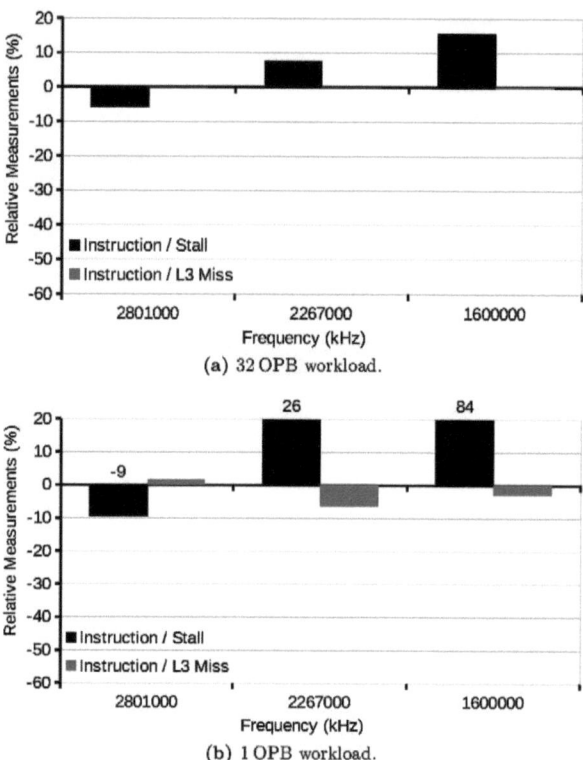

Figure 7.7.: *Instructions per stall and instructions per L3 miss rates performance counters measurements for different processing frequencies of a cpu-bound workload (32 OPB) and a memory-bound workload (1 OPB) on the Intel Xeon nodes. The performance counters are averaged in 10 ms interval steps. The baseline is a run with a fixed processing frequency of 2,800 MHz.*

For the cpu-bound setup, enabling the Turbo Boost results in an increase of the average count of retired instructions (INSTR_RETIRED_ANY counter) per measurement interval and thus the count of resource stalls (RESOURCE_STALLS_ANY counter). If decreasing the frequency to the medium or the minimum frequency, the instruction count also decreases which is reflected in the decreased stalls. In opposition to the cpu-bound setup, the memory-bound setup profits from the frequency decreasing: The number of retired instructions remains constant, while the number of stalls decreases significantly. The explanation is the different ratio of useful work (retired instructions) to useless work (resource stalls) for the two setups. For the cpu-bound setup the portion of useful

7.1. Synthetic Benchmark

work clearly outshines the useless work, for the memory-bound setup the opposite is true. The useful work is highly dependent on the processing frequency, while the useless work (like waiting for data transfered from the memory) is dependent on the memory subsystem frequency, which is not dependent on the processing frequency on the Nehalem architecture. To conclude, with a lower processing frequency the cpu-bound setup gets less useful work done but remains constant for the memory-bound setup because less useless work is required in the same time interval.

Accordingly, the count of L3 cache misses and the total memory bandwidth is decreased with the processing frequency for the cpu-bound setup. For the memory-bound setup the count of L3 cache misses remains constant and the memory bandwidth even increases. Figures 7.7a and 7.7b, respectively, are combining the performance counters measurements to retired instructions per resource stall (IPS) and retired instruction per L3 cache miss (IPM). The Instruction/L3 Miss rate remains for both setups comparable independent of the processor frequency, while the Instruction/Stall rate increases with the frequency decrease. While the latter rate increases with the minimum frequency setup about 15 % for the cpu-bound setup, it increases nearly 85 % for the memory-bound setup.

The outcome of this is: the lower the Instruction/Stall rate the higher is the energy-saving potential for processor frequency switching. Tables 7.1 and 7.2 show the corresponding absolute values for the setups, more detailed tables are in the appendix (Figures A.2 and A.3, respectively).

Table 7.1.: *Measured runtime, energy, mean power and performance counters for the memory bandwidth, Instruction/Stall and Instruction/L3 Miss for different processing frequencies of an cpu-bound workload (32 OPB) on the Intel Xeon nodes. The performance counters are averaged in 10 ms interval steps.*

Frequency MHz	Runtime s	Energy kJ	Power W	Bandwidth MB/s	IPS	IPM
2,801	54.35	14.42	265	23.02	8.09	100.18
2,800	58.26	14.31	245	21.56	8.59	100.14
2,267	72.50	15.61	215	17.61	9.24	100.16
1,600	100.87	19.10	189	12.58	9.92	99.89

7.1.3. Operation-based Instrumentation

In addition to the power saving potential in memory-bound compute phases of applications, communication and I/O phases have a high power saving potential. In this subsection, the communication and I/O benchmarks of the reference run are instrumented to decrease the processor frequency. As discussed in Chapter 3, the power saving potential is dependent on the type of I/O (local or distributed) and communication (inter- or

7. Evaluation

Table 7.2.: *Measured runtime, energy, mean power and performance counters for the memory bandwidth, Instruction/Stall and Instruction/L3 Miss for different processing frequencies of an memory-bound workload (1 OPB) on the Intel Xeon nodes. The performance counters are measured in 10 ms interval steps.*

Frequency MHz	Runtime s	Energy kJ	Power W	Bandwidth MB/s	IPS	IPM
2,801	42.02	10.44	248	17.90	0.16	10.95
2,800	41.99	10.08	241	21.52	0.18	10.77
2,267	41.98	9.00	214	23.52	0.23	10.10
1,600	42.05	8.62	205	24.00	0.33	10.47

intra-node) and the amount of data to be transferred. The amount of data is predefined by the blocksize which is known apriori. The type of I/O is dependent on the selection of the benchset. In the following, the standard benchspec (reference.benchset) is selected which uses MPI I/O. The type of communication is dependent on the placement of the MPI processes to the machines, which is influenced by the distribution parameter specified by the reference run.

The datasizes of the communication benchmarks are 128 MByte (comm1 and comm2) and 96 MByte (comm3), respectively, which should result in noticeable savings in energy under usage of DVFS for at least the inter-node communication. The datasize for the I/O benchmarks is 256 MB, which is too small for 8 processes to avoid I/O caching in the main memory – thus no remarkable results can be expected. The reference run is not modified at this point, since I/O operations are analyzed in detail in real applications in the next section. The type for each function is known when generating the benchmark sources from the template files: If the type is I/O or communication, the processor frequency is reduced via the eeDaemon interface to the minimum.

Figure 7.8 on Page 115 visualizes the relative runtime, energy and power consumption for the communication and I/O benchmarks of the reference run.

The communication benchmark runtime decrease when decreasing the processing frequency (comm3 with fine and roundrobin distribution) results from the fact that the benchmarks are mainly working in different caches. The fine and roundrobin distribution is used, which results in intra-node communication because the communicating processes are located mostly on the same node. Therefore, runtime variations also occur for these setups. However, to see the energy-saving potential for inter-node communication, the focus has to be on the compact distributed setups comm2 and comm3. The results show an energy decrease of about 25 % and 20 %, respectively, with almost no impact on the runtime. The benchmark comm3 does not perform any arithmetic operations between the communication calls in opposition to comm1 and comm2. Thus, the frequency is decreased during the whole benchmark run and the runtime is not increased. The comm2 benchmark consists of long communication operations and short arithmetical

7.1. Synthetic Benchmark

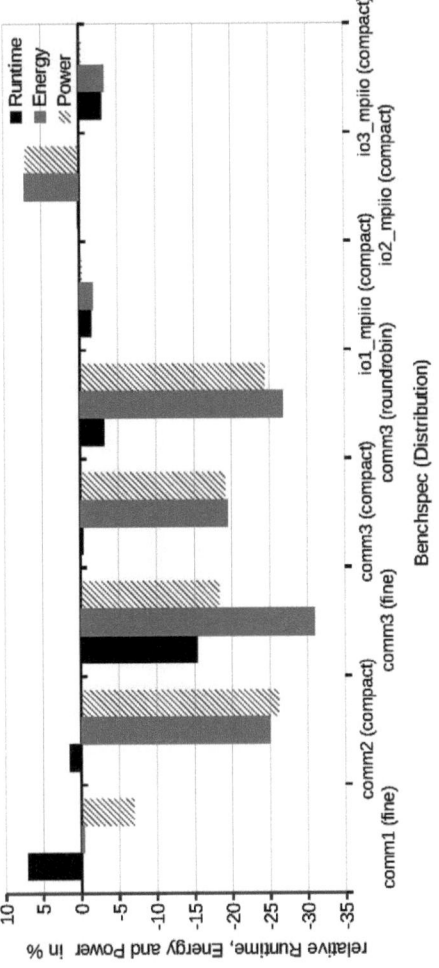

Figure 7.8.: *Relative runtime, energy and power measurements for the communication and I/O benchmarks of the eeMark reference run. The benchmarks are operation-based instrumented. The baseline is the non-instrumented run with a fixed processing frequency of 2,800 MHz.*

operations (see Figure 7.9 on Page 116). This introduces a small overhead visible in the runtime increase of about 3 %, but the total energy still decreases by 25 %.
As already discussed, the I/O benchmark datasize is too small to avoid caching, thus

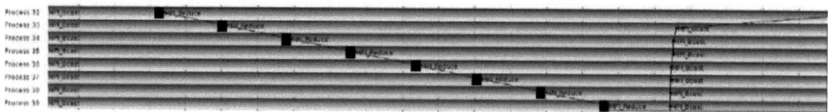

Figure 7.9.: *Vampir screenshot of the operation-based instrumented* comm2 *benchmark.*

runtime (and power, energy) variations occur for all benchmarks. For the io2_mpio benchmark (reads from files and tests every element for abnormal values) the power and energy even increases.

The relative benchmark scores in Figure 7.10 on Page 117 underline these measurements, even if some changes are hidden (e.g. comm3 (compact)) due to the low total values.

Figure 7.11 on Page 118 visualizes the results from instrumenting the combined benchmarks which uses a mix of operations from the compute, communication and I/O benchmarks. The fine distribution changes the communication type to intra-node communication, thus the duration of the communication phases are really short and no significant differences are measureable. However, for all compact benchmark specifications significant power and energy saving are reached. The difference between the combined1 and combined2 benchmarks is the impact on the runtime. The combined2 benchmarks significantly increase the runtime, which also decreases the energy savings even if the power savings are larger than for the combined1 benchmarks. The reason for this different behavior is the different type of used operations – the combined2 benchmark uses collective MPI operations and mainly cpu-bound operations, whereas combined1 uses point-to-point communication and mostly memory-bound operations. Accordingly, the performance impact on the compute phases is smaller.

7.1.4. Energy-Performance Tradeoff

Dynamic Voltage and Frequency Scaling as dynamic power management approach for processors has proven its usefulness in the last two sections. But it also introduces performance overhead: The processor speed is decreased and the transition between the different operating states creates overhead because the voltage has to be increased and decreased, respectively.

Equation 7.1 defines the minimum phase duration t_{min} for an energy-efficient state transition. If the phase duration is longer than the sum of the transition energy divided by the power difference and the transition time, the total phase energy is decreased.

$$t_{min} = \frac{E_{transition}}{P_{difference}} + t_{transition} \tag{7.1}$$

Besides to the state transition itself, the performance decrease has to be considered, too. For analyzing the practical tradeoff between energy and performance exemplary measurements are conducted on memory-bound phases. A memory-bound and a cpu-bound kernel are tailored and repeated in a row with varying datasizes, resulting in different phase durations. The measurement environment described in Section 3.1 is not designed

7.1. Synthetic Benchmark

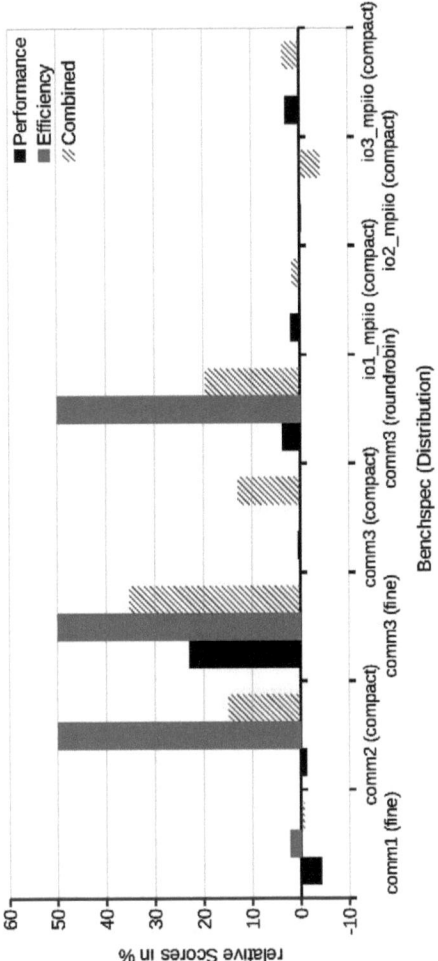

Figure 7.10.: *Relative scores for the communication and I/O benchmarks of the eeMark reference run. The benchmarks are operation-based instrumented. The baseline is the non-instrumented run with a fixed processing frequency of 2,800 MHz.*

to conduct this fine-granular measurements in the range of single milliseconds. With a computesize of 2 GB each phase is executed 2,048 times for the 1 MB datasize setup with a total runtime of $2,048 * (0.7\,\text{ms} + 1\,\text{ms}) \approx 3.5\,\text{s}$. Each benchmark is repeated 10 times and the average values are collected. The relative runtime, energy and performance

7. Evaluation

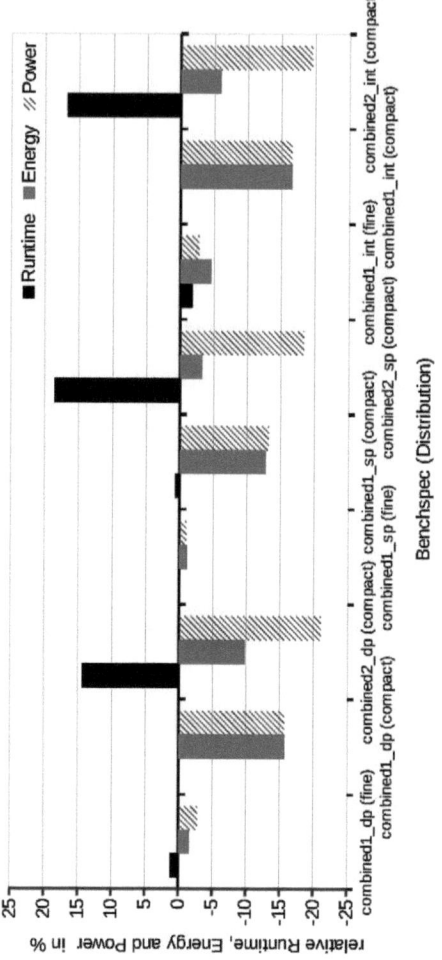

Figure 7.11.: *Relative runtime, energy and power measurements for the combined benchmarks of the eeMark reference run. The benchmarks are operation-based instrumented. The baseline is the non-instrumented run with a fixed processing frequency of 2,800 MHz.*

of the minimum frequency run compared to the maximum frequency run are shown in Table 7.3 and Figure 7.12 on Page 119.

To conclude the measurements: If the phase duration is shorter than 10 ms, the total

7.1. Synthetic Benchmark

Table 7.3.: *Relative runtime, energy and performance for a sequence of an instrumented memory-bound (1 OPB) and an non-instrumented cpu-bound workload (32 OPB) to evaluate the tradeoff between energy and performance. The length of the workloads is varyied with the datasize parameter. The computesize for each workload is 2 GB, 10 iterations are performed. The baseline is the non-instrumented run with a fixed processing frequency of 2,800 MHz.*

Datasize (MB)	Phase duration (ms) 1 OPB	32 OPB	Runtime (%)	Energy (%)	Power (%)
1	0.7	1	2.44	8.94	6.34
2	1.4	2	1.43	1.92	0.47
4	2.8	4	24.04	1.55	-18.14
16	11.2	16	8.60	-5.49	-12.94
32	22.4	32	7.05	-12.37	-18.11
64	44.8	64	4.63	-10.93	-14.93
128	89.6	128	5.17	-17.34	-21.45

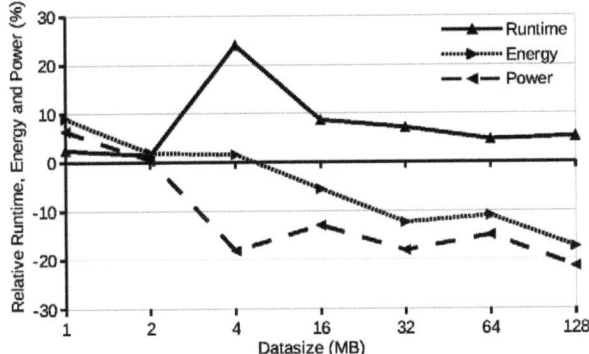

Figure 7.12.: *Relative runtime, energy and performance for a sequence of an instrumented memory-bound (1 OPB) and an non-instrumented cpu-bound workload (32 OPB) to evaluate the tradeoff between energy and performance. The data is based on Table 7.3.*

energy does not profit from manual phase instrumentation. For longer phases, significant energy savings can be reached.

7. Evaluation

7.2. Application Benchmarks

This section focusses on realistic application benchmarks to accomplish the measurements, while the synthetic benchmark is adressed in the last section. The goal is to select a meaningful set of applications that reflect the different workload types identified with eeMark. As analyzed in the last subsections, the applications should be classifiable in terms of compute intensive, communication intensive and I/O intensive. The compute phases should be further classifiable in memory-bound (more memory accesses per processor operation) and cpu-bound (more processor operations per memory acess). Hence, each application should contain at least one out of the aforementioned phases. Additionally, productive applications are preferred.

Four real applications have been selected for evaluation due to their characteristics:

- *partdiff-par*, an I/O-intensive[3] partial differential equation solver in C,
- *swim*, a memory-bound Shallow Water modeling for weather prediction written in Fortran,
- MPIOM, the compute-/communication-intensive Max-Planck-Institute ocean model in Fortran,
- and GETM, the compute-/I/O-intensive General Estuarine Transport Model also written in Fortran.

All applications are available in parallel MPI versions.
Table 7.4 gives a short overview of the applications. Except for *partdiff-par*, all applications are used in productive environments. Even if the first three applications are already sufficient to reach the requirements, a fourth application (GETM) is selected due to its very short and alternating application phases.

Table **7.4.**: *Application benchmarks overview.*

Application	*partdiff-par*	*swim*	MPIOM	GETM
Lines of code	≈ 800	≈ 400	≈ 50.000	≈ 40.000
Productive	−	+	+	+
Memory-bound phases	−	+	+	−
Communication phases	+	−	+	+
I/O phases	+	−	+	+

In the following subsections, each application is introduced and evaluated for itself. Section 7.3 summarizes the measurements, and compares and analyzes the results.

---
[3]Only valid for the used setup

7.2.1. Jacobi PDE Solver

Description

partdiff-par is a parallel partial differential equation solver implemented using the Message Passing Interface [MKL10, Ehm12]. The algorithm uses the iterative Jacobi method to solve the system of equations with a user-specified iteration count or result precision. To update a matrix cell $M_{i,j}$, the directly neighbouring cells $M_{i-1,j}, M_{i+1,j}, M_{i,j-1}$ and $M_{i,j+1}$ are needed for each calculation step.

The matrix is distributed block-wise (contiguous set of rows) among the MPI ranks. For updating the boundary rows of each block, the boundary rows of the corresponding ranks have to be exchanged. After updating the matrix using the stencil operator, the termination condition is checked (count of iterations or result precision reached). The latter includes additional communication to check the precision among all processes.

Thus, the application consists of the initialization phase, a communication phase and a calculation phase. Additionally, the application can write parallel checkpoints which results in an addional I/O phase. The checkpoint frequency can be specified separately and results in a dump of the complete matrix to the I/O system. Every process writes its share of the matrix into the checkpoint file. Figure 7.13 visualizes the different phases for 8 processes on one Intel node.

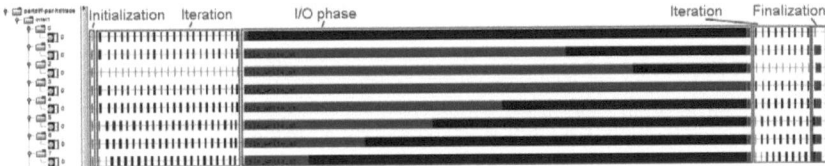

Figure 7.13.: *Sunshot screenshot of partdiff-par phases on one Intel Xeon node [Ehm12].*

Due to the simple and variable structure of the application, particularly with regard to the phase duration, the application is suitable for the manual instrumentation approach as a realistic application benchmark.

Measurements

Figure 7.14 shows the average processor utilization during the phases on one of the Intel nodes.
During the iteration phases (communication and calculation), the average processor utilization is high, but drops at the beginning of the I/O phase. In the I/O phase, the utilization increases from about 5 % up to 100 %. Accordingly, the ondemand governor of the operating system does not reduce the processor frequency. Additional performance counters information (like instructions per stall per socket) shows a low rate in the iteration phase and a high rate in the I/O phase. Generally, the iteration phase is not memory-bound (instructions per stalls are smaller than one), in the I/O phase occur

121

7. Evaluation

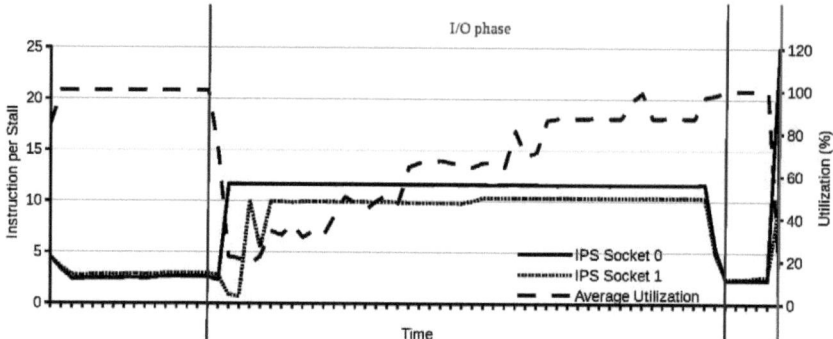

Figure 7.14.: *Average processor utilization and socket instructions per resource stall of partdiff-par phases on one Intel Xeon node.*

less resource stalls. To conclude, the I/O phase has a high potential for operation-based instrumentation.

Figure 7.15 on Page 123 shows an analysis of the setup with Sunshot.
The application spends a high percentage of the total runtime in the I/O phase, thus the I/O phase results in a large block in the screenshot consisting of the two most time consuming functions file_write_at and file_close. The light blue bars reflect the file_write_at operation, while the purple bars visualize the file_close operation for each process. Area 1 visualizes the reduced processor's frequency during the I/O phase, while Area 2 emphasizes the disk write activity. The phase of interest is the internal synchronization in the file_close operation, which seems to be implemented using the busy-wait pattern and thus is predestined for manual instrumentation. Reducing the processor's frequency during this phase results in a reduced power consumption visualized in Area 3.
A rather long MPI_Sendrecv call (that is used to exchange line data) has a duration of about 100 ms on the Intel nodes [Ehm12]; the trace analysis turned out that manual instrumentation does not improve the energy efficiency and thus only the I/O phase is instrumented.
The relative measurement results for the Intel nodes are plotted in Figure 7.16a. The energy savings with the I/O phase instrumentation reach about 8 % while increasing the runtime by about 3 %. Statically reducing the frequency for the whole application or using the ondemand governor (with and without Turbo Boost) is always worse than the static setup with 2,800 MHz.

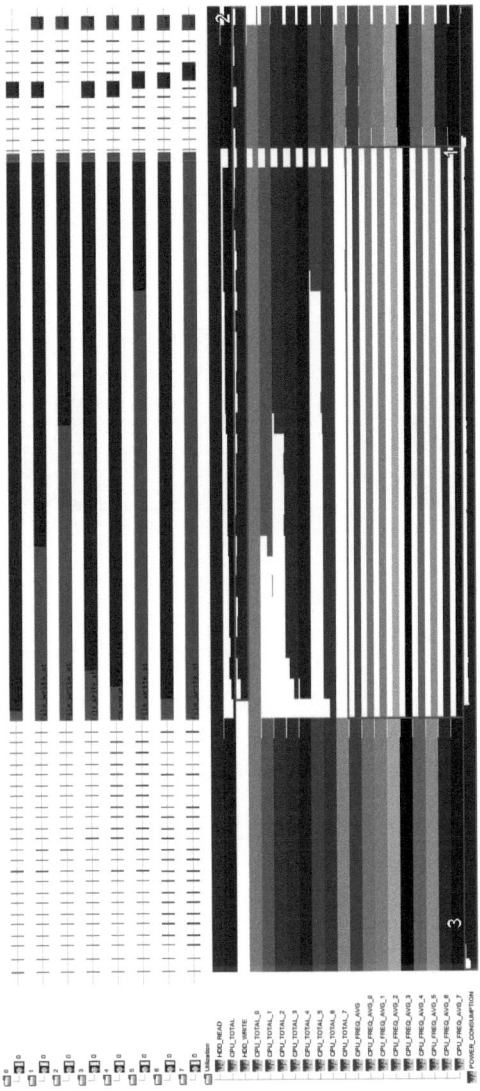

Figure 7.15.: *Sunshot screenshot of an instrumented partdiff-par run on the Intel Xeon nodes [Ehm12].*

7. Evaluation

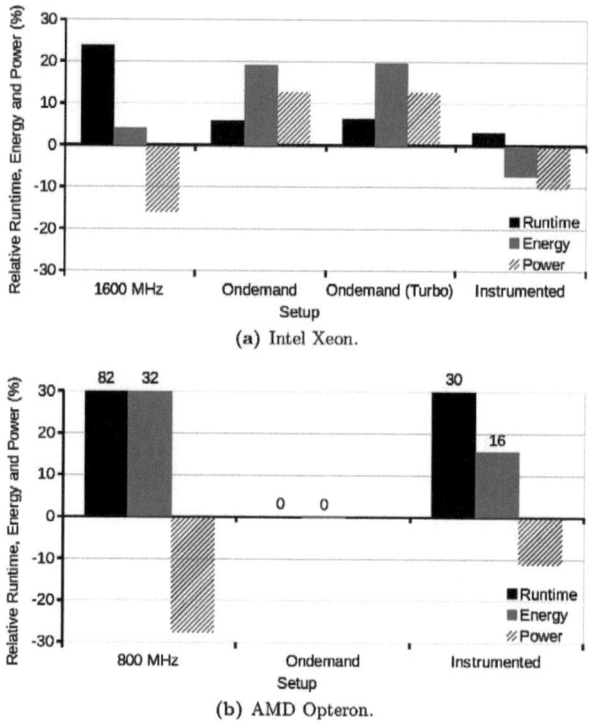

Figure 7.16.: *Relative runtime, energy and power measurements for different frequency setups of partdiff-par. The baseline is the non-instrumented run with a fixed processing frequency of 2,800 MHz.*

The results for the AMD nodes visualized in figure 7.16b show that the frequency reduction during the I/O phase also significantly increases the runtime – which impinges upon the total energy. This corresponds to the I/O write measurements in Chapter 3: For larger block writes, the frequency reduction increases runtime and energy. Further measurements with the application can be found in [Ehm12].

7.2.2. Shallow Water Modeling

Description

Shallow Water Modeling (swim) [Sad75, HSS88] is originally an application in the meteorological field for weather prediction written in Fortran. The application has been extensively used for comparing both the current and poast performance of supercomputers. Amongst others, the application found its way into the SPEC CPU2000 and SPEC OMP2001 benchmark suites as *171.swim* and *312.swim*, respectively. The SPEC CPU200 version creates a $1,335 \times 1,335$ area array of data and iterates over 512 timesteps. It prints the diagonal elements of the velocity field. The reference run has 800 iterations.

The algorithm itself consists of five phases:

- INITIAL: just called once to setup data structures, etc.,

- CALC1: part of the main loop, computes new values for U,V, z and h,

- CALC2: part of the main loop, computes new values for u,v and p,

- CALC3: part of the main loop, time smoothing and update for next cycle,

- CALC3Z: time smoothing for first iteration (only called once instead of CALC3).

The different phases of the main loop are visualized using Vampir in Figure 7.17.
The *312.swim* version used in SPEC OMP2001 is OpenMP parallelized and the reference run has an increased area $(3,801 \times 3,801)$ and increased iterations $(1,200)$. The following measurements focus on the *312.swim* version, since all processes on a node are synchronized with OpenMP. Otherwise, it has to be taken care of the placement of the single-threaded applications in a Multiple-Program Multiple-Data style to adjust processing frequencies in synchronized phases.

Measurements

Table 7.5 shows the detailed duration and various performance counters on phase base for the reference run with the fixed processor frequency of 2,800 MHz on one Intel node. Comparing the memory bandwidth, IPS and IPM to the memory-bound eeMark setup (Table 7.2), the values are in the same order and thus all phases except for the initial phase can be considered memory-bound. The phase length (per iteration) is also in a range that manual processor frequency reduction should decrease the total energy for the phases.

Figure 7.18 on Page 127 exemplarily shows the relative duration, retired instructions, resource stalls and IPS for the CALC1 phase for the minimum core frequency and the ondemand governor with enabled Turbo Boost; baseline is the maximum frequency setup. For the minimum frequency setup, the duration and the retired instructions remain constant, but the number of resource stalls decreases by about 55 %. This clearly shows the memory-boundness of the phase and the potential for energy saving without performance decrease.

A detailed phase counter analysis shows that reducing the frequency for all phases except for INITIAL to the minimum and INITIAL to the maximum is the best setting in terms of total energy. Due to the fact that almost all phases are memory-bound, statically reducing the frequency for the whole application also saves energy. Figure 7.19

7. Evaluation

Figure 7.17.: *Vampir screenshot of the 312.swim main loop phases on one Intel Xeon node. The CALC1 phase corresponds to the OMP loop in source code Line 276, CALC2 to the loop in Line 331 and CALC3 to the loop in Line 415.*

on Page 128 visualizes the runtime, energy and power measurements relative to the maximum frequency setup.

With every frequency step, the total energy is decreased. The manual phase instrumentation achieves the lowest total energy and also small runtime decreases, but the

7.2. Application Benchmarks

Table 7.5.: *Performance counters measurements of swim phases for the reference run on one Intel Xeon node at a fixed processing frequency of 2,800 MHz.*

Phase	Duration (ms)	Bandwidth (GB/s)	IPS	IPM
CALC1	39.37	15.51	0.98	49.82
CALC2	48.42	15.48	0.85	38.99
CALC3	57.32	14.52	0.31	19.27
CALC3Z	52.22	14.37	0.14	10.47
INITIAL	247.69	2.14	1.18	188.06

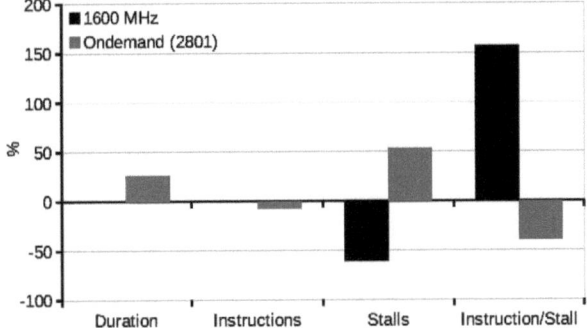

Figure 7.18.: *Relative performance counters measurements of the CALC1 phase of swim on one Intel Xeon node. The baseline is the non-instrumented run with a fixed processing frequency of 2,800 MHz..*

improvements are less significant compared with the minimum frequency setup.

Furthermore, the analysis shows that the measurements are very sensitive to the selected optimization flags of the used gcc compiler. Figure 7.20 on Page 129 visualizes the saving potential for each optimization flag, where the total energy could be reduced in the minimum frequency run. Indeed, the energy-saving potential is the heighest if all flags are enabled (optimized flagset), but compared to the fastest run (O3), the absolute runtime and energy is increased significantly. As a result, the settings are kept constant for each application in this section.

7. Evaluation

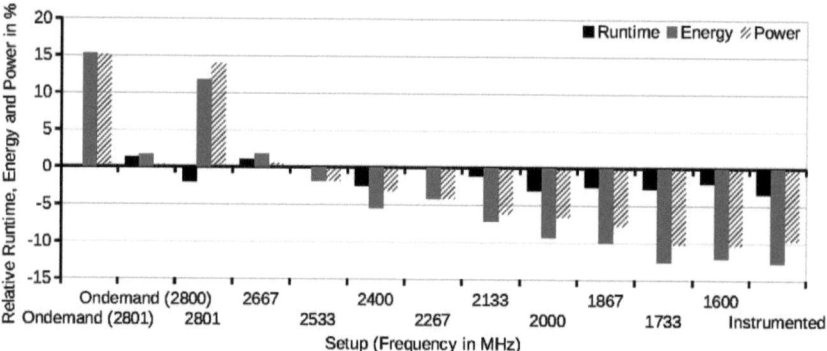

Figure 7.19.: *Relative runtime, energy and power measurements of the swim reference run for different frequencies setups on one Intel Xeon node. The baseline is the non-instrumented run with a fixed processing frequency of 2,800 MHz.*

7.2.3. Max-Planck-Institute Ocean Model

Description

The Max-Planck-Institute ocean model (MPIOM) is the ocean-sea ice component of the Max-Planck-Institute climate model[4].

MPIOM is a primitive equation model (C-Grid, z-coordinates, free surface) with the hydrostatic and Boussinesq assumptions made. It includes an embedded dynamic/thermodynamic sea ice model with a viscous-plastic rheology and a bottom boundary layer scheme for the flow across steep topography. A detailed model description can be found in [MHJ+03].

The standard configuration (GR15) uses a curvilinear orthogonal bipolar grid with poles over Greenland and Antarctica. The horizontal resolution is about 1.5 degrees and therefore gradually varies between a minimum of 12 km close to Greenland and 150 km in the tropical Pacific. It has 40 vertical levels, with 20 in the upper 600 m.

MPIOM is implemented in Fortran and parallelized using message passing for internode and OpenMP for intra-node communication. The domain decomposition for MPI is straight forward. The data is distributed to the processes by the matrix index, i.e. $M_{0,0}$ to Rank 0, $M_{0,1}$ to Rank 1, etc. Additionally, several compute-intensive loops are parallelized using OpenMP.

One model day is subdivided into 24 timesteps (each one model hour). For each timestep, the matrix cell is updated and results are exchanged between the neighboring cells. Based on the output frequency and the user setup, the result of the calculation step is sent to Rank 0 which writes the data to the filesystem using serial *NetCDF*[5]. This

---
[4]http://www.mpimet.mpg.de/en/science/models/mpiom.html, last checked: March 2, 2013

[5]the Network Common Data Form, a set of libraries and a (open, cross platform) file format to exchange scientific data, http://www.unidata.ucar.edu/software/netcdf/, last checked: March

7.2. Application Benchmarks

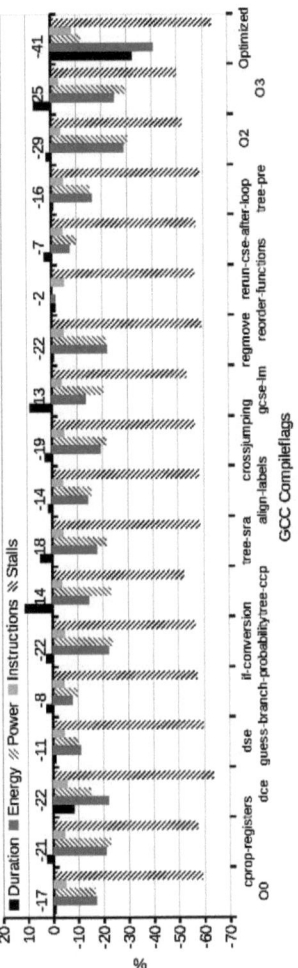

Figure 7.20.: *Performance, energy and power saving potential of optimization flags of the gcc compiler for swim reference runs on one Intel Xeon node. The baseline of each optimization flag is the corresponding fixed processing frequency of 2,800 MHz run. The optimized version (all flags that have power saving potential) has also the highest energy-saving potential.*

implementation results in waiting times for all processes except for rank 0. Because waiting times due to I/O phases are already analyzed with *partdiff-par*, the periodical output of the calculation steps is disabled to focus on the compute phases.

MPIOM is optimized (in terms of scalability and performance) for *blizzard*, the workhorse for the numerical experiments of the German climate researchers located in the German Climate Computing Centre. However, the analysis is started on the *eeClust* test infrastructure, since *blizzard* has no applicable power saving modes and almost no power measurement capabilities.

The maximum number of parallel processes in the Intel test environment is 40, thus the standard configuration is increased as far as possible considering main memory constraints. This results in an increased horizontal and vertical resolution. For all measurements, a processor dimension of 4×10 is used, since measurements for different dimensions are comparable for a 1-day setup in the test environment (see Figure A.2 in the appendix).

Figure 7.21 on Page 131 visualizes one model day with Vampir. Two MPIOM processes on one Intel node are shown in detail, in addition to the retired instructions and L3 cache misses for core 0 and the node power consumption.

Measurements

Figure 7.22 on Page 132 shows the average processor utilization running MPIOM with the ondemand governor. Additionally, the average system frequency and the resulting power consumption is plotted. Due to the full utilization over almost the whole runtime, power savings using the ondemand governor are insignificant.

Unfortunately, the application phase transition is very fast – communication and compute phase have average durations of several microseconds up to a few milliseconds. Out of this, the compute intensive phase are focused trying to allocate memory-bound phases.

Tracing the average instructions per miss rate over the whole application runtime results in Figure 7.23 for the maximum frequency setup. The average instruction per miss rate is $\gg 500$ but should be $\lessapprox 10$ to classify the application as memory-bound.

A more detailed analysis using Vampir shows that the module `occlit` is one of the modules with the lowest IPS and IPM. Results from the measurements with increased time resolution on loop level are shown in Table 7.6 (more details in the appendix in Table A.1).

But also on this fine-granular level, the memory bandwidth and IPS and IPM rates, respectively, are still far above the classified threshold except for LOOP157, which unfortunately has a very small runtime (about 0.16 ms) for manual instrumentation.

Figure 7.24 on Page 133 compares the different frequency setups. With each frequency step, the power consumption is decreasing, but the runtime increases (which corresponds to previous analysis). This results in an increased total energy for the application. Also for the instrumented version, the runtime increase compensates the power decrease and thus the total energy increases. Summing up, the most energy-efficient setup on the Intel nodes is the standard setup with the maximum frequency.

7.2. Application Benchmarks

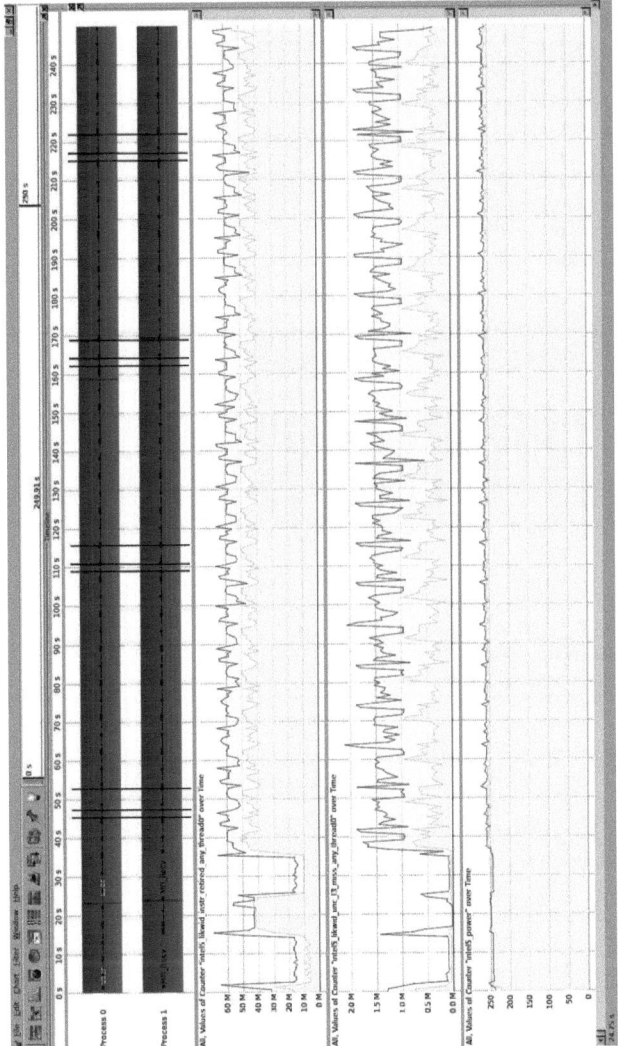

Figure 7.21.: *Vampir screenshot of two MPIOM processes on one Intel Xeon node. The counter timelines display the retired instructions, the L3 cache misses and the node power consumption.*

7. Evaluation

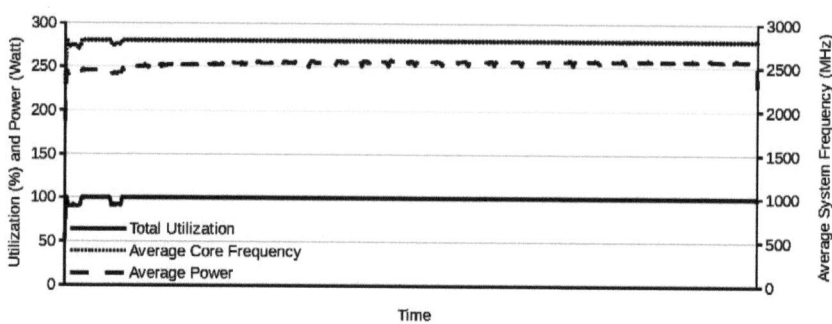

Figure 7.22.: *Average processor utilization, node power and core frequency of MPIOM phases on one Intel Xeon node using the ondemand governor.*

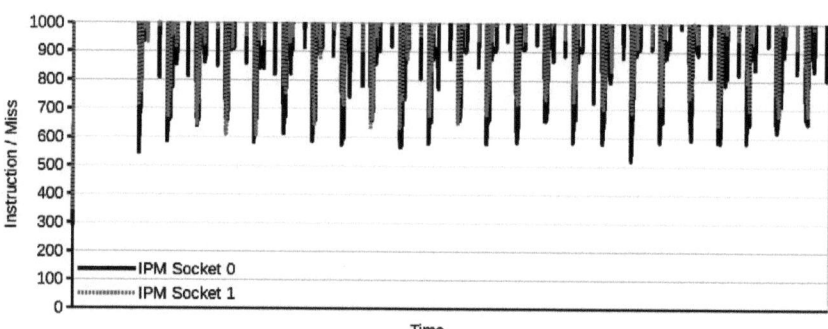

Figure 7.23.: *Average instruction per L3 cache miss rate of MPIOM phases on one Intel Xeon node with a fixed processing frequency of 2,800 MHz.*

Production environment Because MPIOM is optimized to its production environment (*blizzard*, IBM POWER6), the memory-boundness of the application is also analyzed on this architecture. Due to the architectural changes, the total number of processes is increased to 160, which results in 5 *blizzard* nodes (32 processes per node, without SMT). Figure 7.25 on Page 134 visualizes the occlit module and the PM_DATA_FROM_LMEM counter in Vampir. The PM_DATA_FROM_LMEM event describes the processor's data cache was reloaded with data from local memory due to a demand load. Second and third level are remote and distant memory, but the corresponding counters are negligible because these memory levels are not used by the application. The POWER6 architecture has multiple levels in the memory hierachy; the local memory is the first level. With this event, it is possible to calculate the memory bandwidth (to the local memory) in MByte/s using $PM\_DATA\_FROM\_LMEM * MEM\_LINE\_SIZE * CACHE\_LINE\_SIZE/(1,024 * 1,024)/total\_time$. Also in this environment, the ap-

7.2. Application Benchmarks

Table 7.6.: *Performance counters measurements for MPIOM occlit loop instrumentation on one Intel Xeon node with a fixed processing frequency of 2,800 MHz.*

Phase	Duration (ms)	Bandwidth (GB/s)	IPS	IPM
LOOP49	76.50	4.49	34.64	560.53
LOOP105	17.71	5.23	7.53	412.01
LOOP141	26.05	3.88	11.59	423.23
LOOP157	0.16	5.00	4.22	3.79
LOOP212	49.83	6.39	18.38	233.95
LOOP279	18.30	6.80	7.84	278.31
LOOP329	27.28	3.67	12.89	524.17
LOOP369	32.40	3.54	11.46	452.64

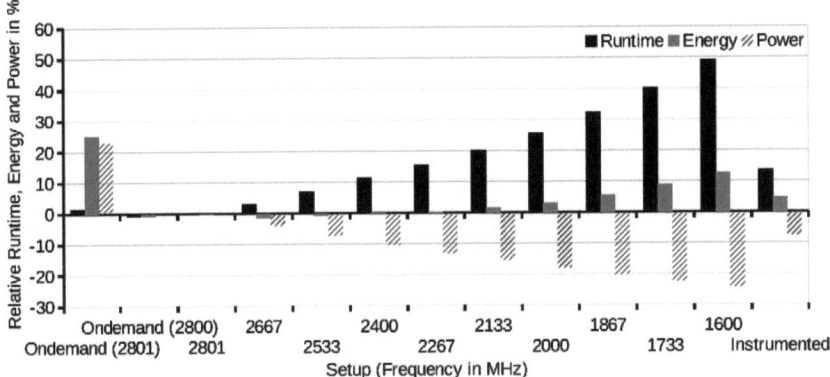

Figure 7.24.: *Relative runtime, energy and power measurements of the MPIOM run for different frequencies setups on five Intel Xeon nodes. The baseline is the non-instrumented run with a fixed processing frequency of 2,800 MHz.*

plication uses (in average) a small percentage of the available memory bandwidth. It appears that the application is presumably L2-cache-bound (see Figure 7.26 on Page 134) due to further brief analysis of the cache usage. L2-cache-bound means in this context that data misses in the L2 cache are usually cought by the L3 cache, thus only a low percentage of data lines resulting from L3 cache misses have to be fetched from the local main memory. Additionally, using data access prediction (prefetching) these waiting times can be minimized if the prefetching engine works well. Because the L2 and L3 cache share the frequency with the core at least for the POWER6, AMD Opteron and Intel Nehalem architectures, reducing the core frequency would also reduce

7. Evaluation

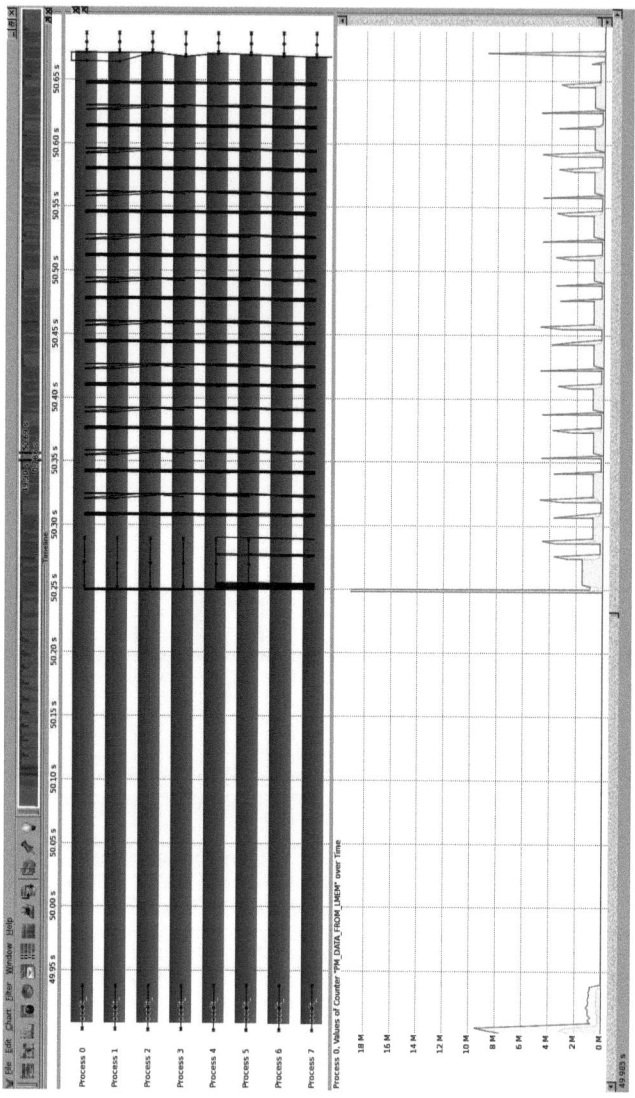

Figure 7.25.: *Vampir screenshot of the MPIOM occlit phase on blizzard. The counter timeline displays the data from local memory counter.*

the cache bandwidth. This definitely reduces the applicability of DVFS corresponding to Chapter 3.

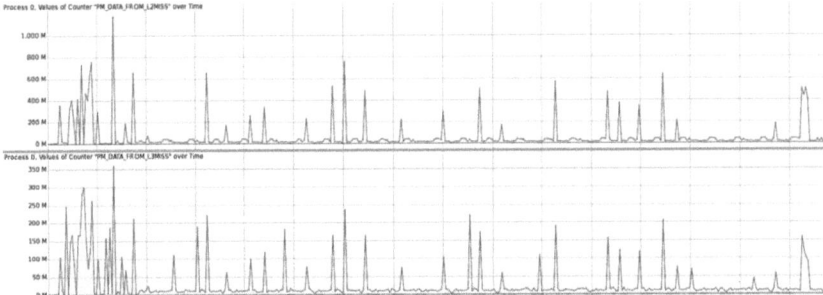

Figure 7.26.: *Vampir screenshot of the MPIOM run on blizzard. The counter timelines display the L2 and L3 cache misses, respectively.*

7.2.4. General Estuarine Transport Model

Description

The General Estuarine Transport Model (GETM) is an open source model and widely used within the geoscientific, oceanographic and operational maritime forecast communities as a regional ocean model[6]. A suite of nested setups of GETM is in operational forecast use at the Danish Maritime Safety Administration (DaMSA) [Bü11]. It is well etablished that the model results generally yield high-quality forecasts. GETM has been sucessfully applied to several coastal, shelf sea and limnic scenarios [Han09].

GETM started in 1997 as a 3D numerical hydrodynamic model including flooding/drying, a k-ϵ turbulence closure model, momentum advection, mass conservation and the general vertical coordinates. Nowadays, GETM is implemented in modular FORTRAN90/95 code and is extended to a fully baroclinic model with transport of active and passive tracers, calculation of density, internal pressure gradients and stratification, surface heat and momentum fluxes and high-order advection schemes. Additionally, horizontal curvilinear coordinates are implemented. A detailed model description can be found in [Han12].

GETM is parallized using MPI and OpenMP. The domain decomposition is similar to MPIOM. The underlying grid is composed into a set of rectangular areas, each process owns one rectangular. For each project setup, the count of rectangulars is predefined, thus the count of MPI processes, too. After each cell update, the boundary regions are exchanged between the neighboring processes. The writing of the calculation results is done by each process using serial netCDF and separate files.

---
[6]http://www.getm.eu/, last checked: March 2, 2013

7. Evaluation

In the following, the parallel version of the box_cartesian setup is used. Due to the static domain decomposition, four MPI processes are used. During all measurements, the unused processor frequency is reduced to the minimum. The test runs the model for 10 days, each day consists of 8,640 timesteps. In total, 86,400 iterations are performed with a runtime of about 223 seconds ($\approx$ 387 iterations per second).

Measurements

Figure 7.27 visualizes the processor frequency of one core on the Intel nodes and the resulting node power consumption using the ondemand governor. Both counters are unsteady – fine-granular frequency changes by the governor result in varying node power consumption. The frequency changes are triggered by the different processor utilization caused by calling the save_2d_ncdf and save_3d_ncdf, respectively, several times per second (see Figure 7.28). Both subroutines contain a call to nf90_sync which synchronizes the *NetCDF* data in the main memory with the data on the harddisk.

Due to the short duration of the I/O phases of in average 10 ms, manual processor instrumentation increases the runtime significantly (by about 10 %) and thus the total energy corresponding to Table 7.7.

Table 7.7.: *Quantification of the instrumentation overhead of GETM on one Intel Xeon node. The four remaining idle cores are set to the maximum frequency. Each setup is executed 10 times [Ehm12].*

Frequency MHz	Duration s	Power W	Energy J
2,800	222	221	48,524
instrumented	245	217	56,230

Profiling of the application to identify further power saving potential shows that all other application phases are very short (in the range of several microseconds), which reduces the applicability of our approach. However, if the output frequency is decreased (it might not be necessary to write the results to disk in every iteration), the total runtime decreases significantly (see Table 7.8 compared to Table 7.7).

But even here the manual instrumentation does not gain any significant energy savings due to the now low I/O to compute ratio in the application (see Vampir visualization in Figures 7.29 and 7.30 on Page 140).

Further measurements with the application can be found in [Ehm12].

7.2. Application Benchmarks

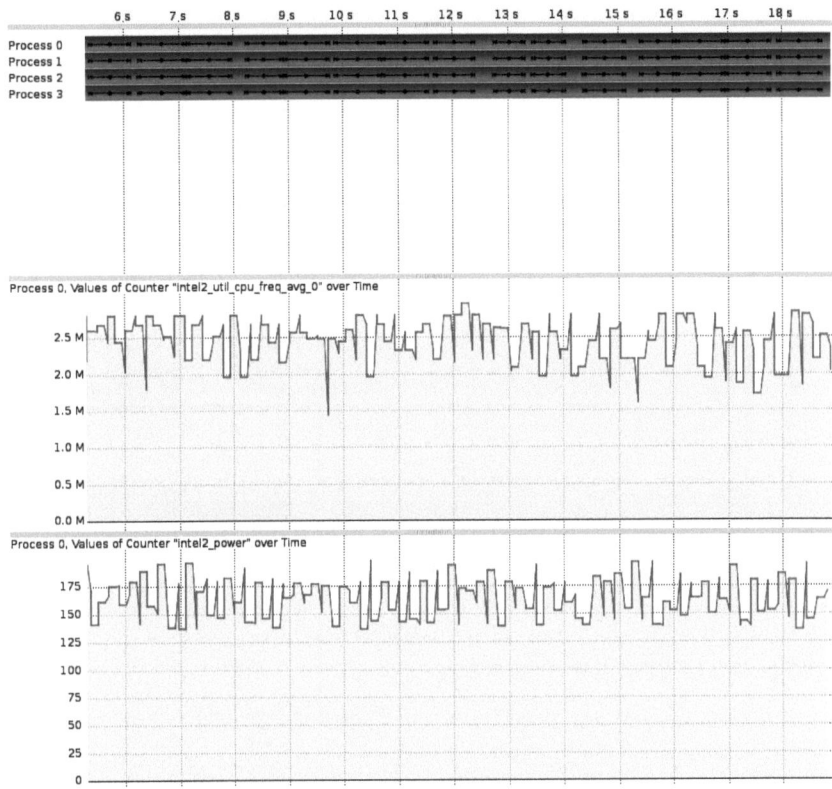

Figure 7.27.: *Vampir screenshot of GETM using the ondemand governor. The counter timelines display the average processor frequency of core 0 and the node power consumption [Ehm12].*

Table 7.8.: *Quantification of the improved instrumentation overhead of GETM on one Intel Xeon node. The output frequency of the model data is decreased to one* ncdf_sync *every 24 hours model time. The four remaining idle cores are set to the maximum frequency. Each setup is executed 10 times [Ehm12].*

Frequency MHz	Duration s	Power W	Energy J
2,800	64.6	195.6	12,612.2
instrumented	64.1	196.4	12,559.7

137

7. Evaluation

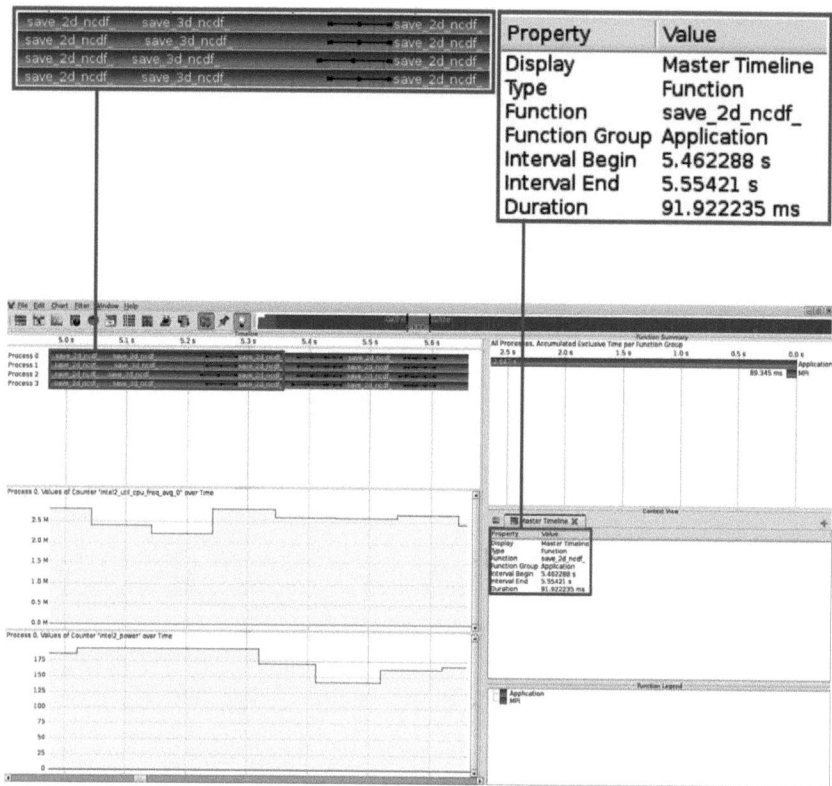

Figure 7.28.: *Detailed Vampir screenshot of GETM's iteration phase using the ondemand governor [Ehm12].*

7.2. Application Benchmarks

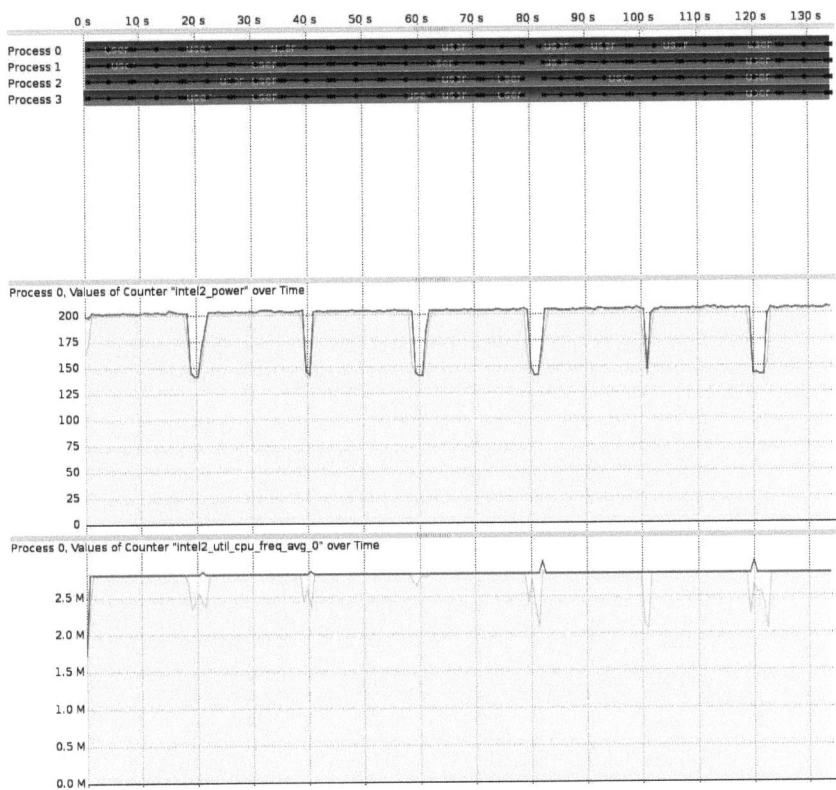

Figure 7.29.: *Vampir screenshot of the improved GETM version (`ncdf_sync` every 24 hours model time). Counter timelines display the node power consumption and the average processing frequency of core 0 [Ehm12].*

7. Evaluation

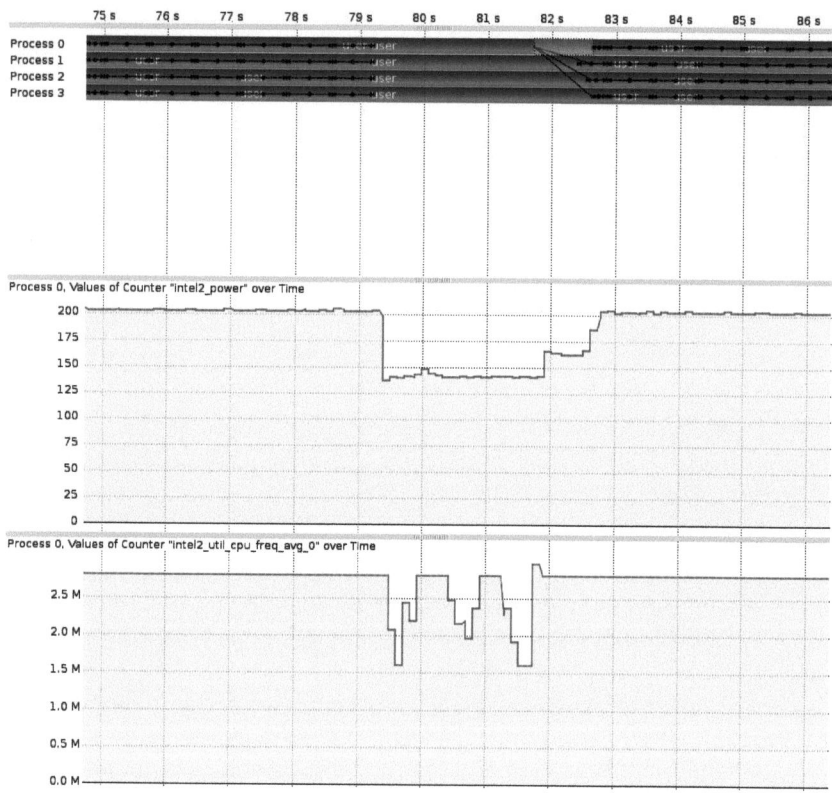

Figure 7.30.: *Detailed Vampir screenshot of the I/O phase of the improved GETM version (*ncdf_sync *every 24 hours model time) [Ehm12].*

7.3. Appraisal of Results

The power saving potential using the appropriate hardware modes is promising as analyzed in Chapter 3. With the introduced tool environment for tracing parallel applications (see Chapter 6) it is possible to identify application phases with power and energy-saving potential. Due to the complex interaction of software and hardware levels such complex tool environments are needed to evaluate power saving strategies. It is essentially to correlate the parallel application with the following metrics to valuate concrete approaches:

- utilization, to analyze the general usage of components and identify low-hanging fruits (e.g. disable harddisk if not used),

- processor Performance Counters, to classify the processor activity and identify especially memory-bound application phases,

- power consumption, to assess the effectiveness of the chosen approach,

- hardware states, to gain detailed knowledge about the usage of device power saving mechanisms to evaluate the tradeoff between energy and performance.

The successfull analysis enables the application developer to monetarily evaluate the economics of the application.

The evaluation of the synthetic benchmark eeMark clearly indicates that trivial power saving strategies like reducing the network card speed or putting the disk to sleep are only limitedly applicable due to long transition times and small power saving potential on device level. Additionally, the caching mechanisms aggravate the usage of power saving mechanisms – I/O and communication is usually shifted by e.g. the operating system which worsens the phase detection on hardware level. Applying these simple power saving strategies is only useful if the devices are unused for almost the whole application run. However, significant energy savings can be reached by reducing the processor frequency in memory-bound application phases. Further, reducing the processor frequency in busy-wait (communication and I/O) application phases can also gain remarkable results. But also here the energy-saving potential depends strongly on the phase duration and the level of memory-boundness. The application analysis using hardware performance counter has been emphasized as suitable method to detect memory-bound phases in applications. In particular, the ratio of retired processor instructions per resource stall (IPS) is appropriate to evaluate the level of memory-boundness and thus the power saving potential.

The evaluation results of the application benchmarks are summarized in Table 7.9.

partdiff-par, the partial differential equation solver is structured in clear compute, communication and I/O phases. The compute phases are not suitable for processor frequency reduction because this phase is strongly cpu-bound. Also the communication phases do not show profitable results for processor frequency reduction due to their short duration. But in the I/O phases processor frequency instrumentation using the eeDaemon results

7. Evaluation

Table 7.9.: *Evaluation results of the application benchmarks.* **Phase ratio** *is the instrumented phase duration compared to total application duration*

	partdiff-par	swim	MPIOM	GETM
Memory-bound phases	-	+	-	-
Communication or I/O phases	+	-	+	+
Instrumented phase	I/O	Compute	Compute	I/O
Phase ratio	0.5	1	0.5	0.8
Average phase duration	variable	variable	300 ms	10 ms
Energy savings	8 %	13 %	-	-

in 8 % savings, mainly based on the busy-waiting in the MPI I/O library. Despite these savings, the overall meaningfullness is not factual, because the I/O phase consumes about 50 % of the total runtime.

In contrast, the I/O (and the communication) phases are negliable for the *swim* application. The weather prediction application consists of multiple strongly memory-bound compute phases. This results in significant energy savings (13 %) using manual application instrumention, but due to the high phase ratio of almost 100 % memory-bound code static frequency reduction reaches comparable results. However, the analysis shows that these measurements are very sensitive to the selected optimization flags of the gcc compiler. The compile flag set with the highest energy-saving potential is not the most energy-efficient setup because the profit from reducing the processing frequency results from inefficient code generated by these special flags.

The Max-Planck-Institute ocean model turns out not to be memory-bound at all, at least with our test infrastructure and the *blizzard* supercomputer. Additionally, the communication phases are too short for manual instrumentation. However, there is still potential in the serial I/O phases of the algorithm due to waiting times of the remaining processes.

Similar results are obtained for the General Estuarine Transport Model. The model consists of even shorter phases, but the approach to increase the output interval results in significant performance (and thus energy) savings. Anyway, the compute phases of the algorithm are cpu-bound and thus inappropriate for saving energy with processor frequency reduction.

In summary, almost all analyzed applications contain phases of interest for manual instrumentation, but every one has also disadvantages (in terms of phase duration etc.). Applications which consist of several, different phases (e.g. memory-bound and cpu-bound) have a huge power and energy-saving potential which cannot be exhausted by the ondemand governor of the operating system. The ondemand governor decisions are only based on the device utilization. The manual instrumentation during busy-wait phases of the application has been proven to be useful. The potential even increases when increasing the process count and thus longer wait times. Anyway, implementation

7.3. Appraisal of Results

alternatives to the busy-wait pattern should be considered by application and library developers. The busy-wait pattern is usually implemented using a spin-lock, which is fast and keeps the overhead low for small waiting times. Interrupt-based approaches, in contrast, introduce overhead for handling the interrupts, which usually results in context switches, processor pipeline stalls and cache flushes. The right implementation choice is – as always – dependent on the specific problem, the hardware and personal preferences. In conclusion, a good library implementation should contain both implementations, for example switchable using a compiler flag.

This chapter evaluated the strategies and tool extensions for reducing parallel application power consumption. This includes detailed analysis of memory-bound application phases as well as various resource intensive application phases like communication and I/O phases. Appropriate application phases are instrumented using the eeDaemon interface and discussed.

8. Related Work and State-of-the-Art

This chapter summarizes related work in the field of green high performance computing. First, tools for assessing the power consumption on system and application level are analyzed and differentiated from this work. Second, approaches for exploiting the hardware power saving mechanisms in high performance computing are briefly summarized.

8.1. Assessing Application Power Consumption

Two common approaches to assess the application power consumption are used in high performance computing environments. The first approach is based on the analysis of the computing system itself, various statistics (like utilization or component power consumption) are collected and analyzed and managed. A detailed correlation of these statistics with the running applications is usually not possible, the focus is clearly on the overall system behavior. In the second approach, the application is analyzed and correlated to (more or less the same) metrics, but the capability to manage on the system level is usually not provided. However, both approaches are very similiar since the same metrics are collected – only the perception for interpretation differs.

8.1.1. System Analysis

Collecting various system statistics with the ability to analyze and manage these values is referred to as *system analysis*. For the Linux operating system, the /proc and /sys interfaces, respectively, can monitor and manage the hardware states. The cpufreq-stats module[1] provides information about the usage of the different processor performance and sleep state usage. For example, the time_in_state file located under /sys/devices/system/cpu includes the amount of time spent in each of the frequencies supported by the processor [MMK+12]. The output has a frequency and time pair in each line, which means this processor spent time (in 10 ms) at the corresponding frequency. The output has one line for each of the supported frequencies.

The main problem when monitoring *P*- and *C-States* are the fast transitions between the states [Int11]. The time it takes for example for the Intel® Xeon X5560 processor to switch between two frequencies is about 10,000 nanoseconds, the *C-States* transition time ranges from 3 to 245 nanoseconds [Int09b].

---

[1] http://www.mjmwired.net/kernel/Documentation/cpu-freq/cpufreq-stats.txt, last checked: March 2, 2013

8. Related Work and State-of-the-Art

A feasible method for monitoring is collecting the data per time step; the smaller the time step the greater the accuracy and the amount of data. This is exactly what PowerTOP does [MMK+12]. PowerTOP is a Linux tool to diagnose issues with power consumption and power management[2]. In addition to being a diagnostic tool, PowerTOP also has an interactive mode where the user can experiment various power management settings for cases where the Linux distribution has not enabled these settings. Additionally, the user gets feedback about the usage of the different idle and performance states of the hardware devices. The software lists the processes polling the devices and thus preventing idle states. So it is possible to analyze the system behavior; for example unnecessary frequent disk polling for journal writing. Furthermore, it is possible to analyze own software to prevent active waiting for resources, which usually results in an inadequate increase of the power consumption.

Further frameworks are available from hardware vendors; for example, the Active Energy Manager Plugin for the IBM Systems Director [IBM09]. The plugin can measure and record power and environmental statistics of IBM systems. Furthermore, thresholds on power and thermal values and events can be created and monitored. Additionally, the tool provides functions to control the system power states on node level.

The *Intel® Energy Checker*[3] is a borderline case between system and application analysis tool. On the one hand, the tool collects various system metrics with the additional capability for integratation of external power meters [Int10a]. On the other hand, the Intel® Energy Checker API provides functions required for exporting and importing counters from an application to measure the real work done by each application [Int10b]. In total, if each running application is instrumented to use the Energy Checker API, the measurement suite provides a system overview correlated to the application work. Consequently, the software faces the problem that all too often activity is measured by how busy a server is while running an application rather than by how much work that application completes. However, this tool is very valuable for accounting energy and resource usage, but it is not possible to correlate application phases with energy-related metrics for classification of utilization.

8.1.2. Application Analysis

Several tools exist for profiling energy usage by applications. These tools measure the hardware power consumption on node or component level. Based on its main purpose, each tool uses different methodologies for correlating the application and the energy-related metrics.

For power-critical fields of computing (e.g. mobile computing), corresponding tools for profiling the cnc.g. usage of mobile applications exist. One of these tools is the *Power-Scope* tool [FS99]. PowerScope maps the measured energy consumption to the application structure, in much the same way that performance profilers map processor cycles to specific processes and procedures. Postprocessing software maps the sampled system

---

[2]http://www.lesswatts.org/projects/powertop/, last checked: March 2, 2013

[3]http://software.intel.com/en-us/articles/intel-energy-checker-sdk, last checked: March 2, 2013

activity and power consumption to the application structure and produces a profile of enery usage by process and procedure.

Chang et al. follow a similiar approach [CFR02] to detect software hotspots. They describe a prototype implementation of this approach for the Itsy pocket computing platform, their experimental results using the prototype show that energy measurement tools that ignore system and kernel effects can give erroneous results about enery hotspots.

Furthermore, *PowerNet* correlates power data with utilization statistics in a building environment [KHLK09]. The deployment includes both wired and wireless sensors and covers offices, networking closets, and server racks. Analyzing PowerNet data traces identifies contexts where electricity consumption can be reduced without cost, and others which call for rethinking system designs altogether.

However, even if these tools provide meaningful insights for its corresponding application areas, the usability for high performance computing environments is very limited.

On the contrary, existing tools for performance analysis of high performance computing applications provide a solid analysis infrastructure. Binding performance and node power analysis has been done for Vampir [MHS$^+$11, MMK$^+$12] and Sunshot [MKL12], as discussed in detail in Chapter 6. VampirTrace supports multiple power meters, while HDTrace supports only the ZES LMG450 power meter. Barreda et al. follow the same approach with *Paraver*[4], developed at the Barcelona Supercomputing Center. They combine the tracing framework with a component power measurement setup to perform a visual analysis of the computational performance and the power consumption of tuned implementations for several key dense linear algebra operations [BDM$^+$12].

The component power measurement infrastructure Barreda et al. use is similar to *PowerPack*. PowerPack [GFC05c, CGF05, GFS$^+$09, SGFC09] is a tool to isolate the power consumption of devices including disks, memory, NICs, and processors in a high performance computing cluster and correlate these measurements to application functions. Additonally, the PowerPack framework enables distributed systems to conserve energy in scientific applications using DVFS [CGF05, GFS$^+$09].

However, the performance analysis capabilities of the tool are not as sophosticated as of Vampir or Sunshot. Indeed, PowerPack provides sophisticated power measurement capabilities but comes with a much more expensive and complicated infrastructure. When it comes to device power consumption, estimation based on performance events is another, more practical approach.

Processor and memory power consumption estimation is mainly done by evaluating processor performance counters [CM05, SBM09]. Additionally, Bircher et al. create power models for the entire system based on processor performance events [BJ07].

This opened a new field for software power meters like *SPAN* [WCS10] and power simulators like *Wattch* [BTM00]. These tools open up the field of power-efficient computing to a wider range of researchers, since no additonal power measurement infrastructure is needed.

---

[4]http://www.bsc.es/computer-sciences/performance-tools/paraver, last checked: March 2, 2013

8. Related Work and State-of-the-Art

However, even if the aforementioned tools increase usability, first the power improvements have to be evaluated at wall level to provide energy-efficiency evaluations and guidelines.

8.2. Exploiting Hardware Power Saving Mechanism

Existing research in exploiting hardware power saving mechanisms in high performance computing focuses mainly on exploiting DVFS to reduce the processor power consumption. The approaches can be roughly subdivided in application and system power management. While the first approach takes place on application level, the second approach is transparent on system level and requires no modifications to the running application. However, especially the latter approach might decrease the application performance due to insufficient information about future hardware utilization.

8.2.1. Application Power Management

Power management for scientific applications is exploited under the general term *power aware high performance computing*. Ge et al. started to exploit parallel performance inefficiencies characteristic of non-interactive, distributed scientific applications for conserving energy using DVFS [GFC05b, GFC05a, Ge07]. The authors analyze and optimize distributed power-performance using various DVFS strategies and achieve application-dependent overall system energy savings as large as 25% with as little as 2% performance impact. The results of Freeh et al. also show that a power-scalable cluster has the potential to save energy by scaling the processor down to lower energy levels [FPK+05]. Furthermore, Freeh et al. developed a model to predict the energy-performance tradeoff of larger clusters estimating the idle times using regression to fit a curve to the measured MPI communication.

Based on this first findings, MPI application profiles are built that can be divided into phases. Free et al. divide the trace files offline into blocks whereat a block is a set of executed statements demarcated by MPI operations and memory pressure changes, indicated by L3 cache misses [FL05]. Two adjacent blocks are merged into a phase if their corresponding memory pressure is within the same threshold. They execute each phase with different DVFS settings and select the right setting based on a user-weighted energy-time trade off. Rountree et al. try to find schedule that realizes energy bounds by dividing the application trace into sections by its communication phases [RLF+07] using a linear programming solver. These first approaches are continued in the *Green Building Blocks* project [Nik09] – the power consumption is sampled to build an application profile that can be divided into phases. Further components can than manage device state based on these phases. Additionally, it is possible to divide traces into phases using performance counters and calculating a solution with specific DVFS settings for program phases via heuristics during execution (online) [HSK+06]. Furthermore, the MPI library itself can be optimized for low power, e.g. exploiting busy-waiting during MPI collective operations [DCY+08]. Using already existing interfaces for phase annotations like the

Adaptable I/O System (ADIOS)[5] interface enables further power management of several devices based on the application phases [KMKL11].
However, the detailed analysis of parallel applications is very promising for reducing the total energy. For example, analysis and optimization of power consumption of sparse [AHA+11, AHR+11] and dense [ADI+12, LLD12] linear algebra operations has gained significant savings.
Additional approaches cover the exploitation of load balancing issues in large scale MPI applications. Zong developed energy-aware load balancing algorithms with the goal to minimize energy consumption while maintaining reasonably high performance by incorporating energy-aware resource management techniques to HPC platforms [Zon08]. Following this approach, Etinski et al. use a trace file as input for Dimemas (a performance simulator) and scale the processors depending on their load (using DVFS and over-clocking to prevent load imbalance) [ECL+09].

8.2.2. System Power Management

On system level, first collaborative efforts to exploit hardware power saving mechanisms are OS-directed [LBM00, LDM01]. The operating system has information about tasks; therefore, the operating system is able to identify hardware idleness and shutdown unused components. But system-level power management is a trade-off among several factors, as this quantitative analysis shows [BBDM00, LDM01].
However, OS-directed power management is designed for a broad variety of workloads and long idle times. For cluster computing systems, the workload is defined by several applications scheduled to a set of computing nodes. A coarse-granular power-saving approach is to completely turn off unused nodes [PBCH01, EKR02]. If new jobs are entered into the workload queue, the necessary amount of nodes is powered on again. This approach introduces comparable large latencies, which are usually only profitable for low-utilized systems. However, through intelligent scheduling of the applications node idle times can be avoided, additional profit is brought into datacenters through virtualization techniques focussing on energy efficiency [RCP+10, VLR+11].
More HPC-specific is to exploit the overhead introduced by parallel applications such as communication phases necessary to synchronize parallel processes and exchange data between processes. Additionally, load imbalances can occur in high performance applications spread over a large number of computing nodes. These characteristics introduce so-called *slack* times. In other words, some of the nodes arrive early at a synchronization point, meaning that one or more (different) bottleneck nodes determine the program execution time. In such a situation, a non-bottleneck node will wait for a message (or other event) from another node, which wastes energy. Exploiting this inter-node slack can result in significant energy saving with insignificant impact on application performance. Kappiah et al. present a system called *Jitter*, which reduces the frequency on nodes that are assigned less computation and therefore have slack time [KFL05]. The system exploits PMPI, the profiling layer of MPI to calculate wait times in blocking MPI routines

---
[5]http://www.olcf.ornl.gov/center-projects/adios/, last checked: March 2, 2013

8. Related Work and State-of-the-Art

which works well for iterative algorithm. Lim et al. follow the same approach, but the algorithm for detection is not limited to iterative algorithm, they designed several training algorithms that demarcate communication regions [LFL06]. This approach is further enhanced by the *Adagio* framework, which focuses on a minimal performance decrease through detection of resources on the critical path of MPI applications [RLS+09].

Besides to the interception of MPI library calls, non-compute intensive phases can be identified by sampling processor performance counters for workload characterization. Hsu et al. propose a power-aware algorithm that automatically and transparently adapts its frequency and voltage settings based on off-chip accesses [HF05]. The same approach is followed by [HF09] based on the processor stall cycles due to off-chip activities. More sophisticated metrics are exploited by Schoene et al. [SH11] and Spiliopoulos et al. [SKK11] which both implemented performance counters based Linux governors, *pe-gov* and *Green Governors*, respectively. The latter governor framework also predicts the effect of frequency scaling in terms of performance loss and processor core energy. Furthermore, the design of online prediction based on the processor performance counters is possible for selecting the right DVFS setting [CMDAN06, LTF+12]. Dhiman et al. propose a online-learning algorithm for system-level power management including DPM and DVFS considering the processor cycles per instruction and miss events [DR09]. However, Nathuji observes the strong need for coordination in managing system power saving modes due to the existence of multiple and independent system layers [Nat08].

Green high performance computing is a very active field of research since a few years which spawned several conferences and workshops[6]. Especially the broad range of power management approaches motivates the further research in tool environments being able to correlate parallel applications with the hardware utilization and energy-related metrics.

---

[6]Including the *Energy-Aware High Performance Computing* conference (EnA-HPC), which was initiated by the research group Scientific Computing of the University of Hamburg: http://www.ena-hpc.org, last checked: March 2, 2013.

9. Conclusion

The demand for high performance computing as a tool for science and industry further increases due to the increasing quest for knowledge and optimization. The increasing demand results in increasing operating costs mainly consisting of power and cooling costs, further accelerated by the applied Jevron's paradox for computing components. In an effort to reduce the energy consumption of the HPC centers, a number of new approaches have been developed in the last few years. One of these approaches is to switch hardware to lower power states in phases of device idleness or low utilization. Even if the concepts are already quite clear, tools to identify these phases in applications and to determine impact on performance and power consumption are still missing. This thesis designs and evaluates tool extensions for power consumption measurement in parallel systems with the final goal to characterize and identify energy-efficiency hot spots in scientific applications. Using offline tracing, the metrics are collected in trace files and can be visualized or post-processed after the application run. The timeline-based visualization tools Sunshot and Vampir are used to correlate Message Passing Interface (MPI) applications with the energy-related metrics. With these new tracing and visualization capabilities, it is possible to evaluate the quality of energy-saving mechanisms, since waiting times in the application can be related to hardware power states.

High performance computing hardware supports multiple power saving mechanisms comparable to mobile devices which are analyzed for its potential for exploitation. A typical high performance computing node is broken down into its components and the fundamental power saving mechanisms for each manageable device are discussed. The component breakdown of promising devices includes the Central Processing Unit, the Input/Output system and the interconnect system between the computing nodes. To adjust the power saving modes of these components, several interfaces including the Advanced Configuration and Power Interface (ACPI) are available. Components with a low power consumption and/or no manageable power saving mode are only briefly discussed. However, the power saving mechanisms of the manageable devices might have impact on the device durability due to frequent mode switches. But the experienced impact is negligible for the moderate count of mode switches.

Based on this first results, a test cluster is designed with 10 high performance computing nodes which support a variety of the introduced power saving mechanisms. Each of these nodes is connected to power measurement equipment to investigate the power saving potential of the specific hardware. Using this infrastructure, the power saving potential of different hardware components is evaluated under different load scenarios. For this investigation, several idle and load measurements are performed for the two different architectures (Intel Nehalem and AMD Magny-Cours) in different power saving

9. Conclusion

modes. The impact of operating system mechanisms like processor governors and processor idle states are analyzed with the SPECPower benchmark. The measured power saving potential significantly differs for different phases of the benchmark – mainly due to the different utilization levels of the processor. Additional processor dynamic voltage and frequency scaling (DVFS) measurements for different application phases result in a coarse classification of memory-bound computation, cpu-bound computation, communication and I/O phases. The memory scaling of the two evaluation systems significantly differs, which results in beneficial characteristics for the Intel nodes. While the evaluated AMD processors scale the memory bandwidth with the core frequency, the Intel processors do not. Thus the energy-saving potential of the Intel nodes in memory-bound compute phases is advantageous.

However, statically switching the power saving mechanisms usually increases the application runtime. On the contrary, dynamic switching strategies consider the hardware usage in the application phases and switch between the different modes. The strategies can roughly be divided into hardware-centric approaches and application-centric approaches. Hardware-centric approaches make the decision about the concrete hardware power state dependent on the hardware utilization. The operating system usually implements several heuristics for a subset of devices like the processor or the hard drive. The most common approach to detect device idle times is utilization sampling. A device is considered idle if the utilization is lower as a specified threshold for a specified time. Based on this historic knowledge, the device is considered idle for the near future and its hardware state is changed. However, especially for scenarios where the device utilization changes frequently, the sampling approach introduces significant performance drawbacks due to device wakeup times. Furthermore, the utilization itself is not classified – it is thus not possible to detect busy-waiting or memory-bound application phases. Even if sampling additional sources for the classification of the utilization (e.g. processor performance counters), the high potential for wrong decisions due to the changing hardware usage pattern still exists. In comparison, the application-centric approach starts the analysis at the application layer which allows decisions to be based on knowledge about future application and system behavior. Following this approach, the different phases can be executed in different power modes via application instrumentation with the advantage of knowing the future utilization of the component. For example, it is possible to reduce the processing frequency and thus the power consumption for profitable (e.g. memory-bound) application phases and increase the processing frequency for application phases with a high demand for processing. If the mode transition is triggered before the processor utilization changes, the mode transition overhead can be reduced to a minimum.

To provide a software interface to instrument the application phases, the *eeDaemon* software is developed. The device requirements are communicated from the application to a server daemon, which runs on each computing node and controls its power modes. Each of the nodes has a fixed set of resources and each of the resources various power saving modes with different performance and power characteristics which have to be managed efficiently. Additionally, the daemon interacts with the cluster resource management system to ensure the undisturbed execution of uninstrumented applications with high performance constraints. However, for a well-founded decision about the application instrumentation a correlation of the application phases and the hardware is necessary. This includes metrics like hardware utilization or processor performance counters to identify and classify application phases of interest, but also the hardware power saving modes to evaluate the application instrumentation and the result on the device performance. The complex environment has a need for analyzing temporal dependencies and event specific information to decrease not only the power consumption, but also the energy. In detail, the following asynchronous tracing extensions are developed to correlate with the parallel application:

- The *PowerTracer* daemon, sampling the node power consumption,

- the *Resource Utilization Tracing* daemon, sampling the device utilization and hardware power states,

- the *Likwid Tracing* daemon, sampling the processor performance counters,

- and the tracing extension of the eeDaemon to log the decisions about the hardware power states.

The process of visual identification of application hot spots in terms of energy and performance is exemplarily illustrated with two tool environments, Sunshot and Vampir. To exploit the developed extensions, several scientific applications are analyzed to evaluate the whole approach. Using the energy-efficiency benchmark eeMark, typical hardware usage patterns are identified to characterize the workload and the impact on the power consumption. This includes detailed analysis of memory-bound application phases as well as various resource intensive application phases like communication and I/O phases. Additionally, the tradeoff between energy and performance is evaluated for the benchmark. Based on this analysis, four parallel applications are examined:

- *partdiff-par*, a partial differential equation solver,

- *swim*, a Shallow Water modeling for weather prediction,

- MPIOM, the Max-Planck-Institute Ocean Model,

- and GETM, the General Estuarine Transport Model.

Appropriate application phases are instrumented using the eeDaemon interface to reduce the power consumption with the final goal of saving energy for the whole application run on the test cluster.
The evaluation of the synthetic benchmark eeMark clearly indicates that trivial power saving strategies like reducing the network card speed or putting the disk to sleep are only limitedly applicable due to long transition times and small power saving potential on device level. Additionally, caching mechanisms limit the capability of power saving mechanisms – I/O and communication is usually shifted by additional software or

9. Conclusion

hardware layers which complicates the phase detection on hardware level. Nevertheless, applying these simple power saving strategies is useful if the devices are unused for almost the whole application run. However, significant energy savings can be reached by reducing the processor frequency in memory-bound application phases. But also here the energy-saving potential depends strongly on the phase duration and the level of memory-boundness. The application analysis using hardware performance counters has been emphasized as suitable method to detect memory-bound phases in applications. In particular, the ratio of retired processor instructions per resource stall (IPS) is appropriate to evaluate the level of memory-boundness and thus the power saving potential.

To sum up, almost all analyzed applications contain appropriate phases for instrumentation, but almost every one has also disadvantages (mainly due to not sufficient phase durations). Applications which consist of several, different phases (e.g. memory-bound and cpu-bound) have a huge power and energy-saving potential which cannot be exhausted by the ondemand governor of the operating system, which is based on the processor utilization. Further, reducing the processor frequency in busy-wait (communication and I/O) application phases can also gain remarkable results. However, implementation alternatives to the busy-wait pattern should be considered by application and library developers. But the right implementation choice is dependent on the specific problem and hardware and performance requirements.

The best energy saving reached for the selected set of application benchmarks is 13 % for a strong memory-bound application. But in general, the energy savings are varying and highly dependent on the type of application:

- I/O bound, memory-bound, cpu-bound, communication-bound and
- phase duration and
- total runtime.

Considering one-digit savings (e.g. 5 %) as realistic for high performance computing applications, this raises one question – is it worth the effort?

From the ecological point of view, the answer is definitely yes. Due to the reduced application energy, less cooling is needed on datacenter level. Figure 9.1 on Page 155 visualizes the resulting CO_2 savings for different PUE values for a HPC center with the annual electricity bill of two million euros.

With a PUE of 2.0, the total CO_2 savings are 1,180 t, which corresponds to a 3,687,500 km flight (about 92 times around the earth). For the best PUE of 1.0, its still about 46 times around the earth.

In addition to the CO_2 savings, Figure 9.1 visualizes the cost savings. The savings range between 100,000 € and 200,000 € per year, which corresponds to 1-3 Full Time Equivalents (FTEs), at least if the center is operated by the government. These amount of FTEs is probably sufficient to reach the energy savings of 5 % via energy-efficiency tuning of the applications. In general, this approach is not dedicated for energy-efficiency tuning, the correlation of application tuning, FTEs and costs is also known as *brainware* [Bal12].

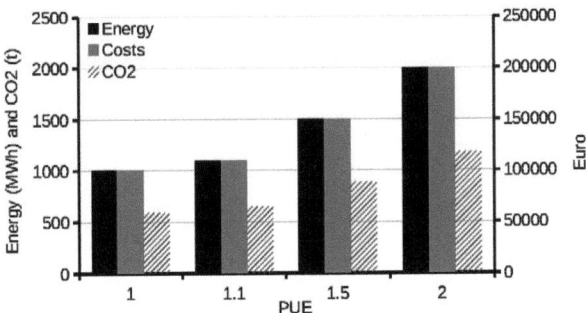

Figure 9.1.: *Savings for energy, costs and CO_2 for different PUEs of datacenters. The values are based on an annual energy consumption of 20 GWh, 0.1 €/kWh and 0.59 kg CO_2/kWh [Umw12].*

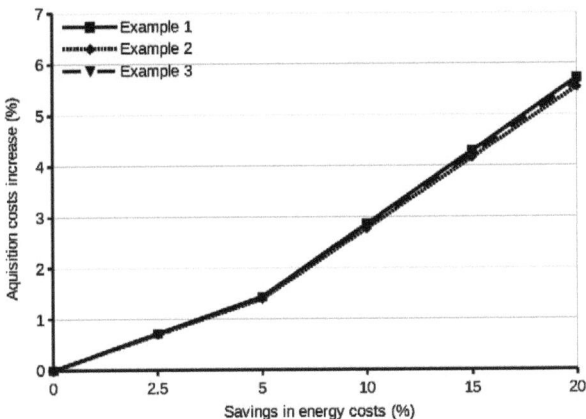

Figure 9.2.: *Relative increase of the acquisition costs based on energy savings without increasing the total cost of ownership.*

Furthermore, the hardware has to be selected carefully for different application types. Even if the acquisition costs seems lower, the total costs of ownership might be higher due to inefficiencies of the hardware or insufficient mechanisms to exploit power saving methodologies. Figure 9.2 shows the relative increase of the acquisition costs based on energy savings without increasing the total cost of ownership (see table 9.1). If saving 10 % of power during runtime, the acquisition costs can be increased by 3 %. To conclude, the answer from the economical point of view is in general yes, but the potential has to be evaluated for each use case.

From the social point of view, the answer should be yes. Revisiting the term *cost of*

9. Conclusion

Table 9.1.: *Composition of the total costs of ownership for three exemplary selected HPC installations. Example 3 is based on the test infrastructure used for this thesis.*

Name	Acquisition costs €	Annual electricity costs €	Operating time years
Example 1	35,000,000	2,000,000	5
Example 2	65,000,000	3,000,000	6
Example 3	32,000	3,000	3

science, high performance computing is an enabling tool and makes several fields of science affordable. Hence, every approach lowering the costs of this tool (including decreasing runtime costs) should be followed. Even more, the global race for exascale computing requires further research in the green HPC area.

The current rank 1 of the TOP500 list, namely the *Titan* supercomputer, has a power efficiency of 2.1 Petaflops per Megawatt[1]. Interpolating the performance of *Titan*, a factor of roughly 50 of the peak performance is required to reach the exascale goal, which results in a power consumption of 400 MW. Keeping HPC as a tool affordable demands for a maximum power consumption of 20 MW[2] which requires a power efficiency of 50 Petaflops per Megawatt. Consequently, the power efficiency has to be improved by a factor of 20. Again, to reach this ambitious goal, every approach has to be evaluated and exploited.

9.1. Future Work

Following the approach of exploiting hardware power saving mechanisms in parallel computing, several points can be addressed. In this thesis, the focus was on applications of the field of climate science. This analysis should be extended to a broader range of applications, covering different classes of applications and resulting resource utilization profiles. Especially HPC centers with a broad range of applications with different, changing behavior (in terms of resource usage) have a higher energy-saving potential since the hardware is usually not perfectly suitable for all these different scenarios. Porting this approach to typical datacenters might not be promising, since different applications classes run interfered (or even in parallel) on multiple subsets of nodes which makes it difficult to detect and predict interesting hardware utilization phases (except for the idle case, which is comparable trivial). Additionally, the aspect of distributed I/O could be analyzed in more detail with a larger count of computing and dedicated I/O nodes in realistic scenarios. Especially the waiting times due to collective operations seems to be promising for power saving and energy reduction. Furthermore, fine-grained

---

[1] http://www.top500.org, last checked: March 2, 2013
[2] as stated by the U.S. Defense Advanced Research Projects Agency (DARPA) in 2007

measurement of the power consumption and performance characteristics at component level should allow improved profiling and analysis of scientific applications. This measurement approach enables the correlation of the software components of the scientific application and the power consumption and thus makes it possible to evaluate interferences in detail. This ambition drives the first workpackage of the *EXA2GREEN*[3] project as continuation of this work.

In general, enhanced measurement capabilities and tool environments make it possible to tune applications for energy efficiency. This includes as well the adaptation of algorithm to specific hardware as also porting of applications to better suitable (in terms of energy-efficient) hardware. The first step – evaluating of the energy efficiency on a given platform via enhanced tool environments – is done is this thesis.

Even if hardware vendors are already improving the efficiency of each new generation of devices, further developments are necessary. The provision of additional counters for the hardware increases the insights for the application developer on the one hand, on the other hand distributed decisions about hardware states could be enabled. Based on different sets of performance counters, the processor could classify an application phase (e.g. memory-boundness) independently and decrease/increase the processor frequency or the memory bandwidth correspondingly. Additionally, modern processors consists of sophisticated and partially dedicated units (like the prefetcher, out-of-order execution unit, etc.), which could be disabled based on this phase detection and resulting usage pattern. Increasing the granularity of the already used power gating would also further decrease the idle power consumption of processor components. Similarly, unused portions of the main memory could be sent to sleep mode for applications with small memory footprints to improve the energy efficiency of the system for special application demands. This could be done by disabling the self-refresh of the memory banks, of course the memory management has to be adjusted to support these kind of resizing of the physical address space.

On software side, the awareness for the *green* topic for application and especially library developer has to be raised. With raising awareness, software energy-saving techniques can be developed, exploited and distributed into well known libraries and applications. Especially the evaluation of the *busy wait* pattern versus interrupts has to be discussed for several use cases. In addition, energy-efficient sets of compile flags have to be evaluated and tuned for several applications, compilers and hardware platforms to maximize the energy efficiency and derive best practices and guidelines. To motivate these steps in the scientific computing community, the resource management system could account the energy on job level (in addition to the job runtime). Hence, the energy efficiency of the whole application/job can be accounted and jobs can be prioritized based on their energy efficiency or energy usage. Furthermore, the system can provide feedback of the application behavior to the developer, especially about costs of the application run or power consumption hot spots. Additional instrumentation of the HPC centers and correlation with the running applications provides further information to the center operator (e.g. room temperature increases during specific application runs). This ap-

---

[3] funded by the EU within the FP7 framework, started in November 2012

9. Conclusion

proach further increases the awareness of the user, because the application costs become transparent which might increase the willingness to optimize the applications for energy efficiency.

Apart from the single cost reduction (cost-effectiveness of science), the ecology should be clearly kept in mind. The ecological impact of building and disposing of these large installations can not be disregarded. At this point, the computing centers have to create a demand for transparency of the whole product life cycle, which the hardware vendor has to fulfill. Additionally, concepts like re-purposing of supercomputers (as introduced by the *PRObE*[4]) project have to be evaluated and possibly adapted to increase the usage period[5] and justify the huge investments, usually supported by the community.

---

[4] http://www.newmexicoconsortium.org/probe, last checked: March 2, 2013
[5] typically four years in Germany

A. Appendix

Listing A.1: *Example PBS run script for example application run instrumented with VampirTrace*

```
1  ##### PBS OPTIONS ######
2  #PBS -q intel
3  #PBS -l nodes=1:ppn=8
4  #PBS -l walltime=01:00:00
5  ##### END PBS OPTIONS ######
6
7  # destinct hostname
8  host=`cat $PBS_NODEFILE | sort -u`
9
10 # setup libraries
11 export LD_LIBRARY_PATH=/sw/DBMetricConnector/lib:/sw/eeDaemon/lib:$LD_LIBRARY_PATH
12
13 # trace power consumption
14 export VT_PLUGIN_CNTR_METRICS=eeClustPlugin_${host}_power:${VT_PLUGIN_CNTR_METRICS}
15 # trace free memory
16 export VT_PLUGIN_CNTR_METRICS=eeClustPlugin_${host}_util_mem_free:${
       VT_PLUGIN_CNTR_METRICS}
17
18 # for all sockets, trace likwid metrics
19 for i in `seq 0 1`
20 do
21     #trace cpi
22     export VT_PLUGIN_CNTR_METRICS=eeClustPlugin_${host}_likwid_cpi_thread${i}:${
           VT_PLUGIN_CNTR_METRICS}
23     #trace L3 request rate
24     export VT_PLUGIN_CNTR_METRICS=eeClustPlugin_${host}_likwid_l3_request_rate_thread$
           {i}:${VT_PLUGIN_CNTR_METRICS}
25     #trace L3 miss rate
26     export VT_PLUGIN_CNTR_METRICS=eeClustPlugin_${host}_likwid_l3_miss_rate_thread${i
           }:${VT_PLUGIN_CNTR_METRICS}
27     #trace L3 miss ratio
28     export VT_PLUGIN_CNTR_METRICS=eeClustPlugin_${host}_likwid_l3_miss_ratio_thread${i
           }:${VT_PLUGIN_CNTR_METRICS}
29 done
30
31 # enable Likwid Tracing daemon with group L3Cache on cores 0 and 4 (socket 0 and 1)
32 /sw/likwid-2.3.0/bin/likwid-perfctr -g L3CACHE -d 50ms -c 0,4 > /dev/null 2>&1 &
33
34 #trace core frequencies for all cores
35 for i in `seq 0 7`
36 do
37     #trace eed core mode
38     export VT_PLUGIN_CNTR_METRICS=eeClustPlugin_${host}_eed_core${i}_mode:${
           VT_PLUGIN_CNTR_METRICS}
39     #trace core frequency
40     export VT_PLUGIN_CNTR_METRICS=eeClustPlugin_${host}_util_cpu_freq_avg_${i}:$
           {VT_PLUGIN_CNTR_METRICS}
41 done
42
43 # start trace unification manually after application run
44 export VT_UNIFY=0
45
```

I

A. Appendix

```
46  # enable Resource Utilization Tracing daemon
47  sudo /sbin/service rut start
48
49  # enable eeDaemon compiled with VampirTrace support
50  sudo /sbin/service eed-dbtrace start
51
52  # run application
53  ./swim_eed_vt < ref.in 2>&1
54
55  # disable eeDaemon
56  sudo /sbin/service eed-dbtrace stop
57
58  # disable Resource Utilization Tracing daemon
59  sudo /sbin/service rut stop
60
61  # disable Likwid Tracing daemon
62  kill -s INT $LIKWID
63
64  echo "Waiting for processes $LIKWID (likwid) to terminate..."
65  wait $LIKWID
66
67  # manual VampirTrace trace unification
68  mpiexec -ppn 8 vtunify-mpi swim_eed_vt -v
```

Listing A.2: *Configuration file for eeMark evaluation*

```
 1  # *************************** Configuration file for eeMark
        ***************************
 2  [general]
 3  prefix=
 4  energylib=powertracer
 5  add_debug_messages=no
 6  # ******************************* Instrumentation settings
        ***************************
 7  # Sets processor eeDaemon mode in compute kernels based ops_per_byte, default = no
 8  # This option needs the eeClust_intel_modes.cfg file containing the modes
 9  #add_cpu_instrumentation=yes
10
11  # Instrumentation on kernel level, default = no
12  # This option puts all processors in MODE_MIN for IO and Communication kernels
13  # Further, the nic and disk are switched into the modes specified in the benchsets
14  #add_instrumentation=yes
15
16  # Sets the default mode for kernel level instrumentation, defaults to MODE_MAX
17  #ee_mode_cpu_default=MODE_MAX
18  #ee_mode_disk_default=MODE_MAX
19  #ee_mode_nic_default=MODE_MAX
20  # ******************************* Compiler settings
        ***************************
21  # cc:       compiler        (e.g. mpicc, vtcc -vt:cc mpicc for VampirTrace support)
22  # ccflags: compiler flags (e.g. -O3), use -std=c99 if available
23  # ldflags: linker flags, -lm is required
24  # defines: definitions,   use -D_POSIX_C_SOURCE=199309L or greater if available
25  #
        ********************************************************************************
26  cc=           mpicc
27  # ******************************* gcc parameters
        ***************************
28  ccflags=    -O3 -funroll-loops -std=c99 -ftree-vectorizer-verbose=0 -ffast-math
29  ldflags=    -lm
30  defines=           -D_POSIX_C_SOURCE=199309L
31  # ******************************* icc parameters
        ***************************
32  #ccflags=   -O3 -std=c99 -vec-report1
33  #ldflags=          -lm
```

```
34  #defines=          -D_POSIX_C_SOURCE=199309L
35
36  #ccflags=          -O3 -std=c99
37  #ldflags=          -lm
38  #defines=          -D_POSIX_C_SOURCE=199309L
39
40  # ******************************* MPI parameters
        ********************************
41  #mpicmd=    mpirun --bind-to-core
42  #np_param=  -np
43  #np_default=  'nproc --all' #if creating a pbs script, this value has to be defined!
44
45  ## ******************************* mpich2-1.3.1 parameters
        **************************
46  mpicmd=    mpirun -binding cpu:cores -print-rank-map
47  np_param=  -ppn
48  np_default= 8
49
50  # ******************************* Batch system settings
        ******************************
51  create_pbs= yes
52  ## ******************************* PBS parameters
        ********************************
53  nodes=    5
54  queue=    intel
55  walltime= 30:00:00
56  mpimodule= mpich2/mpich2-1.3.1
57
58  # *************************** architecture dependent settings
        **************************
59  # simd_width: length of vector registers in Byte (vectors will be aligned
        accordingly)
60  # unroll:    unroll loops to increase amount of independent operations
61  # blocksize: blocksize in KiB for workloads that perform multiple operations per
        Byte
62  #           - should be smaller than L1 cache
63  # [pragma]: add pragmas that will be added before loops
64  #
        ****************************************************************************
65  simd_width= 32
66  unroll=    4
67  blocksize= 8
68
69  [pragma]
70  PRAGMA_VECTOR_ALIGNED="#pragma vector aligned"
71
72  # ******************************* usable functions
        ********************************
73  # the usable functions are omitted for volume reasons
```

A. Appendix

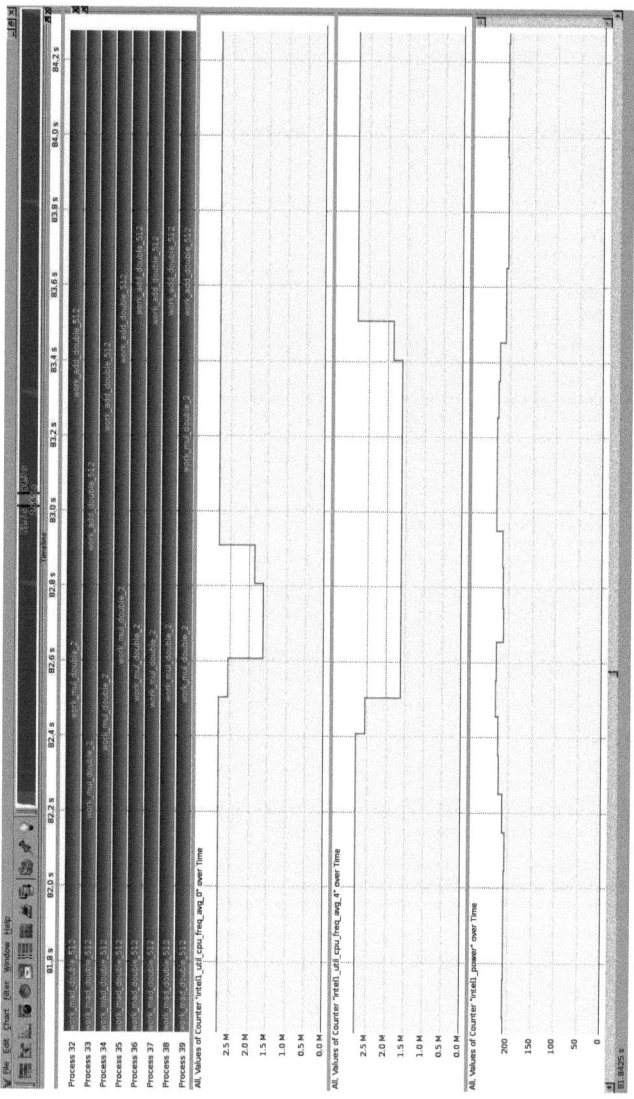

Figure A.1.: *Vampir Screenshot of instrumented eeMark* `compute3` *reference run. Power consumption is increased during memory-bound phases.*

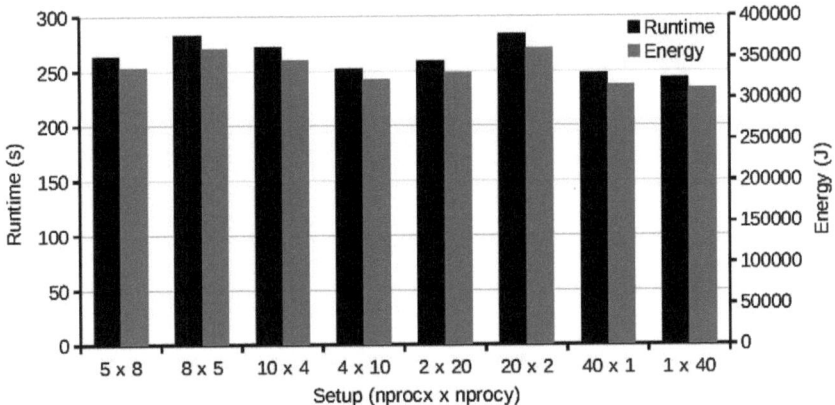

Figure A.2.: *Absolute measurements for different MPIOM tp04l80 setups with 40 processes pinned on the Intel cores. I/O is disabled, the model time is one day. The processor frequency is 2800 MHz.*

Table A.1.: *Performance counters measurements for MPIOM occlit loop instrumentation on one Intel Xeon node with a fixed processing frequency of 2800 MHz. Simulated is one day in a 4 × 10 process setup.*

Loop		LOOP49	LOOP105	LOOP141	LOOP157	LOOP212	LOOP279	LOOP329	LOOP369
Duration (ms)	Socket 0	54.49	16.32	23.86	46.27	16.77	24.85	29.57
Billion Instructions	Socket 0	1.15	0.35	0.56	0.15	1.01	0.41	0.6	0.64
	Socket 1	1.17	0.35	0.54	0.01	1.06	0.39	0.59	0.67
Million L3 misses	Socket 0	2.72	0.95	1.71	0.86	4.51	1.39	1.34	1.42
	Socket 1	2.68	0.94	1.06	0.8	4.34	1.53	0.96	1.49
Instruction/Miss	Socket 0	422.68	369.55	325.72	5.92	223.5	293.27	449.5	448.76
	Socket 1	434.6	375.35	507.52	6.5	244.01	252.58	614.11	453.45
Bandwidth (GB/s)	Socket 0	4.51	5.25	4.75	5.17	6.61	6.83	4.41	3.43
	Socket 1	4.47	5.22	3.02	4.83	6.18	6.78	2.94	3.65
Million Stalls	Socket 0	44.36	51.74	50.32	0.75	56.84	49.71	48.2	58.54
	Socket 1	43.09	51.31	45.67	0.74	55.74	53.77	43.03	56.43
Instruction/Stall	Socket 0	33.62	7.45	11.18	4.16	17.95	8.34	12.29	10.9
	Socket 1	35.66	7.61	12.01	4.28	18.82	7.35	13.48	12.02

Table A.2.: *Measured runtime, energy, mean power and performance counters for the memory bandwidth, Instruction/Stall and Instruction/L3 Miss for different processing frequencies of an cpu-bound workload (32 OPB) on the Intel Xeon nodes. The performance counters are averaged in 10 ms interval steps.*

Frequency (MHz)	2801	2800	2267	1600
Runtime (s)	54.35	58.26	72.5	100.87
Energy (kJ)	4.42	14.31	15.61	19.1
Power (W)	265	245	215	189
Billion Instructions	1.38	1.27	1.04	0.74
Billion Resource Stalls	0.17	0.15	0.11	0.07
Million L3 Misses	13.81	12.72	10.39	7.4
Memory Bandwidth (GB/s)	23.02	21.56	17.61	12.58
Instructions per Stall	8.09	8.59	9.24	9.92
Instruction per L3 Miss	100.18	100.14	100.16	99.89

Table A.3.: *Measured runtime, energy, mean power and performance counters for the memory bandwidth, Instruction/Stall and Instruction/L3 Miss for different processing frequencies of an memory-bound workload (1 OPB) on the Intel Xeon nodes. The performance counters are measured in 10 ms interval steps.*

Frequency (MHz)	2801	2800	2267	1600
Runtime (s)	42.02	41.99	41.98	42.05
Energy (kJ)	10.44	10.08	9	8.62
Power (W)	248	241	214	205
Billion Instructions	0.2	0.2	0.18	0.19
Billion Resource Stalls	1.18	1.05	0.81	0.56
Million L3 Misses	18.27	18.2	18.16	18.02
Memory Bandwidth (GB/s)	17.9	21.52	23.52	24
Instructions per Stall	0.16	0.18	0.23	0.33
Instruction per L3 Miss	10.95	10.77	10.1	10.47

A. Appendix

Table A.4.: *Relative runtime for point-to-point communication using* MPI_Send/MPI_Recv *on the Intel Xeon nodes with varying data sizes and network interface card settings. The baseline is the 1000 Mbit/s and Full Duplex setup.*

Data size	Speed (Mbit/s)	Duplex	Runtime (%)
8	10	half	11277.15
8	10	full	10721.36
8	100	half	1115.23
8	100	full	5327.65
8	1000	half	0.17
16	10	half	11313.51
16	10	full	10772.81
16	100	half	1122.94
16	100	full	4387.91
16	1000	half	0.08
24	10	half	10706.00
24	10	full	10780.18
24	100	half	1133.43
24	100	full	4447.03
24	1000	half	-0.44
32	10	half	10924.9
32	10	full	10825.48
32	100	half	1139.16
32	100	full	4714.10
32	1000	half	0.00

List of Figures

1.1. Amdahl's law and Gustafson's law. 9
1.2. DKRZ supercomputer history. 12
1.3. Increasing efficiency and electricity costs at the DKRZ. 13
1.4. Increasing power consumption of the DKRZ. 13
1.5. Relation between Time-to-Solution and Energy-to-Solution. 15
1.6. Power measurements for different node utilization levels. 16
1.7. Closed loop of optimization and tuning. 18

2.1. DVFS architectures in multicore-processors. 26

3.1. Picture of test infrastructure eeClust. 36
3.2. Physical view on the eeClust infrastructure. 37
3.3. Power consumption for eeClust nodes depending on load. 43
3.4. SPECPower Measurements for AMD Opteron nodes. 45
3.5. SPECPower Measurements for Intel Xeon nodes. 46
3.6. Energy consumption of the eeClust nodes for different workloads. . . . 48
3.7. Memory and L3 cache scaling for the Intel Xeon and AMD Opteron nodes. 49
3.8. Point-to-point communication energy consumption of the eeClust nodes. 50
3.9. Collective communication energy consumption of the eeClust nodes. . . 51
3.10. Disk read operations energy consumption of the eeClust nodes. 53
3.11. Disk write operations energy consumption of the eeClust nodes. 54
3.12. Idle power consumption for eeClust nodes. 56

4.1. Schematic application phases and resulting hardware utilization. 58
4.2. Design overview `cpuidle` and `cpufreq`. 62
4.3. Schematic application and device phases for different power saving scenarios. 65

5.1. eeDaemon mode control based on [MMK+11]. 70
5.2. Instrumented application runtime dependent on eeDaemon interval time. 74
5.3. Scheduling of (un)instrumented applications on processor cores. 75

6.1. HDTrace components. 81
6.2. VampirTrace data sources. 82
6.3. Trace environment with tool extensions. 84
6.4. Application runtime and statistics file size dependent on HDTrace interval. 89
6.5. Statistics file size dependent on HDTrace interval and application runtime. 89
6.6. Main window of Sunshot. 91

IX

List of Figures

6.7. Context view of HDTrace timeline elements. 92
6.8. Sunshot screenshot of `MPI_Barrier` with ondemand governor. 93
6.9. Sunshot screenshot of `MPI_Barrier` at fixed maximum processing frequency. 94
6.10. Sunshot screenshot of `MPI_Barrier` and device power states. 95
6.11. Sunshot screenshot of correlation of memory bandwidth and processor performance states. 97
6.12. Main window of Vampir. 98
6.13. Vampir screenshot of zoomed-in timeline. 99
6.14. Vampir screenshot of `MPI_Barrier` at fixed maximum processing frequency.100

7.1. Vampir screenshot of instrumented `compute3` reference run. 105
7.2. Relative compute benchmarks of the eeMark reference run with ondemand baseline. 106
7.3. Relative compute benchmarks of the eeMark reference run with maximum frequency baseline. 107
7.4. Relative compute benchmark scores of the eeMark reference run. 109
7.5. Instructions and resource stalls for different workload types. 110
7.6. L3 Cache misses and total memory bandwidth for different workload types.111
7.7. Instructions per stall and instructions per L3 miss rates for different workload types. 112
7.8. Operation-based instrumented communication and I/O benchmarks of the eeMark reference run. 115
7.9. Vampir screenshot of the operation-based instrumented `comm2` benchmark. 116
7.10. Operation-based instrumented communication and I/O benchmark scores of the eeMark reference run. 117
7.11. Operation-based instrumented combined of the eeMark reference run. . . 118
7.12. Evaluation of the tradeoff between energy and performance. 119
7.13. Sunshot screenshot of partdiff-par phases on one Intel Xeon node. 121
7.14. Average processor statistics of partdiff-par phases. 122
7.15. Sunshot screenshot of an instrumented partdiff-par run. 123
7.16. Relative runtime, energy and power measurements for different frequency setups of partdiff-par. 124
7.17. Vampir screenshot of the 312.swim main loop phases. 126
7.18. Relative performance counters measurements of the CALC1 phase of swim.127
7.19. Relative runtime, energy and power measurements of the swim reference run for different frequencies setups. 128
7.20. Performance, energy and power saving potential of optimization flags of the gcc compiler. 129
7.21. Vampir screenshot of two MPIOM processes on one Intel Xeon node. . . 131
7.22. Average processor utilization, node power and core frequency of MPIOM phases. 132
7.23. Average instruction per L3 cache miss rate of MPIOM phases. 132
7.24. Relative runtime, energy and power measurements of the MPIOM run for different frequencies setups. 133

7.25. Vampir screenshot of the MPIOM occlit phase on blizzard. 134
7.26. Vampir screenshot of the MPIOM run on blizzard. 135
7.27. Vampir screenshot of GETM processor frequency using the ondemand governor. 136
7.28. Detailed Vampir screenshot of GETM using the ondemand governor. . . 137
7.29. Vampir screenshot of improved GETM version. 139
7.30. Detailed Vampir screenshot of improved GETM version. 140

9.1. Savings for energy, costs and CO_2 for different PUEs of datacenters. . . . 155
9.2. Relative increase of HPC cluster acquisition costs. 155

A.1. Vampir Screenshot of instrumented eeMark `compute3` reference run. . . . IV
A.2. Absolute measurements for different MPIOM setups. V

List of Tables

1.1.	DKRZ supercomputer history from 1988 to 2012.	12
2.1.	Processor power states overview.	27
2.2.	Hard disk power saving modes overview.	28
3.1.	Example power measurement devices overview.	38
3.2.	Power consumption and socket voltage for AMD Opteron 6168.	40
3.3.	Power consumption and socket voltage for Intel Xeon X5560 (C-States enabled).	41
3.4.	Processor C-State power specifications for the Intel Xeon X5560.	41
3.5.	Power consumption and socket voltage for Intel Xeon X5560 (C-States disabled).	42
3.6.	Network card power consumption of the Intel 82574.	55
3.7.	Hard disk power consumption of the Seagate Barracuda ST3500418AS.	55
5.1.	eeDaemon modes and corresponding device mode.	72
7.1.	Performance counters measurements of an cpu-bound workload.	113
7.2.	Performance counters measurements of an memory-bound workload.	114
7.3.	Evaluation of the tradeoff between energy and performance.	119
7.4.	Application benchmarks overview.	120
7.5.	Performance counters measurements of swim phases.	127
7.6.	Performance counters measurements for MPIOM occlit loop instrumentation.	133
7.7.	Quantification of the instrumentation overhead of GETM.	138
7.8.	Quantification of the improved instrumentation overhead of GETM.	138
7.9.	Evaluation results of the application benchmarks	142
9.1.	Composition of the total costs of ownership for HPC installations.	156
A.1.	Detailed performance counters measurements for MPIOM occlit loop instrumentation	VI
A.2.	Detailed performance counters measurements of a cpu-bound workload.	VII
A.3.	Detailed performance counters measurements of an memory-bound workload.	VII
A.4.	Relative runtime for point-to-point communication for different NIC settings.	VIII

XIII

Bibliography

[ADI+12] ALONSO, Pedro ; DOLZ, Manuel F. ; IGUAL, Francisco D. ; MAYO, Rafael ; QUINTANA-ORTÍ, Enrique S.: DVFS-control techniques for dense linear algebra operations on multi-core processors. In: *Computer Science - Research and Development* 27 (2012), p. 289–298. http://dx.doi.org/10.1007/s00450-011-0188-7. – DOI 10.1007/s00450-011-0188-7. – ISSN 1865–2034

[AFK+09] ANDERSEN, David G. ; FRANKLIN, Jason ; KAMINSKY, Michael ; PHANISHAYEE, Amar ; TAN, Lawrence ; VASUDEVAN, Vijay: FAWN: A Fast Array of Wimpy Nodes. In: *Proc. 22nd ACM Symposium on Operating Systems Principles (SOSP)*. New York, NY, USA : ACM Press, 10 2009 (SOSP '09). – ISBN 978–1–60558–752–3, 1–14

[AH03] AEBISCHER, Bernard ; HUSER, Alois: Energy efficiency of computer power supplies. In: *Proceedings of the 3rd International Conference on Energy Efficiency in Domestic Appliances and Lighting*, 2003

[AHA+11] ANZT, H. ; HEUVELINE, V. ; ALIAGA, J.I. ; CASTILLO, M. ; FERNANDEZ, J.C. ; MAYO, R. ; QUINTANA-ORTI, E.S.: Analysis and optimization of power consumption in the iterative solution of sparse linear systems on multi-core and many-core platforms. In: *Green Computing Conference and Workshops (IGCC), 2011 International*, 2011, p. 1–6

[AHC+09] AGARWAL, Yuvraj ; HODGES, Steve ; CHANDRA, Ranveer ; SCOTT, James ; BAHL, Paramvir ; GUPTA, Rajesh: Somniloquy: Augmenting network interfaces to reduce PC energy usage. In: *Proceedings of the 6th USENIX symposium on Networked systems design and implementation*. Berkeley, CA, USA : USENIX Association, 2009, 365–380

[AHR+11] ANZT, H. ; HEUVELINE, V. ; ROCKER, B. ; CASTILLO, M. ; FERNANDEZ, J.C. ; MAYO, R. ; QUINTANA-ORTI, E.S.: Power Consumption of Mixed Precision in the Iterative Solution of Sparse Linear Systems. In: *IEEE International Symposium on Parallel and Distributed Processing Workshops and Phd Forum (IPDPSW)*, 2011. – ISSN 1530–2075, p. 829 –836

[Alc05] ALCOTT, Blake: Jevons' paradox. In: *Ecological Economics* 54 (2005), No. 1, 9-21. http://dx.doi.org/10.1016/j.ecolecon.2005.03.020. – DOI 10.1016/j.ecolecon.2005.03.020. – ISSN 0921–8009

[Amd67] AMDAHL, Gene M.: Validity of the single processor approach to achieving large scale computing capabilities. In: *Proceedings of the April 18-20, 1967, spring joint computer conference.* New York, NY, USA : ACM, 1967 (AFIPS '67 (Spring)), p. 483–485

[ARH10] ANZT, Hartwig ; ROCKER, Björn ; HEUVELINE, Vincent: Energy efficiency of mixed precision iterative refinement methods using hybrid hardware platforms. In: *Computer Science - Research and Development* 25 (2010), p. 141–148. http://dx.doi.org/10.1007/s00450-010-0124-2. – DOI 10.1007/s00450–010–0124–2. – ISSN 1865–2034

[BAEP08] BAO, M. ; ANDREI, A. ; ELES, P. ; PENG, Z.: Temperature-Aware Voltage Selection for Energy Optimization. In: *Proceedings of the conference on Design, automation and test in Europe.* New York, NY, USA : ACM, 2008. – ISBN 978–3–9810801–3–1, 1083–1086

[BaI12] BISCHOF, Christian ; AN MEY, Dieter ; IWAINSKY, Christian: Brainware for green HPC. In: *Computer Science - Research and Development* 27 (2012), p. 227–233. http://dx.doi.org/10.1007/s00450-011-0198-5. – DOI 10.1007/s00450–011–0198–5. – ISSN 1865–2034

[Bar05] BARROSO, Luiz A.: The Price of Performance. In: *Queue* 3 (2005), September, No. 7, p. 48–53. http://dx.doi.org/10.1145/1095408.1095420. – DOI 10.1145/1095408.1095420. – ISSN 1542–7730

[BBDM00] BENINI, L. ; BOGLIOLO, A. ; DE MICHELI, G.: A survey of design techniques for system-level dynamic power management. In: *IEEE Transactions on Very Large Scale Integration (VLSI) Systems* 8 (2000), June, No. 3, p. 299 –316. http://dx.doi.org/10.1109/92.845896. – DOI 10.1109/92.845896. – ISSN 1063–8210

[BDM+12] BARREDA, M. ; DOLZ, M.F. ; MAYO, R. ; QUINTANA-ORTI, E.S. ; REYES, R.: Binding Performance and Power of Dense Linear Algebra Operations. In: *2012 IEEE 10th International Symposium on Parallel and Distributed Processing with Applications (ISPA)*, 2012, p. 63 –70

[BH07] BARROSO, Luiz A. ; HÖLZLE, Urs: The Case for Energy-Proportional Computing. In: *Computer* 40 (2007), 33–37. http://dx.doi.org/http://dx.doi.org/10.1109/MC.2007.443. – DOI http://dx.doi.org/10.1109/MC.2007.443

[BJ07] BIRCHER, W. L. ; JOHN, Lizy K.: Complete System Power Estimation: A Trickle-Down Approach based on Performance Events. In: *ISPASS '07: Proceedings of the 2007 IEEE International Symposium on Performance Analysis of Systems and Software.* Washington, DC, USA : IEEE Computer Society, 2007. – ISBN 1–4244–1082–7, 158–168

Bibliography

[BTM00] BROOKS, David ; TIWARI, Vivek ; MARTONOSI, Margaret: Wattch: A Framework for Architectural-Level Power Analysis and Optimizations. In: *ISCA '00: Proceedings of the 27th annual international symposium on Computer architecture*. New York, NY, USA : ACM Press, 2000. – ISBN 1–58113–232–8, 83–94

[Bü11] BÜCHMANN, BJARNE AND HANSEN, CARSTEN AND SÖDERKVIST, JOHAN: Improvement of hydrodynamic forecasting of Danish waters: impact of low-frequency North Atlantic barotropic variations. In: *Ocean Dynamics* 61 (2011), p. 1611–1617. http://dx.doi.org/10.1007/s10236-011-0451-2. – DOI 10.1007/s10236–011–0451–2. – ISSN 1616–7341

[CFR02] CHANG, Fay ; FARKAS, Keith ; RANGANATHAN, Parthasarathy: Energy-driven statistical profiling: Detecting software hotspots. In: *Workshop on Power-Aware Computer Systems*, 2002

[CGF05] CAMERON, Kirk W. ; GE, Rong ; FENG, Xizhou: High-Performance, Power-Aware Distributed Computing for Scientific Applications. In: *Computer* 38 (2005), 11, 40–47. http://dx.doi.org/10.1109/MC.2005.380. – DOI 10.1109/MC.2005.380

[CM05] CONTRERAS, Gilberto ; MARTONOSI, Margaret: Power Prediction for Intel XScale Processors using Performance Monitoring Unit Events. In: *Proceedings of the 2005 international symposium on Low power electronics and design*. New York, NY, USA : ACM Press, 2005. – ISBN 1–59593–137–6, 221–226

[CMDAN06] CURTIS-MAURY, Matthew ; DZIERWA, James ; ANTONOPOULOS, Christos D. ; NIKOLOPOULOS, Dimitrios S.: On the Design of Online Predictors for Autonomic Power-Performance Adaptation of Multithreaded Programs. In: *Journal of Autonomic and Trusted Computing* 1 (2006)

[CPB03] CARRERA, Enrique V. ; PINHEIRO, Eduardo ; BIANCHINI, Ricardo: Conserving disk energy in network servers. In: *Proceedings of the 17th annual international conference on Supercomputing*. Boston, Massachusetts, USA : ACM Press, 2003. – ISBN 1–58113–733–8, 86–97

[DCY+08] DONG, Yong ; CHEN, Juan ; YANG, Xuejun ; YANG, Canqun ; PENG, Lin: Low Power Optimization for MPI Collective Operations. In: *International Conference for Young Computer Scientists* (2008), 1047–1052. http://dx.doi.org/10.1109/ICYCS.2008.500. – DOI 10.1109/ICYCS.2008.500

[DFG+11] DAVID, Howard ; FALLIN, Chris ; GORBATOV, Eugene ; HANEBUTTE, Ulf R. ; MUTLU, Onur: Memory power management via dynamic voltage/frequency scaling. In: *ICAC '11 Proceedings of the 8th ACM interna-*

XVII

tional conference on Autonomic computing. New York, NY, USA : ACM, 2011. – ISBN 978–1–4503–0607–2, 31–40

[DGMB07] DINIZ, Bruno ; GUEDES, Dorgival ; MEIRA, Wagner Jr. ; BIANCHINI, Ricardo: Limiting the Power Consumption of Main Memory. In: *ISCA '07: Proceedings of the 34th annual international symposium on Computer architecture.* New York, NY, USA : ACM Press, 2007. – ISBN 978–1–59593–706–3, 290–301

[DLP03] DONGARRA, Jack J. ; LUSZCZEK, Piotr ; PETITET, Antoine: The LINPACK benchmark: Past, present, and future. Concurrency and Computation: Practice and Experience. In: *Concurrency and Computation: Practice and Experience* 15 (2003), p. 803—820. http://dx.doi.org/10.1002/cpe.728. – DOI 10.1002/cpe.728

[DR09] DHIMAN, Gaurav ; ROSING, Tajana Šimunic: System-level power management using online learning. In: *IEEE Transactions on Computer-Aided Design of Integrated Circuits and Systems* 28 (2009), 05, 676–689. http://dx.doi.org/10.1109/TCAD.2009.2015740. – DOI 10.1109/TCAD.2009.2015740. – ISSN 0278–0070

[ECL+09] ETINSKI, Maja ; CORBALAN, Julita ; LABARTA, Jesus ; VALERO, Mateo ; VEIDENBAUM, Alex: Power-Aware Load Balancing of Large Scale MPI Applications. In: *IPDPS '09: Proceedings of the 2009 IEEE International Symposium on Parallel and Distributed Processing.* Washington, DC, USA : IEEE Computer Society, 2009. – ISBN 978–1–4244–3751–1, 1–8

[Ehm12] EHMKE, Florian: *Energy-Aware Instrumentation of Parallel MPI Applications*, University of Hamburg, Bachelor's Thesis, 06 2012. http://edoc.sub.uni-hamburg.de/informatik/volltexte/2012/180/, last checked: March 2, 2013

[EKR02] ELNOZAHY, E.N. ; KISTLER, Michael ; RAJAMONY, Ramakrishnan: Energy-Efficient Server Clusters. In: *In Proceedings of the 2nd Workshop on Power-Aware Computing Systems*, 2002, 179–196

[Ele] ELECTRONIC EDUCATIONAL DEVICES: *Watt's up internet enabled power meters.* https://www.wattsupmeters.com/secure/products.php, last checked: March 2, 2013

[FL05] FREEH, Vincent W. ; LOWENTHAL, David K.: Using Multiple Energy Gears in MPI programs on a Power-Scalable Cluster. In: *Proceedings of the tenth ACM SIGPLAN symposium on Principles and practice of parallel programming.* New York, NY, USA : ACM Press, 2005. – ISBN 1–59593–080–9, 164–173

Bibliography

[FPK+05] FREEH, Vincent W. ; PAN, Feng ; KAPPIAH, N. ; SPRINGER, R. ; LOWENTHAL, David K.: Exploring the Energy-Time Tradeoff in MPI Programs on a Power-Scalable Cluster. In: *Proceedings of Parallel and Distributed Processing Symposium.* Washington, DC, USA : IEEE Computer Society, 04 2005. – ISBN 0–7695–2312–9

[FS99] FLINN, Jason ; SATYANARAYANAN, M.: PowerScope: A Tool for Profiling the Energy Usage of Mobile Applications. In: *WMCSA '99 Proceedings of the Second IEEE Workshop on Mobile Computer Systems and Applications.* Washington, DC, USA : IEEE Computer Society, 1999. – ISBN 0–7695–0025–0, 2–9

[Ge07] GE, Rong: *Theories and Techniques for Efficient High-End Computing*, Virginia Polytechnic Institute and State University Blacksburg, VA, USA, PhD Thesis, 2007

[GFC05a] GE, Rong ; FENG, Xizhou ; CAMERON, Kirk W.: Improvement of Power-Performance Efficiency for High-End Computing. In: *Proceedings of the 19th IEEE International Parallel and Distributed Processing Symposium.* Washington, DC, USA : IEEE Computer Society, 2005. – ISBN 0–7695–2312–9

[GFC05b] GE, Rong ; FENG, Xizhou ; CAMERON, Kirk W.: Performance-Constrained Distributed DVS Scheduling for Scientific Applications on Power-Aware Clusters. In: *Proceedings of the 2005 ACM/IEEE conference on Supercomputing.* Washington, DC, USA : IEEE Computer Society, 2005. – ISBN 1–59593–061–2, 34–45

[GFC05c] GE, Rong ; FENG, Xizhou ; CAMERON, Kirk W.: Power and Energy Profiling of Scientific Applications on Distributed Systems. In: *Proceedings of the 19th IEEE International Parallel and Distributed Processing Symposium - Papers - Volume 01.* Washington, DC, USA : IEEE Computer Society, 2005 (IPDPS '05). – ISBN 0–7695–2312–9, 34–44

[GFS+09] GE, Rong ; FENG, Xizhou ; SONG, Shuaiwen ; CHANG, Hung-Ching ; LI, Dong ; CAMERON, Kirk W.: PowerPack: Energy Profiling and Analysis of High-Performance Systems and Applications. In: *IEEE Transactions on Parallel and Distributed Systems* 21 (2009), No. 99, 658–671. http://dx.doi.org/10.1109/TPDS.2009.76. – DOI 10.1109/TPDS.2009.76

[GS07a] GUPTA, M. ; SINGH, S.: Dynamic Ethernet Link Shutdown for Energy Conservation on Ethernet Links. In: *Proceedings of IEEE International Conference on Communications* IEEE, 2007. – ISBN 1–4244–0353–7, 6156–6161

XIX

[GS07b] GUPTA, Maruti ; SINGH, Suresh: Energy Conservation with Low Power Modes in Ethernet LAN Environments. In: *INFOCOM '07: Proceedings of IEEE INFOCOM* IEEE, 2007

[GSKF03] GURUMURTHI, Sudhanva ; SIVASUBRAMANIAM, Anand ; KANDEMIR, Mahmut ; FRANKE, Hubertus: Reducing Disk Power Consumption in Servers with DRPM. In: *Computer* 36 (2003), 59–66. http://dx.doi.org/10.1109/MC.2003.1250884. – DOI 10.1109/MC.2003.1250884

[Gus88] GUSTAFSON, John L.: Reevaluating Amdahl's law. In: *Commun. ACM* 31 (1988), Mai, No. 5, p. 532–533. http://dx.doi.org/10.1145/42411.42415. – DOI 10.1145/42411.42415. – ISSN 0001–0782

[Han09] HANS BURCHARD AND FRANK JANSSEN AND KARSTEN BOLDING AND LARS UMLAUF AND HANNES RENNAU: Model simulations of dense bottom currents in the Western Baltic Sea. In: *Continental Shelf Research* 29 (2009), No. 1, p. 205–220. http://dx.doi.org/10.1016/j.csr.2007.09.010. – DOI 10.1016/j.csr.2007.09.010

[Han12] HANS BURCHARD AND KARSTEN BOLDING AND LARS UMLAUF: *GETM Source Code and Test Case Documentation*. Version pre_2.4.x, 2012. – http://www.getm.eu/data/doc/getm-doc-devel.pdf, last checked: March 2, 2013

[HF05] HSU, Chung-hsing ; FENG, Wu-chun: A Power-Aware Run-Time System for High-Performance Computing. In: *SC '05: Proceedings of the 2005 ACM/IEEE conference on Supercomputing*. Washington, DC, USA : IEEE Computer Society, 2005. – ISBN 1–59593–061–2

[HF09] HUANG, S. ; FENG, W.: Energy-Efficient Cluster Computing via Accurate Workload Characterization. In: *Proceedings of the 2009 9th IEEE/ACM International Symposium on Cluster Computing and the Grid*. Washington, DC, USA : IEEE Computer Society, 2009. – ISBN 978–0–7695–3622–4, 68–75

[HIM+11] HEWLETT-PACKARD CORPORATION ; INTEL CORPORATION ; MICROSOFT CORPORATION ; PHOENIX TECHNOLOGIES LTD. ; TOSHIBA CORPORATION: *Advanced Configuration and Power Interface Specification*, 12 2011. (5.0) . – http://acpi.info/DOWNLOADS/ACPIspec50.pdf, last checked: March 2, 2013

[HOT96] HIRATA, Akio ; ONODERA, Hidetoshi ; TAMARU, Keikichi: Estimation of Short-Circuit Power Dissipation and its Influence on Propagation Delay for Static CMOS Gates. In: *Proceedings of IEEE International Symposium on Circuits and Systems*, 1996, 751–754

[HSK+06]   HOTTA, Yoshihiko ; SATO, Mitsuhisa ; KIMURA, Hideaki ; MATSUOKA, Satoshi ; BOKU, Taisuke ; TAKAHASHI, Daisuke: Profile-based Optimization of Power Performance by using Dynamic Voltage Scaling on a PC cluster. In: *Proceedings of the 20th International Parallel and Distributed Processing Symposium*. Los Alamitos, CA, USA : IEEE Computer Society, 04 2006. – ISBN 1–4244–0054–6, 298–305

[HSRJ08]   HYLICK, Anthony ; SOHAN, Ripduman ; RICE, Andrew ; JONES, Brian: An Analysis of Hard Drive Energy Consumption. In: *IEEE International Symposium on Modeling, Analysis and Simulation of Computers and Telecommunication Systems* IEEE, 2008. – ISBN 978–1–4244–2817–5, 1–10

[HSS88]   HOFFMAN, G.R. ; SWARZTRAUBER, P.N. ; SWEET, R.A.: Aspects of using multiprocessors for meteorological modeling. Version: 1988. http://dx.doi.org/10.1007/978-3-642-83248-2_10. In: *Multiprocessing in Meteorological Models*. Springer Berlin Heidelberg, 1988. – DOI 10.1007/978–3–642–83248–2_10, p. 125–196

[IBM09]   IBM: *Implementing an IT energy management plan for real savings*, August 2009. – http://www-03.ibm.com/systems/software/director/aem/, last checked: March 2, 2013

[Int02]   INTEL CORPORATION: *PCI Express Architecture Power Management*, 11 2002. – http://www.intel.com/content/dam/doc/white-paper/pci-express-architecture-power-management-rev-1-1-paper.pdf, last checked: March 2, 2013

[Int08]   INTEL CORPORATION: *Intel® Turbo Boost Technology in Intel® Core™ Microarchitecture (Nehalem) Based Processors*, 11 2008. – http://www.intel.com/content/www/us/en/io/quickpath-technology/quick-path-interconnect-introduction-paper.html, last checked: March 2, 2013

[Int09a]   INTEL CORPORATION: *An Introduction to the Intel® QuickPath Interconnect*, 01 2009. – http://download.intel.com/design/processor/applnots/320354.pdf?iid=tech_tb+paper, last checked: March 2, 2013

[Int09b]   INTEL CORPORATION: *Intel® Xeon® Processor 5500 Series Datasheet*, 03 2009. (1) . – http://www.intel.de/content/dam/www/public/us/en/documents/datasheets/xeon-5500-vol-1-datasheet.pdf, last checked: March 2, 2013

[Int10a]   INTEL CORPORATION: *Intel® Energy Checker - SDK Device Driver Kit User Guide*. 2.0, Dec. 2010. – http://software.intel.com/file/32935, last checked: March 2, 2013

[Int10b] INTEL CORPORATION: *Intel® Energy Checker - Software Developer Kit User Guide.* 2.0, Dec. 2010

[Int11] INTEL CORPORATION: *Intel® 64 and IA-32 Architectures Optimization Reference Manual*, April 2011

[Jev66] JEVONS, William S.: The Coal Question. In: *Library of Economics and Liberty [Online]* (1866). http://www.econlib.org/library/YPDBooks/Jevons/jvnCQ.html, last checked: March 2, 2013

[KBD+08] KNÜPFER, Andreas ; BRUNST, Holger ; DOLESCHAL, Jens ; JURENZ, Matthias ; LIEBER, Matthias ; MICKLER, Holger ; MÜLLER, Matthias S. ; NAGEL, Wolfgang E.: The Vampir Performance Analysis Tool-Set. In: RESCH, Michael (editor) ; KELLER, Rainer (editor) ; HIMMLER, Valentin (editor) ; KRAMMER, Bettina (editor) ; SCHULZ, Alexander (editor): *Tools for High Performance Computing.* Berlin / Heidelberg, Germany : Springer-Verlag GmbH, 2008. – ISBN 978–3–540–68564–7, 139–155

[KFL05] KAPPIAH, Nandini ; FREEH, Vincent W. ; LOWENTHAL, David K.: Just In Time Dynamic Voltage Scaling: Exploiting Inter-Node Slack to Save Energy in MPI Programs. In: *SC '05: Proceedings of the 2005 ACM/IEEE conference on Supercomputing*. Washington, DC, USA : IEEE Computer Society, 2005. – ISBN 1–59593–061–2

[KHLK09] KAZANDJIEVA, Maria A. ; HELLER, Brandon ; LEVIS, Philip ; KOZYRAKIS, Christos: Energy dumpster diving. In: *Workshop on Power Aware Computing and Systems (HotPower)*, 2009

[KMKL11] KUNKEL, Julian ; MINARTZ, Timo ; KUHN, Michael ; LUDWIG, Thomas: Towards an Energy-Aware Scientific I/O Interface – Stretching the ADIOS Interface to Foster Performance Analysis and Energy Awareness. In: *Computer Science - Research and Development* 27 (2011), p. 337–345. http://dx.doi.org/10.1007/s00450-011-0193-x. – DOI 10.1007/s00450–011–0193–x

[Kre09] KREMPEL, Stephan: *Design and Implementation of a Profiling Environment for Trace Based Analysis of Energy Efficiency Benchmarks in High Performance Computing*, Ruprecht-Karls-Universität Heidelberg, Master's Thesis, 08 2009

[KS92] KAUFMANN, William J. ; SMARR, Larry L.: *Supercomputing and the Transformation of Science.* New York, NY, USA : W. H. Freeman & Co., 1992. – ISBN 0716750384

[LBM00] LU, Yung-Hsiang ; BENINI, Luca ; MICHELI, Giovanni D.: Operating-system directed power reduction. In: *ISLPED '00 Proceedings of the 2000 international symposium on Low power electronics and design*. New York, NY, USA : ACM, 2000. – ISBN 1–58113–190–9, 37–42

[LDM01] LU, Yung-Hsiang ; DE MICHELI, Giovanni: Comparing System-Level Power Management Policies. In: *IEEE Des. Test* 18 (2001), March, No. 2, p. 10–19. http://dx.doi.org/10.1109/54.914592. – DOI 10.1109/54.914592. – ISSN 0740–7475

[LFL06] LIM, Min Y. ; FREEH, Vincent W. ; LOWENTHAL, David K.: Adaptive, Transparent Frequency and Voltage Scaling of Communication Phases in MPI Programs. In: *SC '06: Proceedings of the 2006 ACM/IEEE conference on Supercomputing*. New York, NY, USA : ACM Press, 2006. – ISBN 0–7695–2700–0

[LHL05] LIAO, Weiping ; HE, Lei ; LEPAK, Kevin M.: Temperature and Supply Voltage Aware Performance and Power Modeling at Microarchitecture Level. In: *IEEE Transactions on Computer-Aided Design of Integrated Circuits and Systems* 24 (2005), 07, 1042–1053. http://dx.doi.org/10.1109/TCAD.2005.850860. – DOI 10.1109/TCAD.2005.850860

[LLD12] LTAIEF, Hatem ; LUSZCZEK, Piotr ; DONGARRA, Jack: Profiling high performance dense linear algebra algorithms on multicore architectures for power and energy efficiency. In: *Computer Science - Research and Development* 27 (2012), p. 277–287. http://dx.doi.org/10.1007/s00450-011-0191-z. – DOI 10.1007/s00450–011–0191–z. – ISSN 1865–2034

[LTF[+]12] LIVINGSTON, Kelly ; TRIQUENAUX, Nicolas ; FIGHIERA, Thibault ; BEYLER, JeanChristophe ; JALBY, William: Computer using too much power? Give it a REST (Runtime Energy Saving Technology). In: *Computer Science - Research and Development* (2012), p. 1–8. http://dx.doi.org/10.1007/s00450-012-0226-0. – DOI 10.1007/s00450–012–0226–0. – ISSN 1865–2034

[MFMB02] MARTIN, Steven M. ; FLAUTNER, Krisztian ; MUDGE, Trevor ; BLAAUW, David: Combined Dynamic Voltage Scaling and Adaptive Body Biasing for Lower Power Microprocessors under Dynamic Workloads. In: *Proceedings of the 2002 IEEE/ACM International Conference on Computer-aided Design*. New York, NY, USA : ACM, 11 2002. – ISBN 0–7803–7607–2, 721–725

[MGW09] MEISNER, David ; GOLD, Brian T. ; WENISCH, Thomas F.: PowerNap: Eliminating Server Idle Power. In: *Proceedings of the 14th international conference on Architectural support for programming languages and operating systems*. New York, NY, USA : ACM, 2009 (ASPLOS '09). – ISBN 978–1–60558–406–5, p. 205–216

Bibliography

[MHJ+03] MARSLAND, S.J. ; HAAK, H. ; JUNGCLAUS, J.H. ; LATIF, M. ; RÖSKE, F.: The Max-Planck-Institute global ocean/sea ice model with orthogonal curvilinear coordinates. In: *Ocean Modelling* 5 (2003), No. 2, p. 91–127. http://dx.doi.org/10.1016/S1463-5003(02)00015-X. – DOI 10.1016/S1463–5003(02)00015–X. – ISSN 1463–5003

[MHS+11] MOLKA, Daniel ; HACKENBERG, Daniel ; SCHÖNE, Robert ; MINARTZ, Timo ; NAGEL, Wolfgang E.: Flexible Workload Generation for HPC Cluster Efficiency Benchmarking. In: *Computer Science - Research and Development* 27 (2011), p. 235–243. http://dx.doi.org/10.1007/s00450-011-0194-9. – DOI 10.1007/s00450–011–0194-9

[Min09] MINARTZ, Timo: *eeClust Cluster Manual*. Hamburg, Germany, 2009. – Internal report B1.1 for BMBF project *Energy-Efficient Cluster Computing* (Reference number: 01IH08008E)

[MKJ+07] MÜLLER, Matthias S. ; KNÜPFER, Andreas ; JURENZ, Matthias ; LIEBER, Matthias ; BRUNST, Holger ; MIX, Hartmut ; NAGEL, Wolfgang E.: Developing Scalable Applications with Vampir, VampirServer and VampirTrace. In: *Parallel Computing: Architectures, Algorithms and Applications*, volume 15 of *Advances in Parallel Computing*. Amsterdam, Netherlands : IOS Press, 2007. – ISBN 978–1–58603–796–3, 637–644

[MKL10] MINARTZ, Timo ; KUNKEL, Julian ; LUDWIG, Thomas: Simulation of power consumption of energy efficient cluster hardware. In: *Computer Science - Research and Development* 25 (2010), No. 3, 165–175. http://dx.doi.org/10.1007/s00450-010-0120-6. – DOI 10.1007/s00450–010–0120-6

[MKL12] MINARTZ, Timo ; KUNKEL, Julian M. ; LUDWIG, Thomas: Tracing and Visualization of Energy-Related Metrics. In: *26th IEEE International Parallel & Distributed Processing Symposium Workshops*, IEEE Computer Society, 2012

[MMK+11] MINARTZ, Timo ; MOLKA, Daniel ; KNOBLOCH, Michael ; KREMPEL, Stephan ; LUDWIG, Thomas ; NAGEL, Wolfgang E. ; MOHR, Bernd ; FALTER, Hugo: eeClust - Energy-Efficient Cluster Computing. In: WITTUM, Gabriel (editor) ; Gabriel Wittum (organizer): *Competence in High Performance Computing (CiHPC)*. Berlin / Heidelberg, Germany : Springer-Verlag GmbH, 2011

[MMK+12] MINARTZ, Timo ; MOLKA, Daniel ; KUNKEL, Julian ; KNOBLOCH, Michael ; KUHN, Michael ; LUDWIG, Thomas: Tool Environments to Measure Power Consumption and Computational Performance. In: *Handbook of Energy-Aware and Green Computing*. 6000 Broken Sound Parkway

NW, Boca Raton, FL 33487 : Chapman and Hall/CRC Press Taylor and Francis Group, 2012. – ISBN 978–1–4398–5040–4, Chapter 31, p. 709–743

[MMKK12] MOLKA, Daniel ; MINARTZ, Timo ; KREMPEL, Stephan ; KNOBLOCH, Michael: *eeClust Evaluation*. Hamburg, Germany, 2012. – Internal report B4.2 for BMBF project *Energy-Efficient Cluster Computing* (Reference number: 01IH08008E)

[Mol11] MOLKA, Daniel: *eeMark Manual*. Dresden, Germany, 2011. – Internal report for BMBF project *Energy-Efficient Cluster Computing* (Reference number: 01IH08008E)

[Mud00] MUDGE, Trevor: Power: A First Class Design Constraint for Future Architectures. In: *Computer* 34 (2000), p. 52–57. http://dx.doi.org/10.1.1.16.601. – DOI 10.1.1.16.601

[Nat08] NATHUJI, Ripal: *Mechanisms for coordinated power management with application to cooperative distributed systems*, Georgia Institute of Technology Atlanta, GA, USA, PhD Thesis, 2008

[Nik09] NIKOLOPOULOS, D. S.: Green building blocks - Software Stacks for Energy-Efficient Clusters and Data Centers. In: *ERCIM News* 79 (2009), p. 29–30

[NPI+08] NEDEVSCHI, Sergiu ; POPA, Lucian ; IANNACCONE, Gianluca ; RATNASAMY, Sylvia ; WETHERALL, David: Reducing network energy consumption via sleeping and rate-adaptation. In: *Proceedings of the 5th USENIX Symposium on Networked Systems Design and Implementation*. Berkeley, CA, USA : USENIX Association, 2008 (NSDI 08). – ISBN 111–999–5555–22–1, 323–336

[NVI08] NVIDIA CORPORATION: *PowerMizer® 8.0 Intelligent Power Management Technology*, 06 2008. – http://www.nvidia.de/attach/10153, last checked: March 2, 2013

[OCC+07] OLIKER, Leonid ; CANNING, Andrew ; CARTER, Jonathan ; IANCU, Costin ; LIJEWSKI, Michael ; KAMIL, Shoaib ; SHALF, John ; SHAN, Hongzhang ; STROHMAIER, Erich ; ETHIER, Stéphane ; GOODALE, Tom: Scientific Application Performance on Candidate PetaScale Platforms. In: *Proceedings of the International Parallel & Distributed Processing Symposium (IPDPS)*, 2007

[PBCH01] PINHEIRO, Eduardo ; BIANCHINI, Ricardo ; CARRERA, Enrique V. ; HEATH, Taliver: Load Balancing and Unbalancing for Power and Performance in Cluster-Based Systems. In: *COLP '01: Workshop on Compilers and Operating Systems for Low Power*, 2001

Bibliography

[PLB07] PALLIPADI, Venkatesh ; LI, Shaohua ; BELAY, Adam: cpuidle—Do nothing, efficiently... In: *Proceedings of Linux Symposium*, 2007, 119–126

[PS06] PALLIPADI, Venkatesh ; STARIKOVSKIY, A.: The ondemand governor: past, present and future. In: *Proceedings of Linux Symposium*, 2006, 223–238

[PS07] PALLIPADI, Venkatesh ; SIDDHA, Suresh B.: Processor Power Management features and Process Scheduler: Do we need to tie them together? In: *LinuxConf Europe 2007*, 2007

[Rar10] RARITAN INC.: *Dominion PX-5528 Tech Specs*. http://www.raritan.eu/px-5000/px-5528/tech-specs/. Version: October 2010, last checked: March 2, 2013

[RCP+10] RODERO, I. ; CHANDRA, S. ; PARASHAR, M. ; MURALIDHAR, R. ; SESHADRI, H. ; POOLE, S.: Investigating the potential of application-centric aggressive power management for HPC workloads. In: *International Conference on High Performance Computing (HiPC)*, 2010, p. 1–10

[RLF+07] ROUNTREE, Barry ; LOWENTHAL, David K. ; FUNK, Shelby ; FREEH, Vincent W. ; SUPINSKI, Bronis R. ; SCHULZ, Martin: Bounding Energy Consumption in Large-Scale MPI Programs. In: *Proceedings of the 2007 ACM/IEEE conference on Supercomputing*. New York, NY, USA : ACM Press, 2007. – ISBN 978–1–59593–764–3, 1–9

[RLS+09] ROUNTREE, Barry ; LOWENTHAL, David K. ; SUPINSKI, Bronis R. ; SCHULZ, Martin ; FREEH, Vincent W. ; BLETSCH, Tyler: Adagio: Making DVS Practical for Complex HPC Applications. In: *ICS '09 Proceedings of the 23rd international conference on Supercomputing*. New York, NY, USA : ACM, 2009. – ISBN 978–1–60558–498–0, 460–469

[RMM+01] RONEN, Ronny ; MEMBER, Senior ; MENDELSON, Avi ; LAI, Konrad ; LU, Shih lien ; POLLACK, Fred ; SHEN, P. ; SHEN, John: Coming challenges in microarchitecture and architecture. In: *Proceedings of the IEEE*, 2001. – ISSN 0018–9219, 325–340

[Sad75] SADOURNY, R.: The Dynamics of Finite-Difference Models of the Shallow-Water Equations. In: *Journal of Atmospheric Sciences* 32 (1975), April, p. 680–689. http://dx.doi.org/10.1175/1520-0469(1975)032<0680:TDOFDM>2.0.CO;2. – DOI 10.1175/1520-0469(1975)032¡0680:TDOFDM¿2.0.CO;2

[SBM09] SINGH, Karan ; BHADAURIA, Major ; MCKEE, Sally A.: Real Time Power Estimation and Thread Scheduling via Performance Counters. In: *ACM SIGARCH Computer Architecture News* 37 (2009), 05, No.

	37-2, 46–55. http://dx.doi.org/10.1145/1577129.1577137. – DOI 10.1145/1577129.1577137
[Sey11]	SEYDA, Christian: *Estimation of Power Consumption of DVFS-Enabled Processors*, Ruprecht-Karls-Universität Heidelberg, Bachelor's Thesis, 03 2011
[SGFC09]	SONG, Shuaiwen ; GE, Rong ; FENG, Xizhou ; CAMERON, Kirk W.: Energy Profiling and Analysis of the HPC Challenge Benchmarks. In: *International Journal of High Performance Computing Applications* 23 (2009), 08, 265–276. http://dx.doi.org/10.1177/1094342009106193. – DOI 10.1177/1094342009106193. – ISSN 1094–3420
[SH11]	SCHÖNE, Robert ; HACKENBERG, Daniel: On-line analysis of hardware performance events for workload characterization and processor frequency scaling decisions. In: *Proceeding of the second joint WOSP/SIPEW international conference on Performance engineering*. New York, NY, USA : ACM Press, 2011. – ISBN 978–1–4503–0519–8, 481–486
[SKK11]	SPILIOPOULOS, Vasileios ; KAXIRAS, Stefanos ; KERAMIDAS, Georgios: Green Governors: A Framework for Continuously Adaptive DVFS. In: *Proceedings of International Green Computing Conference and Workshops 2011*, 2011
[SMAb01]	SHENDE, Sameer ; MALONY, Allen D. ; ANSELL-BELL, Robert: Instrumentation and Measurement Strategies for Flexible and Portable Empirical Performance Evaluation. In: *International Conference on Parallel and Distributed Processing Techniques and Applications (PDPTA 2001)*, 2001, 1150–1156
[STHI10]	SCHÖNE, Robert ; TSCHÜTER, Ronny ; HACKENBERG, Daniel ; ILSCHE, Thomas: The VampirTrace Plugin Counter Interface: Introduction and Examples. In: *PROPER 2010 Proceedings*, 2010
[TDZ]	TU DRESDEN, Center for Information S. ; (ZIH), High Performance C.: *VampirTrace 5.12.2 User Manual*. 01062 Dresden, Germany
[Tec09]	TECHNOLOGY, Seagate: *Barracuda 7200.12 Serial ATA Product Manual*, 02 2009. – http://www.seagate.com/staticfiles/support/disc/manuals/desktop/Barracuda%207200.12/100529369b.pdf, last checked: March 2, 2013
[THW10]	TREIBIG, Jan ; HAGER, Georg ; WELLEIN, Gerhard: LIKWID: A Lightweight Performance-Oriented Tool Suite for x86 Multicore Environments. In: *Proceedings of the 2010 39th International Conference on Parallel Processing Workshops*. Washington, DC, USA : IEEE Computer Society, 2010 (ICPPW '10). – ISBN 978–0–7695–4157–0, p. 207–216

[TJYD09]   TERPSTRA, Dan ; JAGODE, Heike ; YOU, Haihang ; DONGARRA, Jack: Collecting Performance Data with PAPI-C. In: *Tools for High Performance Computing, Proceedings of the 3rd International Workshop on Parallel Tools*. Berlin / Heidelberg, Germany : Springer-Verlag GmbH, 2009. – ISBN 978-3-642-11261-4, 157–173

[Tor08]   TORRES, Gabriel: *Everything You Need to Know About the CPU C-States Power Saving Modes*. Tutorial. http://tinyurl.com/atgtt99. Version: 09 2008, last checked: March 2, 2013

[Umw12]   UMWELTBUNDESAMT: *Entwicklung der spezifischen Kohlendioxid-Emissionen des deutschen Strommix 1990-2010 und erste Schätzungen 2011*, 2012. – http://www.umweltbundesamt.de/energie/archiv/co2-strommix.pdf, last checked: March 2, 2013

[VFA+09]   VASUDEVAN, Vijay ; FRANKLIN, Jason ; ANDERSEN, David ; PHANISHAYEE, Amar ; TAN, Lawrence ; KAMINSKY, Michael ; MORARU, Iulian: FAWNdamentally Power-efficient Clusters. In: *Proceedings of the 12th conference on Hot topics in operating systems*. Berkeley, CA, USA : USENIX Association, 2009

[VLR+11]   VISWANATHAN, H. ; LEE, E.K. ; RODERO, I. ; POMPILI, D. ; PARASHAR, M. ; GAMELL, M.: Energy-Aware Application-Centric VM Allocation for HPC Workloads. In: *IEEE International Symposium on Parallel and Distributed Processing Workshops and Phd Forum (IPDPSW)*, 2011. – ISSN 1530-2075, p. 890 –897

[WCS10]   WANG, Shinan ; CHEN, Hui ; SHI, Weisong: SPAN: A software power analyzer for multicore computer systems. In: *Sustainable Computing: Informatics and Systems* 1 (2010), 11, 23–34. http://dx.doi.org/10.1016/j.suscom.2010.10.002. – DOI 10.1016/j.suscom.2010.10.002

[WOS08]   WEHNER, Michael ; OLIKER, Leonid ; SHALF, John: Towards Ultra-High Resolution Models of Climate and Weather. In: *International Journal of High Performance Computing Applications* 22 (2008), No. 2, p. 149–165. http://dx.doi.org/10.1177/1094342007085023. – DOI 10.1177/1094342007085023

[ZES]   ZES ZIMMER ELECTRONIC SYSTEMS GMBH: *Precision Power Analyzer*. http://www.zes.com/english/products/index.html, last checked: March 2, 2013

[Zon08]   ZONG, Ziliang: *Energy-efficient resource management for high-performance computing platforms*, Auburn University Auburn, AL, USA, PhD Thesis, 2008

i want morebooks!

Buy your books fast and straightforward online - at one of world's fastest growing online book stores! Environmentally sound due to Print-on-Demand technologies.

Buy your books online at
www.get-morebooks.com

Kaufen Sie Ihre Bücher schnell und unkompliziert online – auf einer der am schnellsten wachsenden Buchhandelsplattformen weltweit! Dank Print-On-Demand umwelt- und ressourcenschonend produziert.

Bücher schneller online kaufen
www.morebooks.de

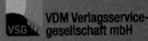

VDM Verlagsservicegesellschaft mbH
Heinrich-Böcking-Str. 6-8   Telefon: +49 681 3720 174   info@vdm-vsg.de
D - 66121 Saarbrücken   Telefax: +49 681 3720 1749 www.vdm-vsg.de

Printed by Books on Demand GmbH, Norderstedt / Germany